Blessings

A Century's Collection of Treasured Recipes

A Blessing

Bless these, Your gifts, our precious God,

From whom all blessings spring.

Make clean our hearts and feed our souls,

With good and healthful things.

Amen.

W. Lee King

Presented by
the Presbyterian Women
of First Presbyterian Church
Pine Bluff, Arkansas

©

Copyright 1996

First Edition   September 1996   3,000 copies
Second Edition   June 1997   4,000 copies

ISBN 0-9659080-1-1

To order copies of 𝔅𝔩𝔢𝔰𝔰𝔦𝔫𝔤𝔰, use order blanks in back of book or write directly to:

𝔅𝔩𝔢𝔰𝔰𝔦𝔫𝔤𝔰
717 West 32nd
Pine Bluff, Arkansas 71603

In the tradition of the Presbyterian Women of the Presbyterian Church, profits may be used to enhance the magnificence and beauty of our church and its programs as deemed necessary and will be determined each year by the Co-ordinating Team.

Printed in the USA by

WIMMER
The Wimmer Companies
Memphis

Special Acknowledgements

We thank the many who shared in preserving our history. The time spent testing and the dedication to this project are truly blessings for which we express our sincere appreciation.

Committee

Leila Wilkins O'Keefe

Monte Atkins

Bettye Hutt

Janie Buckley

Debbie Robinson

Margaret A. Dawson

Liana Siegfried

Claudette Dixon

Jane Stone

Frances Toney Hall

Joan Thompson

Linda VanHook

Cover Design
Kit McDonald

Pen and Ink Drawings
Katherine Ramage Love
Cindy Johnson

History and Research
Frances Toney Hall
Wade Hall

Our Gratitude for Yesterday

We acknowledge our gratitude to Reverend John Ivy Boozer and the small group of men and women who met with him in 1858 and organized our Presbyterian Church.

To the vision, faith and perseverance of the early women leaders of our church and those who followed in their footsteps, we owe the strength of our church today. We are grateful. They stir holy memories for us. Coming together in difficult times, they carried this church through six wars, a devastating flood and a depression. Remembering those wonderful women and what they accomplished, we feel very humble.

This book is dedicated to them. We have tried to recapture through their recipes the spirit of those times in which they lived and also to present our church as it is today. We know their eyes are turned our way and approving our effort.

The committee hopes you enjoy this cookbook as much as we have enjoyed compiling it. In our small way we are trying to pay our debt to them for the blessings they have given us.

The Cookbook Committee

History of Presbyterian Church

Two decades before the Civil War, the term "town" would have been a bit pretentious for Pine Bluff. Though recently incorporated and platted, "village" would perhaps have been a more accurate representation. According to an early description, 1840 Pine Bluff consisted of a total of sixteen structures: Nine log, six frame, and a brick courthouse. The town was still heavily forested; trails connected the houses or businesses with each other with a concentration of the latter along the river front. Many of the mercantile establishments doubled as homes. The only major highway was the Little Rock-Columbia Military Road which bisected town.

By 1857, Pine Bluff had grown to nearly 1,400 people. Into this rough river town came the Reverend John Ivy Boozer, a native of Newberry, South Carolina and a graduate of Columbia Seminary, Columbia, South Carolina. He was sent to Arkansas by the Board of Domestic Missions to tour the state, thinking to establish a mission here. Encouraged by his visit, he petitioned the Presbyterian Committee of Domestic Missions for an appointment and appropriation to establish a mission. The request was granted and Mr. Boozer was appointed to occupy the field as a domestic missionary with an appropriation of $200 to sustain him and the mission for a year.

Mr. Boozer, with his family, moved to Pine Bluff in January, 1858, and commenced his labors. He then asked the presbytery to appoint a committee to organize a Presbyterian church in Pine Bluff, but because of high water the committee failed to arrive. Mr. Boozer then organized the church with seventeen charter members, ten of whom were women. The date was May 15, 1858. In the session records the Sacrament of the Lord's Supper was administered for the first time on "Sabbath, the 16th of May, 1858."

The Cookbook Committee presents our collection of tested recipes combining heritage, tradition, and those new concepts we feel exceptional.

In 1861 the Presbyterian congregation of forty members bought a lot on the corner of South Common and Bonne (Fourth and Chestnut), a location which at that time was on the southern edge of town. Interestingly, the lot was purchased in the name of "Old School Presbyterian Church". After clearing the lot of its corn crop and walnut trees, a small frame church was built at a cost of $5,000. The church featured a sanctuary and vestibule with a servants gallery above. Congregants were seated in fifty-four pews (with doors) which rented for $25 per year or whatever the member was able to pay. Pews were decorated with carved scrollwork on the front and black walnut scrollwork on the back. They were seven feet long, the backs eighteen inches high, and the seats sixteen inches wide. The seatboards and footboards were of the best seasoned pine. The interior and ceiling were plastered and painted white. The two vestibule doors leading to the sanctuary were of grained oak as were the wood frames and facings of the doors and windows. Lighting was provided by four oil chandeliers, three side lamps mounted on brackets and two salon oil lamps. There were 52 book racks. The black walnut pulpit was varnished as were the steps leading to it. The entrance door was of grained oak painted Venetian green and the outside steps were leaden color. There was a stone sidewalk around the church.

During the Civil War years the church building was commandeered for use by occupying Union forces and suffered considerable damage. After the war the scattered congregation returned to restore and reorganize their church. Life returned to normal and the Fourth and Chestnut building continued to serve the congregation until fire destroyed it in August, 1893.

Apache Cheese Loaf

1 (9 inch) Apache loaf bread or
  round loaf bread
16 ounces sharp Cheddar cheese, grated
8 ounces cream cheese, softened
8 ounces sour cream
1/2 cup minced green onions

1 tablespoon Worcestershire
  sauce
2 (4 ounce) cans chopped green
  chilies
1 cup chopped ham

Slice top off the bread; set aside. Scoop out the inside of the loaf; press firmly around the inside. Combine the remaining ingredients; mix well. This will be a very stiff mixture. Fill the bread with the cheese mixture; replace top of bread. Bake on a cookie sheet at 350 degrees for about one hour. Serve with tortilla chips, pita chips, or melba rounds. Serves 10-12. *Works well with low-fat cheeses also!*

Virginia Brown Scriber

Cheese Dip

1/2 cup butter or margarine
1/2 cup plus 2 tablespoons flour
1 can hot jalapeno relish
4 teaspoons cumin
4 teaspoons chili powder

Garlic powder to taste
3-4 cups milk
1 pound mild Mexican Velveeta
Picante sauce (optional)

Melt butter or margarine in a heavy pot. Add flour and make a paste. Add jalapeno relish and seasonings. Slowly add up to three cups of milk to the mixture. Add Velveeta; stir over low heat until well mixed. Add more milk for desired consistency. Serve with tortilla chips and picante sauce. Yields one quart.

Jane G. Starling

In December 1906 and 1907, the session voted for the Sunday School not to have a Christmas tree and presents but to send the money saved to Dr. and Mrs. Bull, our missionaries to Korea. The session promised the Sunday School a picnic the next summer. At the picnic the entire church rode the train to Big Lake in the morning and back that afternoon.

Cold Cheese Dip

1 pint mayonnaise
1-1/2 cups grated Mozzarella cheese
1-1/2 cups grated Cheddar cheese
8 ounces sour cream

4 tablespoons Parmesan cheese
2 tablespoons dried onion flakes
Garlic powder to taste

Mix all ingredients. For a change, serve with pretzels! Serves 10.

Debbie Robinson

Corn Cheese Dip

1 can whole kernel corn, drained
1 can shoe peg corn, drained
1 (10 ounce) can diced Ro-Tel, drained
1 can chopped green chilies
8 ounces cream cheese, softened

5-8 slices jalapeno pepper,
  chopped
1 teaspoon cumin
1 teaspoon garlic powder
1 teaspoon chili powder

Combine ingredients; mix well. Warm slightly. Serve with tortilla or corn chips. *Delicious served warm or cold. Ideal for a Tex Mex meal!*

Jane G. Starling

Deanna's Chili-Cheese Dip

1 pound Hot Mexican Velveeta
1 (10 ounce) can diced Ro-Tel
1 pound ground beef

1 package taco seasoning
  (I use Williams Taco Seasoning)
1/4 cup sliced jalapenos

Melt cheese and Ro-Tel together; set aside. Brown ground beef; drain. Add taco seasonings and jalapeno pepper and combine. For extra heat, add a little jalapeno juice. Serve with tortilla chips.

Deanna Cook

At Christmas time 1947, the young people sent gifts of shoes, toys and money to Bob Rhinehart who was stationed in Germany, so that he could provide Christmas cheer to German children.

Hot Cheese Shrimp Dip

1 can cream of mushroom soup
1 can cream of shrimp soup
1 (6 ounce) roll garlic cheese
1 cup canned chopped shrimp, drained
1 (4 ounce) can sliced mushrooms

1 teaspoon grated onion
1 tablespoon lemon juice
1 cup grated American cheese
Several drops of Tabasco

In top of double boiler, combine ingredients. Heat until cheese is melted and ingredients are well blended. Serve with chips or crackers. *Delicious!!*

Anna Bess Westerfield

Queso Blanco

1 cup mayonnaise
1-1/2 cups grated Parmesan cheese
1 cup Monterey Jack cheese, grated
1/8 teaspoon chili powder

2 (4 ounce) cans chopped green
   chilies, undrained
1/4 teaspoon ground cumin

Combine all ingredients; spoon into a one quart baking dish. Bake at 350 degrees for 20 minutes. Serve hot with tortilla chips. Yields 3 cups.

Ann Bartlett Benton

Guacamole Dip

3 ripe avocados
1/2 cup mayonnaise
1-1/2 tablespoons lemon juice
1 teaspoon grated onion

1 teaspoon salt
1/2 teaspoon chili powder
Cumin to taste

Mash avocados in food processor or blender until smooth. Add remaining ingredients; blend. Serve with your favorite chip. Serves 6-8.

Helen O'Keefe King

The beautiful gold windows on either side of the cross in the sanctuary were given in memory of Mrs. John Harvey Means, Sr., Jane Hardy Means, and Allan Orto Means by their family.

New Years Day Dip

4 cups black-eyed peas, cooked
5 jalapeno peppers, chopped
1 tablespoon jalapeno juice
1 large onion, chopped

1 (4 ounce) can green chilies
1 clove garlic, minced
8 ounces Cheddar cheese, grated
2 ounces butter or margarine

Drain peas; reserve liquid. Mix peas, peppers, pepper juice, onion, chilies, and garlic in blender. Add some of the liquid from the peas, if needed. Melt cheese and butter; add to the pea mixture. Serve hot in chafing dish with chips.

In memory of Cherry Higgins

Salsa

2 (16 ounce) cans whole tomatoes,
 drained
1 tablespoon sliced jalapeno peppers
1/2 teaspoon minced garlic

1 teaspoon minced onion
 (optional)
1 tablespoon sugar
Salt and pepper to taste

Puree three whole tomatoes with jalapeno peppers in blender. Add remaining tomatoes, garlic, and sugar. Pulse just enough to mix and chop tomatoes. Salt and pepper to taste. Serve with your favorite chips. *Great last minute salsa! Most ingredients are stock cabinet items!*

Leah "Pud" Harris

Black Bean and Corn Salsa

1 (16 ounce) can black beans, drained
1 can shoe peg corn, drained
1 tomato, finely chopped
2 green onions, chopped
1/2 purple onion, chopped
1/2 cup chopped fresh cilantro
Tabasco to taste
Garlic powder to taste

3 tablespoons olive oil
Juice of two fresh limes
1-2 tablespoons chopped
 jalapeno (optional)
1 small can sliced ripe olives
 (optional)
1 avocado, chopped (optional)

Combine first 8 ingredients. Add olive oil and lime juice; toss gently to mix well. Add jalapenos according to desired level of "heat." Serve with your favorite chip. Serves 8-10. *My friend, Mary Shannon Fikes, shared this recipe with me.*

Debbie Robinson

Easy Salsa

3/4 cup chopped jalapeno peppers
1-1/2 cups chopped onion
3/4 cup white vinegar
6 cups tomato sauce
3 cups chopped tomatoes
   or 3 (16 ounce) cans diced tomatoes
3-4 cloves garlic or 1/2 teaspoon garlic powder

2 tablespoons sugar
2 tablespoons salt
1 tablespoon dried oregano
1 teaspoon pepper
1 teaspoon dried basil

In a 3 quart (or larger) pot, simmer chopped peppers and onion in vinegar until soft. Add remaining ingredients; simmer 40 minutes. Yield: 11 cups. Will keep in refrigerator several weeks. *Jane Huffstetler shared this recipe with me! Will add zip to anything!*

LeAnn Butts

Fresh Cilantro Salsa

3 (16 ounce) cans tomatoes
2-3 bunches green onions
5-7 jalapeno peppers, chopped
1 bunch fresh cilantro, chopped

1 clove garlic, chopped
2 tablespoons lemon juice
1 teaspoon salt

Mix in food processor until desired consistency; chill. Serve with chips as an appetizer or as an accompaniment. Yields 1 quart. *Delicious! Keeps in the refrigerator several days!*

Linda Burrow VanHook

Fresh Jalapeno Salsa

1 fresh jalapeno
1 (28 ounce) can tomatoes
Fresh cilantro to taste
Salt to taste

Pepper to taste
Garlic powder to taste
Onion powder to taste
Dash of red pepper

Remove stem and seeds from jalapeno. Combine ingredients in a blender or food processor. Process just enough to chop jalapeno and cilantro. Serve with tortilla chips. Yields 3-1/2 cups.

Stacey B. Cook

very good
freezes well

Hot Spinach Dip

16 ounces cream cheese, softened
8 ounces Monterey Jack cheese, grated
4 ounces grated Parmesan cheese
1 can artichoke hearts, drained and
chopped
2 (10 ounce) cans Ro-Tel

2 (10 ounce) packages spinach
thawed
1 onion, chopped
2 teaspoons cumin
2 teaspoons chili powder
1 teaspoon garlic powder

Place spinach in a colander and press out excess water. Mix all ingredients. Bake at 350 degrees for about 30 minutes or until hot. Serve with melba rounds or your favorite chip. Serves 12.

Debbie Robinson

may also microwave

Bacon Sticks

10 slices lean bacon
1 package bread sticks

1 cup Parmesan cheese

Wrap bacon around bread sticks. Roll in cheese. Place on bacon rack (very important) and microwave on HIGH until bacon cooks, approximately 3-4 minutes. *A quick before-dinner treat!*

Jo Neal

Cheese Krispies

1 cup margarine, slightly softened
1/2 pound sharp Cheddar cheese, grated
2 cups flour
Dash of salt

Dash of red pepper
Dash of Tabasco
2 cups Rice Krispies

Cut, using a pie crust tool, the margarine and cheese into the flour. Add remaining ingredients, mixing Rice Krispies in last. Roll into walnut sized balls; flatten with a fork on an ungreased cookie sheet. Bake at 350 degrees for 15 minutes. *These tangy cheese crackers keep well in tins and get crispier as they age.*

Leah "Pud" Harris

Cheese Straws

1/4 cup butter
1 cup flour
1 teaspoon salt
1/2 teaspoon cayenne pepper

1/2 teaspoon paprika
8 ounces aged or sharp
 Cheddar cheese, grated
2 tablespoons water

Mix all ingredients well. Put through cookie press onto ungreased cookie sheet. Bake at 300 degrees until light brown. Cool on cookie sheet.

In memory of Jane Means,
President, Women of the Church 1954-55

Cheese Straws

2 cups flour
2 teaspoons salt
Cayenne pepper to taste

1 cup butter or margarine
16 ounces sharp Cheddar
 cheese, grated

Sift together flour, salt, and cayenne. Mix butter or margarine in with fingers. Add cheese; mix. Put through cookie press onto an ungreased cookie sheet. Bake at 300 degrees for about 12 minutes. Cool straws on the cookie sheet.

Sue Smith

Cocktail Bites

Tiny cocktail sausages
Equal parts:
    Mustard (any kind)
    Jelly (any kind, especially grape or plum)

Boil sausages one minute in water; drain. Heat mustard and jelly to make sauce. Add sausages. Serve warm with picks. *A sure-fire hit with teens - and adults like them too!*

Ellen McClain Nuckolls

The Chrismon tree was first used in 1971. The beautiful Chrismon ornaments were made by the Women of the Church.

Dilly Brussels Sprouts

1 (10 ounce) package Brussels sprouts
1/2 cup Italian dressing

1/2 teaspoon dill weed
1 tablespoon sliced green onions

Cook Brussels sprouts until just done, but still firm; drain. Mix remaining ingredients; pour over Brussels sprouts and chill. Serve with picks.

Mrs. Collins Andrews, Jr.

"Hot" Carrots

1 cup vegetable oil
1 cup cider vinegar
2 tablespoons seasoned salt

1 teaspoon salt (optional)
10 cloves garlic, minced
2 pounds carrot sticks

Mix marinade ingredients well. Add carrots and chill in a zip lock bag for at least two days. Drain to serve.

Jane G. Starling

Marinated Olives and Peppers

1-1/2 teaspoons salt
1 teaspoon sugar
1/2 teaspoon dry mustard
2-1/2 tablespoons lemon juice
2-1/2 tablespoons vinegar

1-1/3 cups salad oil
5 large garlic cloves, minced
2 cans medium pitted black
 olives, drained
1 jar pepperocini peppers, drained

Combine first seven ingredients; pour over olives and peppers. Chill. Marinate 24 hours. Let stand at room temperature and drain before serving.

Pat Lile

Mexican Quiche

1 (4 ounce) can diced green chili peppers
1/2 cup flour
1 teaspoon baking powder
1/8 teaspoon salt
1 pint small curd cottage cheese

10 eggs, slightly beaten
1 pound Monterey Jack cheese,
 grated
1/2 cup butter, melted

Spray a 9 x 13 pan with non-stick cooking spray. Combine all ingredients; mix well. Pour into pan and bake at 400 degrees for 15 minutes. Reduce heat to 350 degrees; bake for 40 additional minutes. Cut into squares

Susan Norton

Roasted Pecans

1/2 cup margarine, melted
2 tablespoons Worcestershire sauce

2 teaspoons salt
2 pounds shelled pecans

Combine margarine, salt and Worcestershire; toss with pecans. Spread in a single layer on baking sheet. Roast 45 minutes in slow oven, rotating at 15 minute intervals. Sample toward the end of roasting time to test for crispness. *Makes a nice gift!*

Ellen McClain Nuckolls

Spinach Tea Sandwiches

1 (10 ounce) package frozen chopped
  spinach, thawed
1/2 (8 ounce) can water chestnuts,
  chopped and drained
2 tablespoons mayonnaise
2 tablespoons sour cream
2 green onions and tops, chopped

1/2 teaspoon salt
1/2 teaspoon white pepper
1/2 teaspoon garlic powder
1/2 teaspoon Worcestershire
  sauce
20 slices of thin bread

Place spinach in a colander and press out excess water. Mix remaining ingredients, except the bread, with the spinach. If desired, remove crusts from bread. Spread 10 slices of bread with a thin layer of butter followed with a layer of the spinach filling. Top with remaining 10 slices of bread. Cut diagonally into fourths to make tea sandwiches. Makes 40 tea sandwiches.

Margaret Dial Dawson

Florentine Sandwiches

1 (10 ounce) package frozen chopped
  spinach
1/2 cup chopped onion
1/2 cup chopped parsley
1/2 teaspoon dill weed
1-1/2 cups mayonnaise

1 (3 ounce) package cream
  cheese
1 tablespoon lemon juice
1 teaspoon Tabasco
20 slices thin bread

Cook spinach 2 minutes; place in a colander and press out excess water. Mix all ingredients thoroughly; let stand overnight in refrigerator. Spread on thin bread with crusts removed. Cut into fourths diagonally. Makes 40 sandwiches.

Helen Pledger Mullins

Stuffed Mushrooms

1 pound large fresh mushrooms
3 tablespoons grated Parmesan cheese
1 small onion, finely chopped
1 cup breadcrumbs,
   preferably Earth Grains Wheat

1 tablespoon chopped parsley
4 tablespoons butter, melted
Salt and pepper to taste

Clean mushrooms; remove stems and chop. Add cheese, onion, bread crumbs, parsley, 2 tablespoons of the melted butter, salt and pepper. Mix well; stuff caps. Place stuffed mushrooms in a pan coated with vegetable spray; drizzle with remaining butter. Bake at 350 degrees for 20 minutes.

Susan Norton

Boursin Cheese

6 ounces cream cheese, softened
1/2 cup butter, softened
1/4 teaspoon garlic salt
1/2 teaspoon Fines Herbs

1/2 teaspoon dill weed
Lemon pepper
Parsley (optional)

Combine first 5 ingredients in a food processor until well blended. Chill until firm enough to form into a loaf or ball. Roll in lemon pepper; garnish with parsley if desired. Delicious with crackers. Serves 12.

Leila Wilkins O'Keefe

Party Cheese Ball

16 ounces cream cheese, softened
8 ounces Cheddar cheese, grated
1 tablespoon chopped pimento
1 tablespoon chopped bell pepper
1 tablespoon finely chopped onion

2 tablespoons Worcestershire sauce
1 teaspoon lemon juice
Dash of cayenne
Dash of salt
1 cup finely chopped pecans

Combine cheeses. Add other ingredients, except nuts; mix until well blended. Shape into a ball; roll in pecans. VARIATION: Omit nuts; roll in 1 cup finely chopped parsley or 1 jar dried beef, finely chopped.

Margaret Dial Dawson

Pineapple Cheese Ball

16 ounces cream cheese, softened
3 tablespoons diced onion
1/4 cup diced bell pepper

1 (8 ounce) can crushed pineapple, drained
2 cups chopped pecans

Mix cheese, onion, bell pepper, pineapple and 1 cup of the chopped pecans with a spoon. Shape into 2 balls. Chill for approximately 1 hour. Roll in remaining pecans on wax paper. Serve with crackers. Freezes well. *This cheese ball is always a hit!*

Melissa Cook

Fiesta Cheese Roll

1 pound Mexican Velveeta cheese
8 ounces cream cheese, softened
3/4 cup pecans, chopped

1 green onion, chopped
1 small jar pimentos, chopped

Divide cheese in half. Roll 1/2 of cheese between two sheets of wax paper. Spread 1/2 of the softened cream cheese over the flattened cheese. Sprinkle with 1/2 of the pecans, green onions, and pimentos. Roll up, jelly-roll fashion. Make another roll with the remaining ingredients. Slice and serve with crackers. Makes two 12-ounce cheese rolls. *An easy last minute appetizer that disappears quickly at a party.*

Cindy Barefield Williams

Garlic Cheese Roll

1 pound hoop or Cheddar cheese
1 cup pecans
3 small cloves garlic

9 ounces cream cheese
Salt to taste
1 teaspoon Worcestershire sauce

Grind Cheddar cheese, pecans, and garlic in a meat grinder. Mix in cream cheese; season with salt; add Worcestershire. Form cheese mixture into a roll approximately 1-1/2 inches in diameter. Wrap in waxed paper and chill. Slice thinly and serve on crackers.

In memory of Frances Lea

Crabmeat Spread

12 ounces cream cheese, softened
2 tablespoons Worcestershire sauce
1 tablespoon lemon juice
2 tablespoons mayonnaise
1/2 onion, finely chopped or
  1 tablespoon minced onion

Dash of garlic salt
1 (6 ounce) bottle cocktail sauce
1 (6 ounce) can crabmeat or
  1 pound fresh lump crabmeat
Fresh parsley
Paprika

Combine first six ingredients; press into pie pan. Spread cocktail sauce over the cream cheese mixture. Top with crabmeat. Garnish with parsley around the edge. Sprinkle with paprika for color. Serve with crackers or melba rounds. *Delicious! Men love it!*

Mari Cousins Eilbott

Duck Pate

3 large wild ducks, cleaned
3 stalks celery, cut into 2-inch pieces
1 onion, sliced
1-1/2 teaspoons salt
1/4 teaspoon pepper
4 stalks of celery, cut into 1-inch pieces
4 green onions, cut into 1-inch pieces

1 green pepper, coarsely
  chopped
2 tablespoons lemon juice
1 tablespoon Worcestershire sauce
3/4 teaspoon salt
1/4 teaspoon hot sauce
1/2 cup mayonnaise

Combine first five ingredients in a large Dutch oven; cover with water, and bring to a boil. Reduce heat; cover and simmer about 1 hour or until ducks are tender. Remove ducks from stock; cool and remove meat from bones.

Grind meat, 1-inch celery pieces, green onion, and green pepper in a meat grinder or food processor; stir in remaining ingredients. Spoon into a 1-quart mold; chill 3 to 4 hours or overnight. Unmold and garnish as desired; serve with whole wheat wafers. Yields about 3-1/2 cups.

Wilma Jane Gillespie

The Women of the Church rolled bandages daily at our church for the Red Cross during World Wars I and II.

Pesto Torta

16 ounces cream cheese   1 pound unsalted butter

Allow cream cheese and butter to come to room temperature; beat together until smooth.

Pesto Sauce
1/4 cup pine nuts   1/2 cup quality olive oil
2 cloves garlic   3/4 cup Parmesan cheese,
1 cup tightly packed fresh spinach   freshly grated
1 cup tightly packed fresh basil   3 tablespoons butter, room
1/2 cup fresh parsley   temperature
1/2 teaspoon salt

Toast pine nuts at 325 degrees for 10 minutes; watch carefully to prevent scorching. Puree, in a food processor, nuts, garlic, spinach, basil, parsley, and salt. Add olive oil and blend. Add Parmesan cheese and butter; pulse briefly. DO NOT OVERBLEND.

Cut an 18" square of cheesecloth; moisten with water. Plastic wrap can be substituted. Wring the cheesecloth dry. Smoothly line a 6 cup plain or Charlotte mold; drape the excess over the rim of the mold. Using a rubber spatula, make an even layer with 1/6 of the cheese mixture in the bottom of the mold. Cover with 1/5 of the pesto sauce extending it evenly to the sides. Repeat layers, finishing with cheese, until mold is filled. Wider molds require fewer layers. Fold ends of cheesecloth over torta; press lightly to compact. Chill several hours or overnight. Invert onto a serving dish; gently unmold. Remove cheesecloth. Present torta with crackers.

To store: Remove cheesecloth, wrap airtight with plastic wrap; refrigerate up to five days. Can be frozen. If desired, cut sun-dried tomatoes into fan shapes and decorate the top of the torta!

Susan Norton

The second kindergarten was started in 1950 with Mrs. Paul Boyer, teacher, and Mrs. Sue Wall, assistant. Tuition was $8 per month with a $5 registration fee. Kindergarten committee: Mrs. Albert Railsback, chairman; Mrs. Clarence Carnahan and Mrs. Warren Means.

Smoked Oyster Spread

8 ounces cream cheese
2 tablespoons mayonnaise
1 teaspoon Worcestershire sauce
1 tablespoon grated onion
Garlic powder to taste

Cayenne to taste
Salt to taste
1 (3-3/4 ounce) can smoked
 oysters

Mix first 4 ingredients. Add garlic powder, cayenne, and salt to taste. Chop oysters; stir into cheese mixture. *My favorite of all dips. I serve this as a spread on melba rounds.*

Frances Toney Hall

Tomato Stuffed Brie

1 (8 ounce) round Brie cheese
1/4 cup butter, softened
1/3 cup sun dried tomatoes
1 small clove garlic, chopped

1/4 cup chopped walnuts,
 toasted
2 teaspoons minced parsley

Place Brie cheese, unopened, in the freezer to chill for approximately 1 to 1-1/2 hours. Soak tomatoes in water; drain. Using a sharp knife, cut the Brie cheese in half horizontally; set aside. Beat butter; stir in tomatoes and garlic; add nuts. Spread over the cut side of the cheese. Gently press the other half of cheese over the filling. Roll in parsley; cover and chill until firm. Present with crackers. Serves 8-10.

Ann Brown Turner

Radish Dip

1 cup chopped radishes
8 ounces cream cheese
1 clove garlic, minced

1 teaspoon lemon juice
3/4 teaspoon salt
1/2 teaspoon dillweed

Combine all ingredients in blender. Add a few dashes of black pepper; pulse briefly. Chill. To serve: scoop out contents of a large green bell pepper. Fill with dip and surround with strips of blanched fresh green beans, strips of red and yellow bell peppers, celery sticks, carrots sticks, broccoli, and cauliflower on a tray. Garnish with rosette radishes and parsley. Serves 8 to 10.

Monte Fitts Atkins

Presbyterian Reception Punch

48 ounces apple juice
48 ounces pineapple juice

48 ounces Sprite

Mix juices together; chill overnight or at least 4 hours. Just before serving, slowly add Sprite. Make ice ring in a ring mold or bundt pan with pineapple slices, cherries, and water. Sprite can be used in the ring instead of water, but it does not freeze clear. *For fewer calories, use unsweetened juices and diet Sprite. Also delicious frozen and served as a slushy punch!*

In memory of Cherry Higgins

Cranberry Christmas Punch

1 (3 ounce) package cherry Jell-O
1 cup boiling water
1 (6 ounce) can frozen lemonade
  concentrate, thawed

3 cups cold water
1 quart cranberry juice, chilled
1 (28 ounce) bottle ginger ale,
  chilled

Dissolve Jell-O in boiling water. Stir in lemonade; add cold water and cranberry juice. Pour into punch bowl with ice ring. Slowly add chilled ginger ale. Serves about 25.

Leila Wilkins O'Keefe

Florence's Southern Punch

2 cups sugar
2-1/2 cups water
Juice of 6 lemons
Grated rind of 2 lemons
Ginger ale

Juice of 2 California oranges
Grated rind of 1 orange
2 handfuls of fresh mint,
  crushed

Syrup: Cook sugar and water together to the boiling point; boil 10 minutes. Pour over juices, rind, and mint; cover and let set for 1 hour. Strain and chill. *For a drink:* Fill glass 2/3 full with crushed ice. Add 5 tablespoons of syrup and equal parts ginger ale (a little more ginger ale, if desired). *For a party:* Fill bowl 1/2 full of ice; add equal parts syrup and ginger ale (more ginger ale, if desired). Garnish with slices of orange or frosted grapes over the side.

Frances Toney Hall

Glenda's White Grape Punch

1 (12 ounce) can frozen white grape juice concentrate, thawed
1 (3-liter) bottle clear carbonated soda (7-Up, Sprite, etc.)

Mix and serve over crushed ice. *Easy to prepare and non-staining. Great for children's parties!*

Ann Rogers

Lemonade Punch

2 (6 ounce) cans frozen lemonade
concentrate, thawed
1-3/4 cups orange juice, chilled
3/4 cup lemon juice, chilled
Ice Ring: Maraschino cherries, orange, lemon, lime slices, and fresh fruit

1 (2-liter) bottle lemon-lime
carbonated beverage, chilled
1 quart club soda, chilled

Combine first 3 ingredients in a punch bowl; stir. Slowly add carbonated beverages; stir. Add ice ring. Serves 18.

The Cookbook Committee

Marlyn's Cooler

1 (6 ounce) can frozen limeade
concentrate, thawed
1 (6 ounce) can frozen orange
concentrate, thawed

1 (6 ounce) can frozen lemonade
concentrate, thawed
1 (3-liter) bottle club soda,
ginger ale, 7-Up or Sprite

Combine, stir, and serve over crushed ice.

Ann Rogers

In the 1800's, nearly all session meetings were held at the parsonage next door to the church.

Mim's Slushy Wedding Punch

5 (12 ounce) cans frozen pink lemonade concentrate, thawed
3 (12 ounce) cans frozen orange juice concentrate, thawed
8 (12 ounce) cans of water

1 (12 ounce) can apricot nectar
1 (10 ounce) box frozen raspberries
1 (3-liter) bottle lemon-lime carbonated beverage, chilled

In a large container (such as a plastic jug), combine all ingredients <u>except</u> lemon-lime beverage. Freeze 2-3 hours before serving. Just before serving chop up partially frozen mixture in a punch bowl. Add lemon-lime beverage. *Refreshing and thirst-quenching as well as pretty.* Serves about 50.

Ann Rogers

Mint Tea

2 cups boiling water
3 large tea bags
6 sprigs of mint, leaves only
1 cup boiling water

1 scant cup sugar
1/2 cup lemon juice
1 quart cold water

Steep tea bags and mint in 2 cups boiling water for 15 minutes. Dissolve sugar in 1 cup boiling water; add lemon juice and stir. Strain tea and mint mixture; add to sugar and lemon juice mixture. Add cold water. Chill. Serve over crushed ice with a spring of mint or lemon slice. *Refreshing on a hot day!*

Joan B. Thompson

On April 28, 1920, the first kindergarten was started in our church, "the teacher promising to teach the children the creed and some of the Psalms and good songs and nothing hurtful." It was held in the upstairs Sunday School rooms.

EGGS, CHEESE and PASTA

After our church at Fourth and Chestnut burned, Temple Anshe Emeth offered the use of their temple and Sabbath school was held there the next day. Main Street Methodist Church also offered their building and some services were held there. However, a committee appointed by the Session rented the upstairs of the Ingram building on the corner of Fourth and Pine for one year but were instructed not to pay more than $25 per month for it. A lot was acquired at Fifth and Walnut and a building committee was appointed.

Under the leadership of Dr. John Livy Caldwell, a graduate of Princeton Theological Seminary, the congregation moved into its new home in 1894. Completely free of debt, the church was dedicated Easter Sunday, April 14, 1895.

The church was a beautiful old brick building with magnificent stained glass windows. It was 102 feet by 70 feet and contained five rooms: An auditorium, a pastor's study and three Sunday School classrooms. Patented rolling partitions separated the classrooms from the auditorium. With the partitions open, the church had a seating capacity of 700. The building was steam heated and had combined electric and gas fixtures. A total of $1,300 worth of stained glass was used in the construction of the building and the pews and woodwork were of solid oak. The ceiling of the auditorium was an octagonal dome resting on eight iron columns with eleven "art glass" windows near the base. Eleven stained glass windows, some of which were memorials, were on the sides of the sanctuary. The exterior was made of pressed brick, both red and buff, and select hand-made brick. The tower was 85 feet tall with granite corners to the roof. One of Arkansas' leading architectural firms, Gibbs and Breysacher, built the church.

Chili Rellenos

3 (7 ounce) cans green chilies
1 pound Cheddar cheese
1 pound Monterey Jack
4 eggs, separated
1 (13 ounce) can evaporated milk

3 tablespoons flour
Salt, pepper to taste
16 ounces tomato sauce

Remove seeds and flatten chilies; put half of chilies in a 1-1/2 or 3 quart casserole. Cover with slices of cheddar cheese; put in rest of chilies and cover with Monterey Jack cheese. Beat egg whites stiff. Beat yolks with milk, flour, salt and pepper. Fold into whites and pour over chilies and cheese. Bake at 325 degrees one hour or less. Pour 2 (8 ounce) cans tomato sauce on top and bake one half hour longer. This is approximate time. It should be good and bubbly. *Mexican entree!!*

Jean Deal

Sausage Coffee Cake

1 pound bulk sausage
1/2 cup chopped onions
1/4 cup grated Parmesan cheese
1/2 cup grated Swiss cheese
1 egg, beaten
1/4 teaspoon Tabasco
1-1/2 teaspoons salt

2 tablespoons chopped parsley
2 cups Bisquick
3/4 cup milk
1/4 cup mayonnaise
1 egg yolk
1 tablespoon water

Brown sausage and onions; drain. Add next 6 ingredients. Make batter of Bisquick, milk and mayonnaise. Spread half of batter in 9X9X2-inch greased pan. Pour in sausage mixture, then spread remaining batter on top. Mix egg yolk and water and brush top. Bake at 400 degrees for 25 to 30 minutes or until cake leaves edges of pan. Cool 5 minutes before cutting into 3-inch squares. This recipe doubles easily in a 9X13-inch pan. Freezes well. *A favorite we love on Christmas morning!*

Bettye Hutt

For 25 years, starting in 1948, the WOC sponsored a child at the Vera Lloyd Home for children, buying clothing, giving spending money and Santa Claus for Christmas. We helped one young lady through college and gave her wedding reception when she married.

Eggs from Hell

10 large hard boiled eggs, peeled
1/2 teaspoon garlic salt
1/2 teaspoon onion powder
2 teaspoons dry mustard
1/4 teaspoon red pepper
1/4 teaspoon chili powder

1/4 teaspoon paprika
1 teaspoon fresh lemon juice
2 jalapeno peppers, seeded
and minced
1/2 cup mayonnaise
1 teaspoon minced cilantro

Cut eggs in half. Remove yolks, mash, and mix with remaining ingredients. Stuff into egg whites. Chill.

Janie Buckley

Deviled Eggs

6 eggs, boiled and peeled
5 tablespoons mayonnaise
2 teaspoons minced onions
1/4 teaspoon salt
3/4 teaspoon prepared mustard

1/2 teaspoon Worcestershire
sauce
1/8 teaspoon pepper
2 tablespoons finely minced
sweet pickle

Hard boil eggs, take from heat and run cold water over to stop cooking. Peel eggs. Cut in half lengthwise. Remove egg yolks and force through sieve. Add next seven ingredients and mix. Put egg yolk filling into egg white halves with pastry tube or with teaspoon. Sprinkle lightly with paprika. Serves 12.

Mary Snavely

Garlic Grits

1/2 cup grits
2 cups water
1/2 teaspoon Worcestershire sauce
Milk, enough to make 1/2 cup with
one beaten egg

1/4 cup oleo
Salt to taste
1 roll of garlic cheese
Shredded cheese, enough to
cover top

Cook grits in boiling water until it thickens (do not overcook). Add Worcestershire sauce, slightly beaten egg, milk mixture, oleo, and garlic cheese. Mix until cheese melts. After cooking 1 hour at 325 degrees, spread shredded cheese over the dish. Cook about 5 minutes more to melt cheese. Serves 4. Ingredients can be doubled to make a larger dish.

Oralee Leslie

Zesty Grits

1 cup of grits
1/2 stick of butter
1/2 pound Kraft old English cheese
   (or 2 glasses)
2 teaspoons Worcestershire

1/2 teaspoon Tabasco (2 or 3
   drops - your taste)
1/2 teaspoon garlic powder
Paprika
1 egg, beaten

Cook grits by directions. Add butter, cheese, Worcestershire, Tabasco, garlic to hot mixture. Mix well, add paprika and a beaten egg. Pour into oven dish (2 or 3 quart) with a top. Bake at 350 degrees for 30 minutes with the last 5 or 10 minutes with top off. Serves 8

Eleanor B. Joerden

Breakfast Pizza

1 pound sausage
1 package crescent rolls
1 cup frozen hash browns
1 cup shredded sharp Cheddar cheese
5 eggs

1/4 cup milk
1/2 teaspoon salt
1/4 teaspoon pepper
2 tablespoons grated Parmesan
   cheese

Cook sausage and drain. Spread rolls on greased pizza pan for crust. Spoon sausage, potatoes and Cheddar cheese on crust. Then mix eggs, milk, salt and pepper together and pour over. Sprinkle with Parmesan cheese. Bake at 375 degrees for 25-30 minutes. Serves 4-6.

Sharon Norton

Chili Quiche

4 eggs, beaten
1-1/2 cups Half and Half
Small (4 ounce) can chopped chilies,
   undrained
1 tablespoon dried ,chopped onions

Dash of salt
Dash of pepper
8 ounces Monterey Jack cheese
1 unbaked pie shell

Beat eggs. Add Half and Half and stir. Add chilies, onions, salt and pepper. Cube cheese and add to mixture. Pour into pie shell and bake at 400 degrees until top is golden brown. Serves 6-8.

Jo and Sam Neal

Basic Quiche

10 inch unbaked pie shell, chilled
1 tablespoon butter, softened
1 cup grated Swiss cheese
1 tablespoon flour
1/4 teaspoon salt
Pepper to taste
Pinch of nutmeg

6 eggs, beaten
1 pint light cream (or milk)
1/4 cup Parmesan cheese, grated
2 tablespoons butter, melted and browned

Spread butter on bottom of pie shell. Sprinkle Swiss cheese in bottom of pie shell. Sift dry ingredients. Add eggs and cream to dry ingredients and beat until mixed, but not frothy. Pour custard over cheese. Bake at 450 degrees for 10 minutes. Reduce heat to 325 degrees and bake 25 minutes longer. Remove from oven and sprinkle with Parmesan cheese and butter. Return to oven for 10 minutes or until a knife inserted in custard comes out clean. Let set 10 minutes before cutting into wedges to serve. Serves 8.

Susan Norton

Basic Quiche - Variations

Quiche Lorraine: 8 slices of crisp bacon, crumbled and added to Basic Quiche.

Shrimp Quiche: 1 - 1-1/2 cups cooked shrimp added to Basic Quiche.

Crab Quiche: 1 - 1-1/2 cups packed and drained crab meat added to Basic Quiche.

Lobster Quiche: 1 - 1-1/2 cups shredded boiled lobster added to Basic Quiche.

Mushroom Quiche: 1-1/2 cups mushrooms sliced and sauteed in 3 tablespoons melted butter, lightly seasoned, added to Basic Quiche.

Asparagus Quiche: Arranged cooked asparagus (1 box frozen or 1/2 pound fresh asparagus) in a pinwheel design in bottom of pie shell.

Susan's Quiche: 8 slices of crisp bacon crumbled and one 4 ounce can of sliced mushrooms, drained, added to Basic Quiche.

Susan Norton

Easy Does It Quiche

1-1/3 cup cream sauce
3 (10 ounce) packages frozen spinach
24 ounces shredded Swiss cheese
1/2 pound sharp Cheddar cheese, shredded
2 cans fried onion rings, crushed

1/2 cup chopped onion
4 eggs
Salt and pepper to taste
1/2 teaspoon nutmeg (optional)
2 9" shallow pie shells, unbaked

Make a medium thick cream sauce using: 1 tablespoon oleo, 1 tablespoon flour, 1 cup milk. Set aside. Cook spinach according to package. Drain well and mix into cream sauce. Add cheeses, crushed onion rings, and chopped onion. Mix together. Beat in 4 eggs with wooden spoon, and add salt and pepper. Divide into the 2 pie shells. Bake 45-55 minutes at 350 degrees. Cut each shell, as you would a pie, into 6 pieces. A Greek salad or fresh fruit salad compliments this quiche. Can be made a day ahead and refrigerated overnight. Serves 12.

Shirley Lynch

Hash Brown Quiche

3 cups loose-packed frozen shredded
    hash brown potatoes
1/4 cup butter or margarine, melted
1 cup diced cooked, lean ham, or
    3/4 cup fried, crumbled bacon
1 cup shredded cheese

1/4 cup diced green pepper
2 eggs, beaten
1/2 cup milk
1/2 teaspoon salt
1/4 teaspoon pepper

Press thawed potatoes between paper towels to remove moisture. Press into bottom and sides of an ungreased 9" pie plate. Drizzle with the melted butter. Bake at 425 degrees for 25 minutes. Combine ham (or bacon), grated cheese, and bell pepper and spoon over crust. In small bowl beat eggs with milk, add salt and pepper. Pour over other mixture. Bake at 350 degrees for 25 to 35 minutes until knife comes out clean when inserted into center. Let stand 10 minutes before cutting. Serves 6 - 8.

Norma Roberts

In 1938, more than 1200 visits were made to the hospital by ladies of First Presbyterian Church.

Spinach Quiche

1 9" pie shell
3 eggs, beaten
Large can Carnation milk
1 teaspoon dry minced onion
1/2 teaspoon nutmeg

1 teaspoon salt
Pepper to taste
1 (10 ounce) frozen chopped
   spinach, thawed
1/2 cup Parmesan cheese

Preheat oven to 400 degrees. Bake pie shell 10 minutes. Remove. Meanwhile, combine eggs and milk. Add onion and seasonings. Stir in thawed spinach and cheese. Bake at 375 degrees for 20 to 30 minutes, until knife inserted in center comes out clean. Serves 6 to 8.

Betty Abbott

Blender Hollandaise Sauce

3 egg yolks
1 tablespoon fresh lemon juice
Dash of cayenne pepper

1/2 cup melted, unsalted butter
1/8 teaspoon salt
Dash white pepper

Put egg yolks, lemon juice and cayenne into a blender; cover. Quickly turn blender on and off. Melt butter until bubbling. Slowly pour hot butter through opening in the top while blender is on high. Blend until thickens and fluffy. Do not double recipe. Makes 2/3 cup. *Wonderful on asparagus and also on poached eggs!*

Cookbook Committee

Sausage Strata

8 slices bread, crusts removed
2 pounds pork sausage
4 teaspoons prepared mustard
1/2 pound Swiss cheese, grated
6 eggs, slightly beaten
2 cups milk

2 cups Half and Half cream
4 teaspoons Worcestershire
   sauce
1/4 teaspoon grated nutmeg
1/2 teaspoon black pepper
1 teaspoon salt

Fit the 8 slices of bread evenly into a greased 3 quart casserole (13X9). Brown the pork sausage and drain off all excess fat. Stir in the mustard, then sprinkle evenly over bread layer. Sprinkle Swiss cheese over sausage layer. Combine the eggs, milk, cream, Worcestershire, nutmeg, salt and pepper and pour over entire mixture. Let sit until bread absorbs liquid. Bake at 350 degrees for 35 minutes, or until set and browned. Serves 8 to 12.

Pat Lile

Egg and Sausage Casserole

(Must be prepared 1 day ahead)

6 eggs
1/2 cup flour
1 teaspoon baking powder
1 cup milk
1 (3 ounce) package cream cheese
1 (8 ounce) carton small curd cottage
  cheese
10 ounces Monterey Jack cheese, grated
6 ounces mild Cheddar cheese, grated

1 pound sausage, cooked and
  drained
1/8 teaspoon salt
1 bunch green onions, chopped
12 ounces sliced mushrooms,
  drained
6 tablespoons butter
Paprika

In a large bowl, beat eggs well with a wisk. Add flour, baking powder and milk. Cut cream cheese in small cubes. Add cream cheese and cottage cheese to egg mixture. Next add Monterey Jack and Cheddar cheeses, along with the cooked, crumbled sausage, salt, chopped green onions and mushrooms. Pour mixture into a buttered 9X13 casserole. Dot with butter and sprinkle with a little paprika. Cover and refrigerate overnight. The next day, bring to room temperature and bake at 350 degrees for 45 minutes. Serves 8 to 10.

Leila Wilkins O'Keefe

Cheese Soufflé

Softened butter
4 slices very fresh bread
1/2 pound Cheddar cheese, grated
4 eggs
2 cups milk
1 teaspoon Worcestershire sauce

1 teaspoon Tabasco
1 teaspoon dry mustard
1 teaspoon salt
1 teaspoon pepper
1 clove garlic

Butter bread, then trim and cut into cubes. Rub casserole with garlic and butter. Layer bread cubes and cheese, ending with cheese. Beat the rest of the ingredients well and pour over the other ingredients in the casserole. Refrigerate at least 6 hours. Then bring to room temperature. Bake 1-1/2 hours at 350 degrees in pan of water.

Jodie Henslee

Apricot Pasta

3/4 cup of quality olive oil
15 cloves garlic (yes, 15!), pressed or
   finely chopped
1 cup of dry white wine
1-1/2 teaspoons rosemary

1 cup dried apricots, cut
   into slivers
Salt and freshly ground black
   pepper, to taste
1 pound linguine
1/2 cup chopped fresh parsley

Heat the olive oil in a skillet over medium heat. Add the pressed garlic. Saute just until browned. Stir in the white wine. Reduce the heat and simmer uncovered for 5 minutes. Add the rosemary and apricots. Season with salt and pepper. Simmer 5 to 10 minutes longer. Cook the pasta in boiling salted water until tender and drain. Place the pasta, sauce and parsley in a serving bowl and toss to coat. Serve hot but it is good cold too. Doubles and triples well. Serves 4 to 6.

Connie Mullis

Macaroni and Cheese

3 quarts water
1 tablespoon salt
1 package macaroni (8-9 ounces)
4-1/2 tablespoons margarine
3 tablespoons flour
1-1/2 teaspoons salt
1/4 teaspoon pepper
1/2 teaspoon dry mustard

3 cups milk
1/4 pound grated cheese
1 tablespoon grated onion
1 teaspoon Worcestershire
Grated cheese, for topping
1/2 cup buttered crumbs
Dash paprika

Bring to boil water and salt and add package of macaroni. Boil for 9-1/2 to 12 minutes. Drain and rinse with cold water. Make white sauce by melting margarine in heavy sauce pan. Add flour, salt, pepper and dry mustard. Stir to mix well. Add 3 cups milk. Stir constantly and cook until thickened. Add 1/4 pound grated cheese, onion and Worcestershire sauce. Add cooked macaroni and mix. Placed in greased casserole - top with grated cheese and crumbs. Add dash of paprika. Bake 25 to 30 minutes in 375 degree oven. Serves 6 to 8.

Mary Snavely

LaNelle's Favorite Macaroni Casserole

5 Stouffer's 15 oz. or Swanson's frozen
  macaroni & cheese (75 ounces), thawed
1 (10 ounce) chopped frozen spinach,
  thawed
12 ounces sharp Cheddar cheese
1 bunch green onions, chopped
1/2 teaspoon oregano
Salt, white pepper, cayenne pepper to taste

Topping:
1 can French fried onion rings
Grated Cheddar cheese
Cayenne pepper to taste

Combine all ingredients except the topping. Put in large sprayed casserole. Sprinkle onion rings on top, then the cheese. Sprinkle a little cayenne on if desired. Bake at 350 degrees for 45 to 50 minutes. Serves 12 to 16.

Montine McNulty and Debbie Robinson

Spicy Sesame Noodles

2 tablespoons salt
1 pound thin linguine or other thin pasta
1/4 cup peanut oil
2 cups sesame mayonnaise
Szechwan hot chili oil

8 scallions, trimmed, cleaned &
  cut diagonally into 1/2 pieces
2 bundles of fresh blanched
  asparagus tips

Bring 4 quarts of water to a full boil in a large pot, stir in salt, drop in the linguine, and cook until tender. Drain, toss in a mixing bowl with the peanut oil, and let cool to room temperature. Whisk together the sesame mayonnaise and chili oil in a small bowl. Try 1/2 tablespoon at first then taste and add more. Add the scallions to the pasta, pour in the sesame mayonnaise, and toss gently but well. Cover and refrigerate until serving time. Toss the noodles again and add additional sesame mayonnaise. garnish with asparagus.

SESAME MAYONNAISE:

1 whole egg
2 egg yolks
2-1/2 tablespoons Oriental soy sauce
2-1/2 tablespoons rice vinegar

3 tablespoons Dijon mustard
1/4 cup dark Oriental sesame oil
2-1/2 cups corn oil
1/2 to 1 tablespoon Szechwan
  hot and spicy oil

In a food processor fitted with a steel blade, process the whole egg, egg yolk, vinegar, soy sauce and mustard for 1 minute. With the motor still running, drizzle in the sesame oil and then the corn oil in a slow stream. Season with drops of the hot and spicy oil. Begin with 1/2 tablespoon and taste. Remember that the noodles will take up some of the heat of the oil and you may want to add more. Put in a bowl, cover and refrigerate until ready to use. Serves 6.

Connie Mullis

Forty-Five Minute Meat Sauce

1 medium yellow onion, sliced thin
1 bell pepper, seeded and cut into
  small slivers
2 cups mushrooms, sliced
3 tablespoons extra virgin olive oil
2 (15 ounce) cans tomato sauce
1 (15 ounce) can whole tomatoes, crushed
1-1/2 teaspoons dried oregano (fresh
  is best, if possible)
1 teaspoon dried basil (fresh is best, if possible)
1 teaspoon granulated garlic

2 tablespoons fresh parsley,
  chopped coarsely
1/2 teaspoon black pepper
1 teaspoon salt
1 pound lean hamburger meat,
  well-browned and with fat
  drained off (use colander)
Grated Parmesan or Romano
  cheese
1 (16 ounce) package vermicelli

In a 4-quart pot, saute onions, bell pepper and mushrooms in olive oil for 7 to 8 minutes. Add remaining ingredients and bring to a slow boil; cover and simmer for 30 minutes. Uncover and cook for 5 more minutes. Cook one pound of pasta al dente, which will be tossed with 1/4 of the sauce. Sprinkle with cheese. Serves 6 to 8. Remaining sauce may be frozen.

Ann Rogers

Twenty Minute Pasta Sauce

3 tablespoons extra virgin olive oil
1 medium onion, sliced thin
1 (16 ounce) can tomato sauce
1 (16 ounce) can whole tomatoes, crushed
1-1/2 teaspoons dried oregano, better fresh
1-1/2 teaspoons dried basil, better fresh
1/2 teaspoon granulated garlic

2 teaspoons fresh parsley,
  chopped
1 teaspoon salt
1/2 teaspoon black pepper
16 ounces of favorite pasta

In a 10" skillet over medium high heat, add oil. Saute onions for 5 minutes; add remaining ingredients and blend. Reduce heat and simmer 15 minutes uncovered. Meanwhile, have a large pot of boiling water to cook 1 pound of your favorite pasta until done. Drain pasta and toss with 1/2 of the sauce. Serve with grated Parmesan or Romano cheese. Serves 4 to 6.

Ann Rogers

Blessed are the merciful; for they shall obtain mercy.   Matthew 5:7

Pesto Sauce

1/2 cup extra virgin olive oil
1/2 teaspoon salt
1/4 teaspoon pepper
2 cloves garlic
1 tablespoon pine nuts

2/3 cup fresh dry basil leaves
tightly packed, (2-1/2 oz.
packed)
1/4 cup grated fresh Parmesan
cheese (imported preferred)
1 pound pasta

In a blender, set at medium speed, add all ingredients except basil and cheese. Blend for 1 minute, then slowly add basil and blend for 2 minutes. Slowly add cheese and blend an additional 1 minute. Cook one pound of angel hair pasta or fettuccine al dente. Shells or twists pasta work very well also. Blend pesto sauce with pasta and serve immediately. Serves 6 to 8.
VARIATION: Substitute 2/3 cup (4 oz.) fresh spinach for basil - will give a different flavor - just as good!!

Ann Rogers

Pesto Sauce

4 cups washed, torn basil leaves,
(or spinach)
3 cloves garlic
1/2 teaspoon dried basil (if using
spinach leaves)

1/4 cup olive oil
3 tablespoons pine nuts
1/2 cup Parmesan cheese, grated
1/4 teaspoon salt
Pasta (vermicelli)

Puree basil leaves a few at a time in food processor along with garlic and olive oil. Keep adding leaves until all are pureed. Add pine nuts last so that there is some crunch to them. Add cheese and salt. Whirl one more time. Serve over hot pasta cooked al dente (firm).

Pat Brown

Through the years these people from our congregation have gone into the ministry or, are attending seminary:
Roberts (Rob) A. Anderson, Susan Matthews Arnold, David Howard Bonds, Norwood Verne Brown (Woodie), Oris L. (Lee) Holiday, Joel Lucke, Margaret McLellan (married Al Henager), Grady Perryman, Charles W. Roberts (Chuck), Ron Stone, Paul M. Thompson, Thomas Andrew Ulrich, Walter J. Wilkins, III (Jay), and Russell Anderson Wilkins.

Suzy's Stuffed Shells

4 dozen jumbo pasta shells
Olive oil
1 onion, diced (can use more)
1 pound mushrooms, diced
2 medium zucchini, diced
2 cloves garlic, pressed

1 (10 ounce) box frozen spinach
2 pounds cottage or ricotta cheese
1 pound grated Mozzarella cheese
1/2 pound grated Parmesan cheese
1-1/2 quarts tomato sauce (I use
(Paul Newman spaghetti sauce)

Cook shells until just pliable enough to work with. Saute diced onion, garlic, mushrooms, zucchini in a little olive oil. Cook spinach and drain. Combine with cheese and sauteed vegetables; mix all together. Spoon mixture into shells so they are "stuffed." Cover bottom of pan with a generous amount of spaghetti sauce and arrange shells snugly to fill pan, filled side up. Cover entirely with sauce and sprinkle additional Parmesan on top. Bake for 20 minutes or so in a 325-350 degree oven. Serves 16 to 20.

Ann Bartlett Benton

Summer Spaghetti

2 pounds VERY RIPE tomatoes
   (Roma tomatoes are best, if available)
1 large Vidalia onion, finely chopped
2 cloves garlic, finely minced
3 tablespoons finely minced fresh parsley
1 tablespoon fresh basil, minced
1/4 cup extra virgin olive oil

1/2 cup tarragon wine vinegar
Salt to taste
Pepper to taste - black, red and
   white peppers
1 pound spaghetti
Freshly grated Parmesan cheese

Peel and dice the tomatoes. Add the onions, garlic, parsley, basil and olive oil to the tomatoes and season to taste with vinegar, salt and peppers. Set aside. Boil the spaghetti until al dente and drain. Toss the hot spaghetti with the tomato mixture. Serve immediately topped with Parmesan cheese. The tomato mixture may be prepared ahead, but if it is refrigerated, bring it back to room temperature before mixing with the hot spaghetti. Yield: 6 to 8 servings.

Ann Rogers

BREADS

One of the finest evidences of our love and devotion to God is the determination to erect a suitable edifice in which to worship Him. In all the great crises confronting us as a people we have resorted to the house of God for comfort and guidance.

First Presbyterian Church is not only our place of worship, it is the Holy place to which we come with our burdens and problems to face a loving God and a living Christ. Here the dross is refined from our lives, the highest inspirations come and the noblest resolves are made.

— *William Lewis McColgan, D.D.*

In 1950 the needs of the First Presbyterian Church began to change to a residential area worship center. Recognizing the necessity for larger facilities, a Research and Planning Committee was formed with Mr. M. Stanley Cook as chairman. Mr. Harvey Hogg was chairman of the committee for financing and general planning of the new church. Mr. Harold E. Wagoner, nationally recognized church architect, drew the plans of the entire church complex. Completely free of debt, the church was dedicated in the Fellowship Hall on November 15, 1957. The Youth Building was completed in 1971.

Mr. Benny Hatcher of Hatcher Construction Company built the beautiful sanctuary which was dedicated on March 31, 1974. Mr. Arl V. Moore was chairman of the Sanctuary Building Committee. When completed, it was free of any indebtedness. Had it not been for Dr. McColgan, we might never have undertaken the building of this sanctuary. It was his dream for his congregation.

Marcella's Struedel

2 cups milk
1/2 cup shortening
1/2 cup sugar
1 egg
1-1/2 tablespoons yeast
(dissolve in 1/4 cup warm water)
6 cups flour

Topping:
4 tablespoons butter
4 tablespoons shortening
Sugar
Cinnamon
Nutmeg
Raisins
Nuts

Cream sugar and shortening. Add egg and yeast mixture with 3 cups flour in a large bowl. Cover and let rise in a warm place until bubbly. Add remaining flour, put on floured board and knead until it forms a soft ball. Put in greased bowl, cover and let rise until doubled. Half dough and roll on floured surface into a rectangle 1/8" thick. Brush surface with mixed melted butter and shortening. Cover with sugar and sprinkle with cinnamon, nutmeg, raisins and chopped nuts. Starting on long side, roll into log, join ends to make circle. Slash with scissor cuts at even intervals. Bake at 375 degrees for 30 to 40 minutes. Ice if desired. Icing: 1 tablespoon milk, 1/2 teaspoon vanilla or almond flavoring, 1 cup powdered sugar. Makes 2 coffee cakes, each serves 12.

Katherine Love

Apricot-Almond Coffee Cake

1 cup butter (softened)
2 cups sugar
2 eggs
1 cup sour cream
1 teaspoon almond extract
2 cups flour

1 teaspoon baking powder
1/4 teaspoon salt
1 cup sliced almonds
1 (10 ounce) jar apricot
preserves

Cream butter and sugar. Beat in eggs one at a time. Fold in sour cream and almond extract. Sift flour, baking powder and salt and fold in. Place 1/3 of batter in greased and floured bundt pan. Put 1/2 the preserves over the batter and sprinkle with half the almonds. Spoon in rest of batter, add remaining preserves and almonds. Bake at 350 degrees for 1 hour or until done. Cool before turning out of pan. *Do not let the preserves touch edge of pan. They may burn.*

Frances Toney Hall

Easy Coffee Cake

1 package frozen Bridgeford rolls or
   1-1/2 loaves cut in cubes
1 small package butterscotch pudding
1/2 cup sugar

1/2 cup brown sugar
1/2 cup nuts, chopped
1 stick butter or oleo
1-1/2 teaspoons cinnamon

The night before, put rolls in a bundt pan sprayed with Pam. Mix rest of dry ingredients and spread over top of rolls. Slice butter and place over top of mixture. Cover with a towel overnight. In the morning preheat oven to 350 degrees and poke the dough down. Bake 20 to 25 minutes at 350 degrees.

Nena Busby

Fruit Coffee Cake

1 (18-1/4 ounce) package yellow cake
   mix (divided)
1 cup all purpose flour
1 package dry yeast
2/3 cup warm water to activate yeast
2 large eggs
1 (21 ounce) can fruit pie filling
1/3 cup butter or margarine

Glaze:
1 cup powdered sugar
1 tablespoon light corn syrup
2 tablespoons water

Combine and drizzle over cooled cake.

Combine 1-1/2 cups cake mix, flour and yeast. Add warm water, mix till smooth. Stir in eggs. Spread in 9 X 13 pan. Spread pie filling evenly over mixture. Cut butter into remaining cake mix till crumbly. Sprinkle over pie filling. Bake at 350 degrees for 28 to 32 minutes. Cool cake. Drizzle glaze over and cut in squares. Serves 15 to 18.

Jackie Quinn

Blessed is the man that feareth the Lord, that delighteth greatly in His commandments.

Psalms 112:1

31

Sour Cream Coffee Cake

Enough pecan halves for each notch
  in bundt pan
2 sticks butter
2 cups sugar
2 eggs
2 cups cake flour
1 teaspoon baking powder

1/8 teaspoon salt
1 cup sour cream
1/2 teaspoon vanilla
Filling:
1/2 cup chopped pecans
2 tablespoons sugar
1 tablespoon cinnamon

<u>Generously</u> coat a bundt pan with butter or Crisco. Begin placing a pecan half in each notch. Cream 2 sticks butter and 2 cups sugar until smooth. Beat in eggs. Sift together cake flour, baking powder and salt. Add gradually to creamed mixture. Blend well. Fold in 1 cup sour cream and the vanilla. Prepare filling and sprinkle 2 tablespoons in bottom of pan. Cover with 1/3 of cake batter, filling, cake batter, continue until all cake batter is gone, ending with filling on top. Bake at 350 degrees for 55 to 60 minutes or until cake pulls away from pan. Cool 10 minutes in pan before turning out to cake plate. *Given to me by my grandmother, Mrs. T. E. Rhine.*

Ann Brown Turner

Florence's Orange Rolls

2-1/2 cups hot tap water
1/2 cup melted shortening
2 cups flour
2 teaspoons salt
1/3 cup powdered milk

1/2 cup sugar
3 heaping tablespoons fast
  active dry yeast
6 cups flour

In large mixing bowl, add the first 3 ingredients. Mix for 2 minutes with beater. Add next 4 ingredients and continue to blend. Slowly add remaining flour until mixture is blended well. Cover and let double in size. Punch down and roll dough out long and narrow to 1/4 inch in thickness. Spread thin layer of orange frosting over dough. Roll up and cut in 1-1/2 inch rolls. Place in greased pans. Let rise to top of pans and bake at 375 degrees for 18 minutes or until golden brown. Makes 20 rolls.

ORANGE FROSTING:

1 cup soft margarine
2 cups sugar

1 orange

Cream margarine in mixing bowl until soft and smooth. Add sugar, juice from one orange and grated peel of orange. Blend well.

Frances Toney Hall

Tea Ring

Susan Norton's refrigerator roll recipe
1/2 cup sugar
1-1/2 teaspoons cinnamon

Melted butter
Pecans, chopped

Roll 1/2 of roll recipe to 16 X 8 inch rectangle 1/4 inch thick on floured board. Spread melted butter on top of dough. Combine cinnamon and sugar and sprinkle heavily on top of butter. Sprinkle with pecans to taste. Roll lengthwise and seal edge. Cut diagonally halfway through the roll 2 to 3 inches apart. Put ends together to make a circle. Cover and let rise until double in size. Cook at 375 degrees 15 to 20 minutes until lightly browned. 1/2 of roll recipe makes two tea rings. *I put these on cardboard doilies, wrap with plastic wrap and tie with ribbon for Christmas gifts.*

Susan Norton

Butter Babies

2 cups Bisquick
1 cup whipping cream

1/2 stick butter

Combine Bisquick and cream, stirring until well mixed. Turn dough onto surface lightly sprinkled with more Bisquick and pat out to 1/2 inch thickness. Dough will be sticky. Cut with small biscuit cutter. Place butter on a baking sheet with low sides. Melt butter in 350 degree oven. Arrange biscuits on baking sheet not touching and bake at 350 degrees for 15 minutes or until lightly browned. Do not butter. They absorb plenty while cooking. Serves 12.

Frances Toney Hall

Garlic-Cheese Biscuits

3 cups Bisquick
2/3 cup milk
1/2 cup fine shredded Cheddar cheese

1/2 cup margarine, melted
1/4 teaspoon garlic powder

Mix all ingredients together. Beat vigorously for 30 seconds. Drop by tablespoonfuls on lightly greased cookie sheet. Bake at 450 degrees for 8 to 10 minutes. Yields 12 biscuits.

Jane Eddins Stone

Susan's Homemade Biscuits

2 cups sifted flour
4 teaspoons baking powder
1/2 teaspoon salt

4 tablespoons shortening
2/3 to 3/4 cup milk

Sift together dry ingredients. Cut in shortening until like coarse meal. Add milk until batter is moist but not gooey, then knead on floured surface. Pat out about 1 inch thick. Cut with biscuit cutter and place a pat of butter on top of biscuits that have been placed close together in greased pan. Bake at 450 degrees for approximately 12 minutes.

Susan Norton

Nannie's Biscuits

2 cups flour
1 pinch baking soda
2 tablespoons baking powder

1 teaspoon salt
1 tablespoon shortening
1 cup buttermilk

Sift 2 cups of flour, 2 tablespoons of baking powder, 1 teaspoon of salt and very small amount of baking soda together. Combine with 1 tablespoon of shortening or until flour mixture will adhere to itself. You may have to add a teaspoon more of shortening, being sure not to get mixture too "short". Add cup of buttermilk or a bit more until mixture will hold together. Place on floured counter and pat out to 3/4" thick and cut biscuits in any size (I prefer 2"). Place on greased cookie sheet and bake at 450 degrees until brown, about 20 minutes. Serves 10 to 12. *From Helen Zappe, my mother-in-law. Served these at men's breakfast every month.*

Lara Hutt, III

Sweet Potato Biscuits

2 cups flour (self-rising)
2/3 cups granulated sugar

1/2 cup shortening
2 cups mashed sweet potatoes

Preheat oven to 350 degrees. Sift flour. Mix flour and sugar together until well blended. Cut in shortening. Add sweet potatoes. Knead until blended. Pinch off balls and pat out biscuits. Bake at 350 degrees until brown. Makes about 2 dozen.

Brenda Norsworthy

Sweet Milk Biscuits

2 cups sifted flour
2 teaspoons baking powder
1 teaspoon salt

2/3 cup sweet milk
1/3 cup corn or canola oil

Sift dry ingredients into bowl. Combine milk and oil and pour in all at once. Mix with fork to make soft dough. Place on waxed paper and knead lightly 10 times or until smooth. Pat out to 1/2 inch thickness or roll between 2 squares waxed paper. Remove top paper, cut biscuits with unfloured 2 inch cutter. Place on ungreased cookie sheet close together with sides touching for soft biscuits or well apart for crusty biscuits. Bake at 450 degrees 12 to 15 minutes. *Can increase milk to 3/4 cup and drop dough by spoonfuls onto cookie sheet. Easy and quick - I like them crusty.*

Frances Toney Hall

Apricot Bread

1 cup dried apricots
1 cup sugar
1/4 cup shortening or oleo
1 egg
2 cups sifted flour
2 teaspoons baking powder
1 teaspoon salt (or less)

1/4 teaspoon baking soda
1/4 cup water reserved from
   soaking apricots
1/2 cup orange juice
1/2 cup walnuts or pecans,
   chopped

Cut up apricots in small pieces and soak in warm water to cover for at least 15 minutes. Drain and reserve 1/4 cup of the water. Cream sugar and shortening. Add egg and beat well. Sift flour, baking powder, salt and baking soda together. Mix the 1/4 cup water and orange juice. Add alternately the flour mixture and the liquid. Then stir in apricots and nuts. Put in well greased 9 inch loaf pan and let stand 20 minutes. Bake at 375 degrees for 60 minutes or until done and slightly browned.

Marion Ryland Love

Blessed is he that shall eat bread in the kingdom of God.

Luke 14:15

Apricot-Pumpkin Bread

1-1/2 cups pumpkin
1 cup sugar
3/4 cup oil
3 large eggs
2-1/4 cups flour
1-1/2 teaspoons baking soda
1-1/2 teaspoons baking powder
3/4 teaspoon cinnamon

3/4 teaspoon nutmeg
3/4 teaspoon salt
1 (3.4 ounce) instant vanilla
  pudding mix
1-1/2 cups dried apricots,
  (6 ounces), chopped
1-1/2 cups chopped walnuts,
  (6 ounces)

Combine pumpkin, sugar, oil, eggs, mix until blended. Combine in separate bowl flour, salt, soda, baking powder and spices. Add to pumpkin mix and blend. Fold in vanilla pudding mix. Stir in chopped apricots and nuts. Put mixture into two greased and floured 8-1/2 X 4-1/2 X 2-1/2 inch bread pans. Bake 1 hour at 350 degrees. Check with tester after 50 minutes. Cool 10 minutes. Remove from pans. Slice when cool. May be frozen up to 3 months. Makes 2 loaves. If using smaller pans (7-1/2 X 3-1/2 X 2), will make 3 loaves. Reduce cooking time.

Grace Mebane

Banana Nut Bread

1/2 cup shortening
1 cup sugar
2 eggs
2 cups flour
1 teaspoon baking soda

1/8 teaspoon salt
1 cup mashed banana (about 3)
1/2 cup chopped walnuts or
  pecans

Cream shortening and sugar. Add eggs and beat well. Sift flour, baking soda and salt together and add alternately with mashed bananas. Stir in nuts. Bake in 350 degree oven in two greased 6 X 3 loaf pans for 45 to 60 minutes. *Can be made in mini loaf pans and used for gifts.*

Mary Snavely

Bishop Bread

3 eggs, well beaten
1 cup sugar
1-1/2 cups sifted flour
1-1/2 teaspoons baking powder
1/4 teaspoon salt

1 (6 ounce) chocolate chips
2 cups chopped nuts
1 cup chopped dates
1 cup candied cherries

Beat eggs and sugar. Sift flour, baking powder and salt. Add dates and cherries to flour mixture, then add nuts and chips. Fold into egg and sugar combination. Cook in 9" loaf pan lined with wax paper. Bake 325 degrees for 1 hour.

Eleanor B. Joerdan

Cranberry Bread

2 cups all-purpose flour, sifted
1 cup sugar
1/2 teaspoon salt
1-1/2 teaspoons baking powder
1/2 teaspoon baking soda
1 cup walnuts, coarsely chopped

1 cup whole raw cranberries
2 tablespoons oil, add hot water
  to make 3/4 cup
1 tablespoon grated orange peel
1/2 cup orange juice
1 egg, slightly beaten

Sift dry ingredients together. Combine walnuts and cranberries with 1/2 cup dry ingredients. Put oil in measuring cup and add hot water to make 3/4 cup. Add orange peel and juice to hot water. Stir into flour mixture with egg. Mix just enough to moisten. Gently stir in walnuts and cranberries. Grease and flour two small loaf pans or 1 large pan. Bake 1 hour at 325 degrees. Remove from pans and cool completely. Wrap in foil overnight before slicing. Freezes well.

Grace Hoffman

Dilly Casserole Bread

2-1/2 to 3 cups flour
2 tablespoons sugar
1 tablespoon instant minced onion
2 teaspoons dill seed
1-1/4 teaspoons salt
1/4 teaspoon soda
1 package dry yeast

1 cup creamed cottage cheese
1/4 cup water
1 tablespoon butter (margarine)
1 egg
Butter, softened
Coarse salt

Combine 1 cup flour, sugar, onion, dill seed, salt, soda and dry yeast. Heat cottage cheese, water, and butter until warm. Add egg and warm liquid to flour mixture. Blend at lowest speed in mixer until moistened. Beat 3 minutes at medium speed. By hand stir in remaining flour to form a stiff dough. Cover. Let rise until double in size (about 1 hour). Stir down batter. Turn into well greased 8 inch round casserole. Cover and let rise (3o to 45 minutes). Bake at 350 degrees for 35 to 40 minutes or until done and brown. Brush with softened butter and sprinkle with salt. *This was a Pillsbury "bake-off" recipe winner years ago. This is the original recipe and we are repeating it by request - very good.*

Cookbook Committee

37

Eggnog Christmas Bread

3 cups flour, sifted
1 cup sugar
1 tablespoon baking powder
1/2 teaspoon salt
1 teaspoon ground nutmeg
1-1/2 cups commercial egg nog

1 egg
1/4 cup melted butter
3 cups chopped pecans
3/4 cups chopped, mixed,
  candied fruit

Combine dry ingredients; add eggnog, egg and butter mixing well. Stir in pecans and fruit. Spoon batter into a greased and floured 9 X 5 X 3 loaf pan. Bake at 350 degrees for about 60 minutes or until bread tests done. Do not over-cook.

Frances Toney Hall

Pumpkin Bread

1 pound can pumpkin
2/3 cup milk
1 cup oil
4 whole eggs
3 cups sugar
3 cups sifted flour
1/2 teaspoon salt

1 teaspoon cinnamon
1 teaspoon nutmeg
1/4 teaspoon cayenne pepper
3 teaspoons baking soda
1/2 cup chopped dates
1/2 cup chopped pecans

Combine pumpkin, milk, oil, eggs and sugar. Sift flour with salt, nutmeg, cinnamon, pepper and baking soda. Stir into pumpkin mixture. Fold in dates and pecans. Grease and flour bread pans Fill 1/2 full and bake at 350 degrees for about 1 hour or until bread tests done. Cool slightly in pans, then turn out on rack to finish cooling. Makes 2 to 3 loaves.

Nancy Ryland Williamson

Strawberry Bread

1-1/2 cups flour
1/2 teaspoon soda
1/4 teaspoon salt
1 tablespoon ground cinnamon
1 cup sugar

2 eggs, beaten
1/2 cup vegetable oil
1 (10 ounce) package frozen,
  sliced strawberries, undrained
1/2 cup walnuts, chopped

Combine the flour, soda, salt, cinnamon and sugar and mix well. Combine the eggs, oil and thawed strawberries. Add dry ingredients and nuts; mix. Grease and flour a 9 X 5 X 3 loaf pan. Bake at 350 degrees for 60 minutes or until done. Makes 1 loaf.

Betty Perryman

Walnut Delight Bread

3/4 cup brown sugar
1/2 stick oleo
1 egg
2 cups sifted flour
1 teaspoon soda
1/4 teaspoon salt

1/3 cup frozen orange juice
    concentrate, thawed
1 (8-1/4 ounce) can crushed
    pineapple in heavy syrup
1/2 cup chopped walnuts

Cream the sugar and oleo. Add egg. Sift the flour, soda and salt together. Alternately add the orange juice and dry ingredients to the creamed mixture. Stir in pineapple with juice and walnuts. Put in greased loaf pan and bake at 350 degrees for 50 to 60 minutes. Cool slightly on rack and remove from pan. Makes 1 loaf.

Mrs. John Ingram

Betty's Hot Water Cornbread

2 cups white corn meal
1 heaping teaspoon salt

2 tablespoons flour
2-1/2 cups boiling water

Mix corn meal, salt and flour. Pour boiling water over mixture until all the meal is wet. Wet hands and shape into pones. Cook six minutes in deep hot oil.

Janie Buckley

Broccoli Cornbread

2 boxes of Jiffy corn muffin mix
2 sticks of oleo, melted
4 eggs, beaten
1 medium onion, chopped fine

1 (10 ounce) package frozen,
    chopped broccoli, thawed
1 (8 ounce) cottage cheese

Mix all ingredients well. Cook in greased 9 X 13 pan 30 to 35 minutes at 350 degrees. Serves 16.

Betty Bell

Mexican Cornbread

3 cups cornbread mix
2-1/2 cups milk
1/2 cup vegetable oil
3 eggs, beaten
1 medium onion, chopped
2 tablespoons sugar
1 cup creamed corn

1-1/2 cups grated Cheddar
cheese
1/4 pound cooked bacon,
crumbled
Chopped jalapeno peppers,
to taste

Combine mix and milk. Add all other ingredients and mix well. Pour in 3 greased 8 inch round pans. Bake at 400 degrees for about 35 minutes. Freezes very well. Serves 6 to 8. *I use frozen, chopped onions and real bacon bits to save time.*

Jackie Quinn

Mexican Cornbread

1 cup self-rising cornmeal
1 (4 ounce) can green chilies
1/4 cup Wesson oil

3 eggs, beaten
1 (8 ounce) carton sour cream
1 teaspoon salt

Combine all ingredients and cook in greased muffin tins or small iron skillet. Bake at 350 - 375 degrees until brown. Serves 6.

In memory of Rose Cook Hutt

Cornbread Dressing Patties

2 cups chopped celery
3 cups chopped onion
1/2 pound butter
2 (9 inch) pans baked cornbread
4-6 slices white bread, toasted

2-3 cups chicken or turkey broth
2 eggs beaten
1/4 teaspoon sage
1/3 cup chopped fresh parsley
Salt and pepper to taste

Saute onion and celery in butter until limp and yellow. Crumble cornbread into mixture and add torn pieces of toast. Add broth slowly, 1 cup at a time, until mixture is moist. Add beaten eggs, sage and salt and pepper. Lightly grease a large cookie sheet. Shape dressing into 3 inch patties (approximately 24-30) and bake at 375 degrees until lightly brown and crispy. Serves 8. *Nice way to serve, surrounding turkey on platter.*

Bettye Hutt

Billy's Hush Puppies

1 cup flour
1 cup white cornmeal
3 teaspoons baking powder
1 teaspoon salt
1 tablespoon sugar

1 egg
3/4 cup sweet milk
1 medium onion, chopped
1/2 pound Cheddar cheese,
   grated

Mix dry ingredients together. Add egg, sweet milk, onion and cheese. Form into small balls. Drop in hot fat and cook until golden.

Jane Eddins Stone

Bran Muffins

15 ounce box Raisin Bran
3 cups sugar
5 cups flour
5 teaspoons soda
2 heaping teaspoons nutmeg
2 heaping teaspoons cloves
2 heaping teaspoons cinnamon

3 teaspoons vanilla
4 beaten eggs
1 cup oil
1 quart buttermilk
1 cup white & dark raisins,
   mixed
1 cup pecans, chopped

Mix dry ingredients together. Add buttermilk, oil, eggs and vanilla. Fold in raisins and pecans. Bake in greased muffin tins in 400 degree oven for 15 minutes or until edges are light brown. Batter may be kept in refrigerator and cooked as needed. Makes about 3 dozen.

Joan B. Thompson

Fudge Muffins

1 cup margarine
2 (1 ounce) squares unsweetened
   baking chocolate
2 cups sugar
1-1/2 cups flour

4 eggs
1-1/2 teaspoon vanilla
1/2 teaspoon salt
1 cup chopped nuts (optional)

Melt the margarine and chocolate in a 1 quart saucepan, stirring to blend well; remove from heat. Add the sugar, flour, eggs, vanilla and salt; mix well. Stir in nuts if used. Spoon into greased muffin cups. Bake at 325 degrees for 25 to 30 minutes or until a toothpick inserted in the center comes out clean; do not overbake. Remove immediately to a wire rack to cool. Makes 1 dozen.

Frances Toney Hall

Graham Cracker Muffins

1 cup sugar
1 cup graham cracker crumbs
1 teaspoon baking powder
3 eggs, beaten

Large pinch of salt
1-1/2 cups raisins
1-1/2 cups chopped pecans

Lightly mix together sugar, graham cracker crumbs, baking powder, and salt. Add beaten eggs. Fold in raisins and nuts. Put in mini-muffin pans. Bake at 350 degrees for 15 to 20 minutes. *Freezes well; recipe doubles easily.* Yield 3 dozen.

Corinne Hunter

Heavenly Muffins

1 (8 ounce) package Philadelphia
  cream cheese

1/2 cup margarine
1 cup self-rising flour

Beat cream cheese and margarine at medium speed of mixer, about 2 minutes or until creamy. Gradually add flour beating at low speed until just blended. Spoon dough into miniature muffin pans filling them 2/3 full, or refrigerate dough for up to 3 days and then bake. Bake at 400 degrees for 17 minutes or until golden brown. Serve immediately. Makes 24 muffins.

Jane Eddins Stone

Melba's Muffins

1 stick butter
1 cup sour cream

2 cups Pioneer Biscuit Mix

Melt butter and mix with sour cream and biscuit mix. Drop by teaspoons in small greased muffin tins. Bake at 350 degrees for 15 minutes or until light brown. Makes 36 muffins.

Frances Toney Hall

Blessed is the man whose strength is in Thee.

Psalms 84:5

Oatmeal Muffins

1 cup quick-cooking oats
1 cup buttermilk
1 cup flour
1 teaspoon baking powder
1/2 teaspoon salt

1/2 teaspoon soda
1 egg, slightly beaten
1/3 cup brown sugar
1/3 cup cooking oil

Soak oats in buttermilk for 15 minutes or longer. Sift together flour, baking powder, salt and soda; stir into oat mixture. Add egg, brown sugar and oil; stir until just blended. Fill muffin pans 2/3 full and bake at 400 degrees for 20 to 25 minutes. *Not a sweet muffin - a dinner muffin.* Yields 12 large muffins.

Mrs. Collins Andrews, Jr.,
President, Women of the Church 1963-64

Sausage Muffins

1 pound hot sausage
1/2 cup chopped onion
1 egg, beaten
1 tablespoon parsley
2/3 cup milk
1/2 teaspoon hot sauce

1/2 cup Parmesan cheese
1 cup grated Swiss cheese
1 teapoon salt
2 cups Bisquick
1/4 cup mayonnaise

Saute sausage and onion and drain. Mix all other ingredients. Add sausage and onions. Bake in greased muffin tins at 400 degrees for 20 to 25 minutes.

Janie Buckley

Popovers

1 cup milk
2 eggs
1/4 teaspoon salt

1 tablespoon melted margarine
1 cup flour

Mix first 4 ingredients and then stir in flour. Do not beat. Fill greased Pyrex cups 2/3 full. Bake in 450 degree oven for 20 minutes and turn oven down to 350 degrees for 15 minutes or until brown. Do not open oven door. Makes 6.

In memory of Virginia Walker,
President, Women of the Church 1955-56

The Best Blueberry Muffins

1/2 cup butter or margarine, softened
1 cup sugar
2 large eggs
1 teaspoon vanilla
2 teaspoons baking powder
1/4 teaspoon salt
2 cups flour
1/2 cup milk

2-1/2 cups fresh blueberries
or 1 (12 ounce) package
frozen blueberries

Topping:
1 tablespoon sugar mixed with
1/4 teaspoon nutmeg

Heat oven to 375 degrees; grease 24 regular size muffin cups or line with paper muffin cups. Cream butter, add sugar and beat until fluffy. Add eggs one at a time beating after each addition. Beat in vanilla, baking powder and salt. With a rubber spatula fold in half the flour, then half the milk. Repeat with remaining flour and milk. Fold in blueberries either fresh or frozen. Spoon into muffin cups. Sprinkle with topping. Bake 25 to 30 minutes until golden brown.

Joan B. Thompson

Oatmeal Pancakes

1/2 cup all-purpose flour
1/2 cup quick-cooking oats
3/4 cup buttermilk
1/4 cup milk
1 tablespoon sugar

2 tablespoons vegetable oil
1 teaspoon baking powder
1/2 teaspoon baking soda
1/2 teaspoon salt
1 egg

Whisk all ingredients in a medium bowl until smooth. Grease a heated griddle. For each pancake, pour about 1/3 cup of batter onto the hot griddle. Cook until pancakes are puffed and dry around edges. Turn and cook other side until golden brown. *Blueberries can be sprinkled on pancake before serving.* Serves 2 to 3.

Diane Fisk

In 1955, the Women of the Church exchanged Green Stamps for a silver service. They also got their first deep freeze, a present from Mrs. Fred Ingram.

Pancakes

1-1/4 cups flour
2 teaspoons baking powder
1/2 teaspoon salt
1 teaspoon sugar

2 eggs, separated
1 scant cup milk
2 tablespoons melted butter

Sift dry ingredients. Mix well beaten egg yolks and milk and add melted butter. Beat egg whites and fold in. Cook on griddle until small bubbles form, turn and cook other side a minute or so.

Mrs. Grover Roberts

Raised Waffles

1/2 cup lukewarm water
1 package yeast
2 cups lukewarm milk
1/2 cup butter
1 teaspoon salt

1 teaspoon sugar
2 cups flour
2 eggs
Pinch of soda

Put in large mixing bowl the lukewarm water and yeast. Let stand five minutes; add the lukewarm milk, butter, salt and sugar. Beat in the flour. Cover the bowl and let stand overnight or at least 8 hours (not in refrigerator). When time to cook waffles add the eggs and soda. Beat well. Batter will be thin. Cook in waffle iron. Makes 6 large waffles.

Mildred Andrews Bradley

Anne's Spoon Bread

3/4 cups corn meal
1 teaspoon salt
2 tablespoons butter
1 cup boiling water

2 eggs, separated
1/2 cup sweet milk
2 teaspoons baking powder

Mix meal, salt and butter and pour in boiling water. Beat well. Add egg yolks well beaten. Add milk and baking powder. Beat whites until stiff and fold in. Pour mixture into greased baking dish and bake in 350 degree oven for about 40 minutes. Serve hot with a spoon.

Anne Huff Monroe

Howell Spoon Bread

2 cups milk
3/4 cup white corn meal
1/2 stick butter

1 teaspoon salt
1 teaspoon sugar
4 eggs, separated

Lightly boil milk and stir in corn meal. Cook over medium heat, stirring until mushy. Remove from heat and add butter, salt and sugar. When melted and cool, beat in egg yolks. Whip egg whites until stiffened and fold in mixture. Pour into greased Pyrex casserole. Bake at 350 degrees for 25 minutes until slightly brown on top. Serves 4 to 6. *Delicious with fish.*

Shirley Lynch

Spoon Bread

2 cups milk
3/4 cup white corn meal
3/4 teaspoon salt

1/2 stick unsalted butter
4 eggs, separated

In large, heavy saucepan scald milk. Moisten corn meal well with water and add to warm milk. Add salt. Cook to a "mushy" consistency, stirring often. Remove from heat. Add butter and stir until melted. Beat egg yolks slightly. Beat egg whites until soft peaks form. Add egg yolks to cooled corn meal mixture and stir. Fold in egg whites carefully lifting from the bottom and taking care to preserve the air trapped in beaten whites. Bake in a 350 degree oven for 45 minutes in an 8 cup souffle pan. Spoon bread will be puffed and beautifully browned. Serve with butter. Serves 4. *This has been a favorite in the Martin family forever. Your family will love it with fried fish.*

In memory of Mrs. Rufus Martin (Helen)

Bruschetta

French bread, sliced 1" thick
1/4 cup extra virgin olive oil
2 cloves of crushed garlic
3 cups chopped tomato pulp

5 tablespoons of fresh basil
1 tablespoon minced garlic
1/4 cup olive oil
Salt and pepper to taste

Rub one side with olive oil and garlic and toast; mix remaining tomato, basil, garlic, oil and seasonings and marinate 45 minutes. Spoon on toasted bread and let stand 15 minutes. Serves 6.

Bettye Hutt

French Bread

2-1/2 cups warm water
2 fresh packages dry yeast
2 tablespoons sugar

1 teaspoon salt
7 cups all purpose flour in all
2 egg whites

Mix first 4 ingredients and stir until well dissolved. Add 5 cups flour and mix with a spoon until you have a sticky glop. Stir in 1 more cup flour. Place on floured surface and knead with hands, adding more flour as needed, probably about 1 cup. Do this a minimum of 10 minutes. If you use a mixer and dough hook, it will take more flour and change the texture of the bread. Place in greased bowl, cover and let rise. Beat the dough down and pour out. Knead and roll out into elongated loaves. Place in greased French bread pans and cover tops with a mixture of egg white and water, using a brush. Let rise. Bake at 400 degrees for 10 minutes, then 350 degrees for 30 minutes or until done. Cool on racks.

Wayne Buckley

Parmesan Garlic Bread

1 large loaf French Bread
2 sticks butter
3 cloves garlic, chopped
1 cup Parmesan cheese

1/2 teaspoon salt
1/4 teaspoon red pepper
Dill weed

Put all ingredients except bread in food processor. Process until creamy. Spread on bread which is halved lengthwise. Slice in diagonal slices, but keep loaf halves intact. Bake until very hot and sprinkle with dill weed. Serves 8.

Janie Buckley

Stuffed French Bread

1 stick margarine
1-1/2 teaspoons garlic powder
1 small can chopped green chilies

1/4 lb. Monterey Jack cheese, grated
1/2 cup mayonnaise
1 loaf French bread

Soften oleo and mix with garlic powder and green chilies. Mix cheese and mayonnaise separately. Split loaf of bread longways. Spread the oleo, garlic and chilies on one half and the cheese and mayonnaise mixture on the other half. Put loaf back together. Wrap in foil and heat at 400 degrees until bread is crispy and filling is very hot and cheese is melted. Slice and serve.

Cookbook Committee

Monkey Bread

2 packages dry yeast
1 cup lukewarm water
1 cup shortening
1 cup boiling water
3/4 cup sugar

1-1/2 teaspoons salt
2 eggs
6 cups of flour
2 sticks melted oleo

Mix yeast with 1 cup lukewarm water. Mix shortening in 1 cup boiling water. When cold, add to yeast mixture. Combine with sugar, salt, eggs and flour. Let rise until doubled in size. Knead and pinch off in egg-size balls. Dip in melted oleo. Put in 2 bundt pans or deep pans lightly greased and let rise until doubled. Cook at 350 degrees for 30 to 40 minutes. Makes 2 pans.

Jane Alexander Keathley

Pull-Apart Bread

1 cup milk
1-1/2 sticks butter
1-1/2 teaspoons salt
1/2 cup sugar
1 package yeast

1/4 cup warm water
1 teaspoon sugar
3 eggs, beaten
4 cups sifted flour
2 sticks butter
Sesame seed

Scald one cup milk. Add the 1-1/2 sticks butter, salt and sugar. Let cool. Add the yeast which has been dissolved in the 1/4 cup lukewarm water with the 1 teaspoon sugar. Add the beaten eggs and flour. Cover and let rise until double in bulk. Punch down and refrigerate overnight. Melt 2 sticks butter and grease three 8" round cake pans. Take 1/3 of dough and roll out 6" square & 1/2" thick on floured wax paper. Cut in 1/2" strips. Dip strip in butter and wind around finger. Center in pan. Dip other strips in butter placing them around pan. Sprinkle with sesame seeds and let rise 2 hours. Bake at 350 degrees for 15 minutes. Can be wrapped in foil and frozen. Before serving remove from pan, place on folded foil and bake 15 minutes at 350 degrees. Brush with melted butter.

Ann Benton

Edward Howell Smith was the first baby baptized in the present church on July 1, 1957.

Whole Wheat Bread

2 packages yeast
1/4 cup warm water
1/2 cup honey
2-3/4 cups water
1 tablespoon salt

7 to 8 cups whole wheat flour
(or use combination you
desire)
1/2 cup oil or melted butter
or margarine

Dissolve yeast in 1/4 cup warm water and let sit till bubbly. Put honey in a bowl and add yeast mixture, rest of water, salt and 3 to 4 cups of flour, and the oil or butter. Beat for 7 minutes with wooden spoon. Add rest of flour and knead till smooth - at least 10 minutes. Let rise in large bowl till doubled, then punch down and shape into 2 loaves. Place in greased standard size loaf pans; let rise till double again. Bake at 350 degrees for 45 minutes or so, till browned on top and done. Brush with melted margarine and cool on rack. Can make into great cinnamon rolls too.

Pat Lile

Bran Bud Rolls

1 cup shortening
3/4 cup sugar
1 cup All Bran Buds
1-1/2 teaspoons salt
1 cup boiling water

1 cup lukewarm water
2 packages yeast
2 eggs
6 cups flour

Mix shortening, sugar, All Brand Buds and salt. Pour 1 cup boiling water over this and let set for a few minutes. Dissolve yeast in a cup of lukewarm water and add to shortening mixture. Add eggs (slightly beaten) and flour. Mix well. Let rise double; pinch off enough dough for one roll, press flat then fold in half. Let rise until double in size and bake in 350 degree oven for 15 minutes. Makes 4 dozen rolls.

Sue Deneke

Mrs. John Spears, a member of the church who lived in a beautiful home at Fourth & Walnut, had a greenhouse and the church at Fifth & Walnut always had fresh flowers on Sunday morning.

Mother's Wonderful Rolls

2 packages dry yeast
1/4 cup lukewarm water
1 cup sugar plus 1 tablespoon
1 cup milk

1-1/2 teaspoons salt
1/2 cup butter
5 cups sifted flour
3 eggs, well beaten

Dissolve yeast in lukewarm water with one tablespoon sugar. Combine milk with remaining sugar and butter in large bowl. Beat until sugar is dissolved. Add the yeast mixture, three cups flour and the salt. Mix well by hand. Add the eggs and the remaining two cups flour. Mix well. Let rise until double. Roll out on floured board and cut in desired shapes. Dip in butter and fold over and let rise again. Bake in 400 degree oven about 10 minutes. *Sinfully delicious!*

Mari Cousins Eilbott,
Co-Moderator 1995-96

Refrigerator Rolls

2 packages dry yeast
1 cup warm water
1 cup shortening
1 cup sugar
1 cup boiling water

2 eggs
6 cups unsifted flour
1 tablespoon salt
Melted butter

Mix yeast and warm water. Cream shortening and sugar in large bowl. Add boiling water. Beat the eggs until thick and add to shortening and sugar mixture. Stir in lukewarm yeast mixture. Sift in flour and salt and mix well. Tightly cover bowl and set in refrigerator overnight or until needed - will keep a week. To use - roll out dough to 1/2" thickness and cut with biscuit cutter. Place small bits of butter on round, fold over and pinch edge. Place close together on greased pan. Brush with butter and let rise for 2 or 3 hours. Bake in 400 degree oven 10 minutes or until brown. Makes 5 to 6 dozen rolls.

Susan Norton

Angel Biscuits

5 cups unsifted flour
1/2 cup sugar
3 teaspoons baking powder
1 teaspoon soda
2 teaspoons salt

1 cup shortening
1 package dry yeast
2 tablespoons warm water
2 cups buttermilk
1 stick melted butter

Sift dry ingredients together. Cut in shortening. Dissolve yeast in warm water; combine with buttermilk and dry ingredients. Mix well. Turn on floured board (adding flour if necessary). Roll out and cut with biscuit cutter; dip in melted butter. Place on greased baking sheet and bake at 400 degrees for 15 minutes.

Sue Smith

SOUPS and SANDWICHES

Katherine W. Ramage 1986

The gold Budding Cross behind the pulpit was given in memory of Mrs. Adam B. Robinson, Sr. by her family.

The carvings on the left side of the cross symbolize the following:

Alpha — *Beginning*

Griffin — *Incarnation*

Pelican — *Atonement*

Phoenix — *Resurrection*

The carvings on the right side of the cross symbolize the following:

Omega — *End*

Cock — *Passion*

Peacock — *Eternal Life*

Eagle — *Spread of Gospel*

Bean Soup

2 cups beans (dry, mixed)
1 teaspoon salt
2 quarts water
Ham bone, or 1 pound of ham, diced
1 (10 ounce) can Ro-Tel

1 large onion, diced
1 clove garlic, minced
1 pound Polish sausage, sliced thick
Cayenne pepper, if needed

Wash beans, cover with water, add salt and soak overnight or bring to a boil for 5 minutes, remove from heat and soak 1 hour. Drain. Place beans in the 2 quarts water, add ham and simmer for 3 hours. Add Ro-Tel, onion, garlic, sausage and simmer for 1 more hour. Serves 8 to 10.

Leila Wilkins O'Keefe

Black Bean Soup

1/4 cup bacon grease or oil
2 medium onions, chopped
4-5 garlic cloves, minced
2 cans beef broth
2 cans chicken broth
1 pound dry black beans, rinsed
1 ham hock with meat
2 tablespoons cumin

2 teaspoons oregano
1 teaspoon thyme
1/4 teaspoon ground cloves
3 pickled jalapenos - sliced
2 cups water
1/2 cup sour cream
1/2 cup green onions

Saute onions and garlic in oil until soft. Add beef and chicken broth, beans, ham and seasonings. Add water, bring to a boil and simmer for 2 hours. Puree half of mixture in blender then return to pot. Garnish with sour cream and onions when serving. Serves 6. *Keeps several days.*

Bettye Hutt

Broccoli Cheese Soup

3 tablespoons butter
1/2 cup onion, chopped
2 cans chicken broth
1 (5 ounce) package thin noodles
2 (10 ounce) boxes chopped broccoli, cooked

1 teaspoon salt
Pepper to taste
3-4 cups milk, heated
1 pound American cheese, cubed

Saute onions in butter. Add broth and bring to a boil. Add noodles and cook 5 minutes. Mix in broccoli, salt, pepper and milk. Add cheese and stir until completely melted. Serves 6 to 8. *May be frozen.*

Grace Hoffman

Broccoli Cheese Soup

3 tablespoons butter
1 onion, chopped
2 packages chopped frozen broccoli, thawed
2 cans cream of chicken soup

1 can cream of celery soup
4 soup cans milk
1 (8 ounce) jar jalapeno Cheese Whiz

Saute onions lightly in butter. Add remaining ingredients. Simmer for 30 to 40 minutes. Stir well. Serves 10.

Corinne Hunter

Cabbage Soup

2 pounds ground round
3 tablespoons butter
1 large onion, chopped
2 stalks celery, chopped
1 head cabbage, chopped

2 packages Italian dressing mix
1 large can V-8
1 can Ro-Tel, diced
1 can (15 ounce) tomato sauce
2 cups pinto beans, drained

Brown meat with butter, onion and celery. Boil cabbage 15 minutes then drain. Combine all ingredients and bring to a boil. Simmer for 1 hour. Serves 12.

Ann Brown Turner

Cheese Vegetable Soup

1 pound stew meat
1 pound lean ground beef
3 strips bacon, browned
2 potatoes, cubed
4 carrots, cut in 1 inch pieces
1 large onion, chopped
1 can tomatoes
1 can green beans

1 can English peas
1 can yellow corn
1 can white corn
3/4 pound Velveeta cheese, chunked
Salt and pepper to taste
Tabasco to taste

Brown the stew meat and ground beef together. Add the bacon, potatoes, carrots and onions. Add enough water to cover well. Cook over medium heat 40 to 45 minutes. Add next five ingredients and cook for 1 hour. Twenty minutes before serving, add the cheese, salt, pepper and Tabasco. Serves 10 to 12.

Jackie Perryman Hart

Chicken Taco Soup

1 pound chicken breasts, skinned
2 tablespoons olive oil
1 onion, chopped
1 clove garlic, minced
1 package taco seasoning
1 can stewed tomatoes
1 (4 ounce) can green chilies, chopped

1/2 cup chicken broth
1 (8 ounce) jar green chili salsa
1 can black beans
1 can jalapeno pinto beans,
  undrained
Corn chips
Sharp Cheddar cheese, grated

Cover chicken in water and season to taste. Boil chicken and reserve broth. Cut chicken into bite size pieces. Saute onions and garlic in olive oil then add taco seasoning. Add chicken and next six ingredients. Additional chicken broth can be added if needed. Heat thoroughly. Top with corn chips and cheese before serving. Serves 4.

Cathy Kennedy

Chicken Vegetable Soup

1 whole chicken
1 quart water
4 tablespoons Cavender's seasoning
2 onions, chopped
2 bell peppers, chopped
5-6 stalks celery, chopped
1/2 pound carrots, sliced
3-4 cups baby lima beans

3-4 cups whole kernel corn
3 large cans tomatoes, chopped
2-3 cans green beans
1 package frozen okra
1 cup brown rice
Several dashes Worcestershire
  sauce

Boil chicken in water with seasoning until tender. Remove skin and bone and chop into large pieces. Add raw vegetables (onions, celery, bell pepper and carrots) to chicken broth and rice and cook 30 minutes. Last of all add chicken and remaining ingredients. Cook a little longer. Makes about 2 gallons.

Eloise Fitts

The memory of the just is blessed.

Proverbs 10:7

Cold Beet Borscht

1 can beef bouillon
1 cup beet juice
1 cup buttermilk
1 pint sour cream
1 can beets, sliced

1 cucumber, sliced
3 green onions, sliced
1 teaspoon salt
1 teaspoon sugar
Juice of 1/2 lemon

Blend together in a bowl the first 4 ingredients. Add the remaining ingredients. Chill. Nice garnished with fresh dill weed. Serves 4.

Pat Brown

Cold Cucumber Soup

1 large cucumber, peeled and seeded
12 ounces cream cheese
3 or 4 green onions with 3" tops
1/2 bunch fresh parsley, stems removed

3 tablespoons sour cream
3/4 teaspoon salt
White pepper
Heavy or light cream

Cut cucumber, cheese and onions into 1" pieces and place in food processor with parsley, sour cream and salt. Blend for 6 seconds. Scrape sides and blend until a smooth texture is achieved. Refrigerate for 4 hours. Thin with cream to desired consistency. Pour into chilled bowls and sprinkle with white pepper. *Shared by Agnes Hughes.* Serves 4.

Mildred Andrews Bradley

Cold Orange Tomato Soup

2 cups tomato soup
2 cups orange juice
1/2 cup white wine
Juice of 1 lemon

1 teaspoon sugar
1-1/2 teaspoons salt
3 dashes cayenne pepper
Chopped parsley

Combine first seven ingredients. Serve very cold, sprinkled with parsley.

Monte Atkins

Crabmeat Bisque

4 tablespoons butter
1/2 small onion
1 pound lump crabmeat
4 tablespoons flour

3 or 4 cups chicken broth
3 or 4 cups Half and Half
1/2 cup sherry
Salt and pepper to taste

Saute finely chopped onion in butter. Add crabmeat and cool. In another pot add flour, chicken broth, Half and Half and sherry (a little at a time) stirring constantly so it will be smooth. Add sauteed onion and crabmeat. Heat for 10 more minutes stirring constantly. Season with salt and pepper. Serves 4 to 6.

Bettye Hutt

Hearty Vegetable Soup

3 quarts water
2 packages dried onion soup mix
2 pounds cubed chuck roast
1 (16 ounce) can tomato sauce
1 can tomatoes, diced
1-1/2 teaspoons marjoram
1-1/2 teaspoons basil
1-1/2 teaspoons pepper

1 teaspoon garlic powder
1 tablespoon salt
2 bay leaves
1-1/2 teaspoons parsley flakes
1 large bag frozen mixed
    vegetables
1 box frozen cut okra
Parmesan cheese, grated

Bring water with meat and onion soup mix to a boil and simmer 30 to 40 minutes. Add other ingredients except frozen vegetables and cook 15 minutes. Add frozen vegetables and cook 2 to 2-1/2 hours. Sprinkle Parmesan cheese over top before serving. Serves 12.

In memory of Cherry Higgins

Heavenly Three Bean Soup

1 can red beans
1 can great northern beans
1 can black beans
1 medium onion, chopped
1 can tomatoes, chopped

1 teaspoon sugar
1 cup water
4 dashes Tabasco
Salt to taste

Combine ingredients. Bring to a boil, reduce heat and simmer for 45 minutes. Serves 6.

Donald Angus Tatman

Homemade Chicken Noodle Soup

1 whole chicken
Salt, pepper and garlic to taste
1 large onion, chopped
5 carrots, sliced
1 package vegetable soup mix

5 medium potatoes, chunked
1 package wide egg noodles
1 can green beans, drained
1 can corn, undrained
1 can chicken broth

Cook chicken with salt, pepper, garlic and onion. Simmer 1 to 1-1/2 hours, then debone. Cook carrots in this broth for 30 minutes. Add vegetable soup mix, potatoes and noodles; cook until soft. Add chicken, green beans, corn and canned chicken broth. Add water to thin, if needed. Salt and pepper to taste. Serves 8 to 10.

Jana Roberts

Hot Madrilene Soup

1/4 cup onion, chopped
1/4 cup butter
2 (18 ounce) cans tomato juice
1 or 2 bay leaves

2 tablespoons dried parsley
flakes
2 (10 ounce) cans beef broth
Grated Parmesan cheese

Saute onions in butter until tender. Add next 4 ingredients and simmer for 5 minutes. Remove bay leaves. Sprinkle cheese over soup before serving. *Served at the first Wednesday luncheon at our church.* Serves 6.

In memory of Juanita Atkins Bohnert,
President, Women of the Church 1962-63

Jane's Zucchini Soup

2 tablespoons green onion, chopped
1 garlic clove, minced
1 pound zucchini, sliced thin
2 tablespoons butter

1/2 teaspoon salt
1/2 cup whipping cream
1-3/4 cups chicken broth

In heavy covered pan, simmer onion, zucchini and garlic in butter for 10 to 12 minutes, until barely tender. Stir frequently. Place zucchini mixture in blender for about 20 seconds. Put in heavy pan with salt, cream and broth. Simmer 5 minutes. May serve cold or hot. Serves 4.

Leila Wilkins O'Keefe

Minestrone Soup

2 pounds boneless chuck, cubed
1 tablespoon salt
1 (16 ounce) can tomato wedges
1 medium onion, chopped
2 stalks celery, chopped
1/3 cup parsley, chopped
1/2 teaspoon oregano
1/4 teaspoon pepper
1 clove garlic

2 cups tomato juice
1 cup chopped cabbage
1 cup sliced carrots
1 small can cut green beans
1 can kidney beans
1 cup elbow macaroni
1 cup sliced zucchini
Parmesan cheese, freshly grated

Add chuck to 8 cups of water and salt. Bring to boil and skim. Simmer until meat is tender in covered pot. Remove meat from broth. Add next 7 ingredients and simmer 20 minutes. Add next 5 ingredients and simmer 20 minutes, stirring occasionally. Add meat and macaroni and simmer 10 minutes, dropping in zucchini for last 4 minutes. Add salt and pepper to taste and add more water if soup seems too thick. Serve in bowls with cheese and a little extra parsley sprinkled over soup. *This is a meal in itself. Serve with hard rolls or Italian breadsticks and a leafy salad.* Serves 16.

Helen Claire Brooks

Potato Cheese Soup

2 tablespoons butter
1/4 onion, chopped
2 tablespoons parsley, chopped
3 cans potato soup
1 can chicken broth

8 ounces grated Cheddar cheese
1/2 carton or more sour cream
Dash of Tabasco
1 small packaged chopped
   broccoli, cooked and drained

Saute onion and parsley in butter in a heavy pan. Add soup and broth. Cook 15 minutes. Add cheese, sour cream, Tabasco and broccoli. Cook for 15 minutes, stirring often. Do not add salt! *Shared by my friend, Sally Holmes.* Serves 4 to 6.

Helen O'Keefe King

> *Blessed are they that dwell in Thy house.*
>
> Psalms 84:4

She-Crab Soup

1 can Harris She-Crab Soup
2 cans cream of celery soup
1 can tomato soup
4 cups milk
1 carton cream cheese with chives

Pepper
3/4 cup sherry
1 (6-1/2 ounce) can crabmeat

Mix first 7 ingredients well, using wire whisk. Heat slowly. Add sherry and crabmeat toward the end. Do not boil. Serves 8 to 10.

Mildred Andrews Bradley

Texas Soup

2 pounds ground chuck or turkey
1 onion, chopped
1 can kidney beans, undrained
1 can pinto beans, undrained
1 can yellow hominy, undrained
1 can stewed tomatoes

1 can Ro-Tel
1 package dry taco seasoning
  mix
1 small package Ranch dressing
  mix
1-2 cups water

Brown meat and onions. Add other ingredients except water and mix well. Add water to desired consistency. Simmer for 30 minutes, stirring frequently. Serves 6 to 8.

Jackie Quinn

Tortilla Soup

1 small onion, chopped
1 (4 ounce) can chopped green chilies
2 cloves garlic, crushed
2 tablespoons oil
1 cup tomatoes, peeled and chopped
1 can condensed beef bouillon
1 can condensed chicken broth
1-1/2 cups water
1-1/2 cups tomato juice
1 teaspoon ground cumin

1 teaspoon chili powder
1 teaspoon salt
1/8 teaspoon pepper
2 teaspoons Worcestershire
1 tablespoon steak sauce
2-3 chicken breasts, cooked
  and deboned
3 tortillas, cut in 1/2" strips
1/4 cup shredded Cheddar
  cheese

Saute onion, chilies and garlic in oil until soft. Add tomatoes, bouillon, chicken broth, water, tomato juice, cumin, chili powder, salt, pepper, Worcestershire sauce and steak sauce. Cut chicken into strips and add also. Bring soup to a boil; lower heat and simmer covered for 1 hour. Add tortillas and cheese and simmer 10 minutes longer. *Try topping with sour cream, fresh cilantro or avocado slices before serving.* Serves 4 to 6.

Ann Bartlett Benton

Tuesdays Together Gumbo

3 quarts water
3 pounds chicken
1 bunch celery
1 onion, cut in quarters
1/3 cup oil
1/2 cup flour
1 pound frozen cut okra
1 cup chopped onion

1 cup celery, chopped
1 large can V-8 juice
1/2 pound cubed ham
2 cans tomatoes
1 pound smoked sausage, sliced
2 pounds shrimp, shelled
Salt and pepper to taste
Rice, cooked

Boil water. Add the chicken, celery and quartered onion. Simmer 30 minutes or until done. In another pot make roux* with oil and flour. Add okra, chopped onion and chopped celery to roux and cook 15 minutes. Then add the V-8 juice, ham, tomatoes and sausage. Combine the two pots. Add shrimp and simmer until done. Prepare rice and put in bowls. Cover with gumbo and season to taste. Serves 12.
* To make a roux: Heat oil and gradually add flour, stirring constantly. Cook until caramel color.

Don A. Eilbott

Turkey Bone Gumbo

Turkey bones
Water
1/2 cup bacon drippings
1 cup flour
2 onions, chopped
3-5 cloves garlic, minced
1 bell pepper, chopped
2 celery stalks, chopped
2 quarts turkey broth
Salt and pepper to taste

Tabasco
2 bay leaves
1 teaspoon dried basil
1 tablespoon parsley
2 cups turkey, chopped
1 pound smoked sausage,
  cooked and cut in bite size
  pieces
Green onion tops

Put turkey bones in water and boil slowly until meat is almost off of bones. Make a roux with bacon drippings and flour, stirring until caramel colored. Add onions, garlic, bell pepper and celery and cook until wilted. Add hot broth, salt, pepper, dash of Tabasco, bay leaves, basil and parsley. Cook 1 hour. Add turkey and sausage and cook 30 minutes longer. Add green onion tops and cook a few minutes longer. Serve over cooked rice. Serves 6 to 8.

LaNelle Roberts

Vichyssoise

7 large potatoes, peeled and cubed
2 medium onions, diced
4 celery stalks, diced
Salt
1 pint well seasoned chicken broth

Half and Half cream
Butter
Garlic Salt
Sherry (optional)

Boil potatoes, onion and celery in just enough salted water until soft. Drain well. Put in blender or processor and blend until smooth and thick. Add chicken broth and some cream. Mixture should be rather thick. Add a little butter, garlic salt and sherry, if desired. Top with chives or onions. Serve cold or warm

In memory of Eugenia Oudin Cook

Zesty Mexican Chicken Chowder

1/4 cup chopped onion
1 clove garlic, finely chopped
3 tablespoons margarine or butter
1-1/2 pounds skinned boneless
    chicken breasts, cut into bite-size
    pieces
1 cup water
2 tablespoons chicken-flavor instant
bouillon or 2 chicken-flavor bouillon
    cubes

1 teaspoon ground cumin
2 cups (1 pint) Half and Half
1 (16 ounce) can cream-style
    corn
1 (4 ounce) can chopped green
    chilies, undrained
1 cup (4 ounces) shredded
    Monterey Jack cheese
Hot pepper sauce to taste
Chopped tomatoes, sliced green
    onions and cilantro

In large saucepan, cook onion and garlic in margarine until tender; add chicken, water, bouillon and cumin. Bring to a boil Reduce heat; cover and simmer 15 minutes. Add Half and Half, corn, chilies, cheese and hot pepper sauce. Cook and stir until cheese melts and mixture is hot. Garnish with tomatoes, green onions and cilantro. Refrigerate leftovers. Makes about 2 quarts.

Cookbook Committee

Cheesy BLT's

3 English muffins (split, buttered
   toasted)
12 slices bacon (cooked and halved)
6 lettuce leaves
6 tomato slices
Cheese sauce
Paprika

Cheese Sauce:
2 tablespoons butter
2 tablespoons flour
1 cup milk
1/2 cup shredded cheese
4 olives, sliced
1/4 teaspoon dry mustard
Salt

Top each muffin half with 2 slices bacon, lettuce leaf, tomato and cheese sauce.
Sprinkle with paprika.
Cheese Sauce: Melt butter, add flour, stir until smooth. Add milk and cook about
1 minute stirring constantly until thick and bubbly. Add cheese, olives, mustard
and salt. Stir until cheese melts. Serves 6.

Helen O'Keefe King

Cream Cheese and Olive Spread

1 (8 ounce) package cream cheese
1/2 cup mayonnaise
1 can chopped black olives, drained

1/2 cup pecans, chopped
Salt to taste

Combine cream cheese and mayonnaise. Add olives, pecans and mix well.
Spread on buttered bread to make sandwiches, then trim crust. Makes about 10
sandwiches.

Claudette Dixon

Egg Olive Sandwich

4 hard boiled eggs
12 large stuffed olives
Mayonnaise

Salt and pepper
Softened butter
Bread slices

Chop eggs and olives very fine. Mix with mayonnaise and season with salt and
pepper. Mix well and spread on buttered bread.

Liana Siegfried

Lara's Steak Sandwich and Sauce

2 pounds sirloin steak, 1-1/2" thick
Cracked black pepper
1 stick butter

Juice of 1 large lemon
2-3 tablespoons Worcestershire
4-6 hamburger buns

Generously sprinkle pepper on steak before grilling. Grill steak. Melt butter and combine with lemon juice and Worcestershire sauce. Brush on grilled steak. Cut meat into strips and layer on warmed grilled buns. Add extra sauce if desired. *A family favorite!* Serves 4 to 6.

Bettye Hutt

Ground Ham Salad

10 cups ground baked ham
1-1/4 cups mayonnaise
1-1/2 tablespoons mustard

1/3 cup sweet pickle juice
Soft butter

Mix ingredients blending well. Spread soft butter very thinly on both slices of bread. Spread ham salad well to the edges of bread. Trim crust. Makes about 20 sandwiches.

Joan B. Thompson

Green Pepper Cheese Sandwiches

6 tablespoons margarine, melted
2 tablespoons flour
1/2 teaspoon salt
1 cup milk
1 cup American cheese, shredded

3 medium green peppers, cut
   into thin rings
6 slices bread, toasted and
   buttered
12 slices bacon, cooked

Combine 2 tablespoons margarine, flour and salt. Gradually add milk, stirring until smooth over low heat. Cook slowly until thickened. Add cheese and stir until cheese melts. Saute green peppers until tender in remaining 4 tablespoons margarine, drain. Arrange green pepper on toast, cover with cheese sauce and garnish with bacon. Serves 6.

Margaret Dial Dawson

It is more blessed to give than to receive.   Acts 20:35

Olive Salad Muffalettas

2 grated carrots
30 ounces green olives, drained
  and chopped
3 (15 ounce) cans ripe olives, drained
  & chopped
2 stalks celery, finely chopped

4 cloves crushed garlic
1 cup olive oil
1/2 cup red wine vinegar
1 teaspoon oregano
1/2 teaspoon pepper
1 teaspoon basil

Mix together. Refrigerate overnight. Serve as a dressing with deli sandwiches like muffalettas. Keeps at least 2 weeks in refrigerator.

Ellen Nuckolls

Pimento Cheese Spread

1 pound sharp Cheddar cheese, grated
1 tablespoon Worcestershire sauce
1 handful dried parsley
1 (4 ounce) jar pimento

1 small onion, minced
3 tablespoons lemon juice
1 small handful celery seed
Mayonnaise to taste

Process the grated cheese in a food processor; continue adding remaining ingredients until well mixed. Will keep in refrigerator up to two weeks. Yield: 3 cups. Serve with crackers or on thin bread as tea sandwiches. *May also be mixed by hand!*

Laura Richardson Norsworthy

Razorback Spread

2 cups sharp Cheddar cheese, shredded
  fine
1/2 cup mayonnaise
1/3 cup chopped ripe olives
1/4 cup pimento, chopped

2 tablespoons green onions,
  chopped
2 teaspoons Worcestershire
1/4 teaspoon garlic powder
Cayenne pepper to taste

Combine ingredients, mixing well. Chill. Use for sandwiches or serve with crackers. Serves 10 to 12.

Frances Toney Hall

Tomato Salad Sandwich

4 Holland Rusks (or toast)
Anchovy paste
4 baked ham slices
4 chicken breast slices
4 tomato slices
Salt

4 hard boiled eggs, deviled
Russian salad dressing
4 artichoke hearts or stuffed
  olives for garnish
Shredded lettuce

Spread Holland Rusks with anchovy paste. Cover each with slice of baked ham, chicken breast, and tomato. Sprinkle with salt. Put 2 halves of deviled egg on top of each tomato, flat side down. Pour a generous portion of Russian salad dressing over each salad, covering completely. Place open artichoke heart or large stuffed olive on top of each sandwich. Serve on shredded lettuce. Serves 4.

In memory of Juanita Atkins Bohnert

Grilled Reubens

Rye bread
Butter
Durkees
Swiss cheese, sliced

Corned beef, cooked and thinly
  sliced
Sauerkraut, drained

Butter outsides of bread slices. Spread Durkees on "insides" of bread slices (spread to edges). On one slice put Swiss cheese, several slices of corned beef and top with drained sauerkraut. Put slice of bread on top and grill on preheated griddle or skillet. Press down with spatula and brown on both sides. *A family favorite!*

Dutch King

Christmas 1876 - Snow fell on Christmas Eve and by Christmas Day there was a heavy accumulation. The Presbyterian Church at Fourth and Chestnut was filled with hundreds who were there to see the children receive their gifts. The tree was the most handsome seen. The activities began with the choir singing several Christmas hymns accompanied by Mrs. W. E. Owens on the organ. The tree was "unladen" by Mayor P. H. Buford, M. J. Colburn and the minister, Joseph Dodds. The press said "an exquisitely attired doll was given to Colonel C. Pitts' little daughter."

PINE BLUFF COMMERCIAL

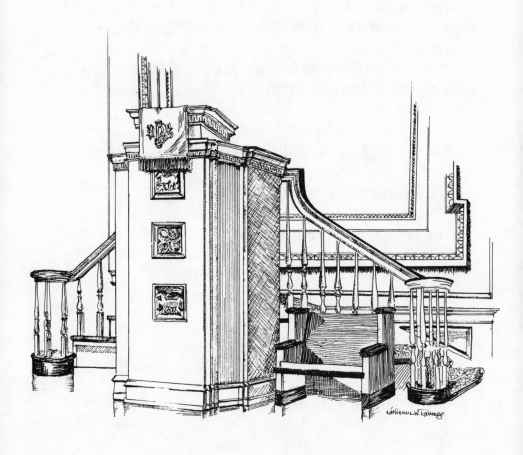

The pulpit was the gift of Mr. and Mrs. Leo Andrews Nichol in memory of their father, Mr. William Nichol.

The first needlepoint falls for the pulpit and lectern were gifts of Mrs. Laurence Gilmore and were designed by Mrs. Henry Gregory.

The carvings on the pulpit symbolize the following:

The Unicorn — *Virgin Birth*

The Quatrefoil — *Four Evangelists*

    Matthew — *Christ's Humanity (Man)*

    Mark — *Christ's Royalty (Lion)*

    Luke — *Christ's Sacrifice (Ox)*

    John — *Christ's Divinity (Eagle)*

The Agnus Dei — *The Lamb of God*

Apricot-Pear Salad

2 boxes lemon Jell-O
1-1/2 cups apricot nectar
1-1/2 cups pear juice
Large can (20 ounce) pears
1/3 cup blanched almonds

3/4 cup fresh orange juice
1-1/2 cups fresh orange
  sections
1 package Knox gelatin

Dissolve Jell-O in hot pear and apricot nectar. Add Knox gelatin softened in 1/4 cup pear and apricot nectar. Add sliced pears and orange sections. Next add orange juice and sliced almonds. Mold in individual molds or ring mold. Serve on lettuce. Serves 16.

In memory of Dorothy Ann Benton Mead.

Ann's Frozen Fruit Salad

2 (3 ounce) packages cream cheese
1 (10 ounce) package frozen
  strawberries, thawed and drained
1 cup mayonnaise
1 (15 ounce) can crushed pineapple, drained

1 cup chopped pecans
16 quartered marshmallows
1/2 pint whipping cream,
  whipped

Soften cream cheese and mix in enough juice drained from strawberries to make smooth and creamy. Add mayonnaise and mix well. Add pineapple, pecans, marshmallows and strawberries. Fold in whipped cream. Spoon into mold and freeze. Serve on lettuce leaf. Serves 14 to 16. *Pretty for a summer party and can be made ahead.*

Helen Clement

Frozen Cranberry Salad

1 (8 ounce) package cream cheese
1 cup whole cranberry sauce
1/2 cup mayonnaise

1 (18 ounce) can crushed pineapple, drained
1/2 cup whipping cream
1/2 cup chopped pecans

Soften cream cheese and mix with cranberry sauce and mayonnaise. Add remaining ingredients. Mix and pour in individual molds and freeze. Serves 8 to 9.

Jodie Henslee

Frosty Apricot Salad

1 (3 ounce) package apricot Jello-O
1 cup orange juice
1 cup buttermilk

1 small can Mandarin oranges,
   drained

Heat orange juice and dissolve gelatin in warm juice. Cool. Add buttermilk and oranges. *The tart flavor is great with pork or game.* Serves 4.

Bettye Hutt

Apricot-Pineapple Mold

1 (17 ounce) can apricot halves
1 (8 ounce) can pineapple tidbits
1/4 cup cider vinegar
1 teaspoon whole cloves

2 sticks cinnamon
1 (3 ounce) package orange
   Jell-O

Drain apricot and pineapple, reserving juices. Add vinegar, cloves and cinnamon to juices and enough water to make 2 cups. Bring to a boil and add fruit and simmer 3 minutes. Strain to remove fruit, discarding cloves and cinnamon sticks. Add Jell-O to juice. Chill until "jelly-like". Add apricots and pineapple and pour into a 1 quart mold or 6 individual molds. Serves 6.

Joan B. Thompson

Apricot and Almond Salad

1/2 cup orange juice
1 (12 ounce) can apricot nectar
1 (3 ounce) package apricot Jell-O
1 teaspoon fresh lemon juice

Dash salt
1/4 cup sliced almonds, lightly
   toasted

Heat orange juice and 1/2 cup apricot nectar to boiling. Dissolve Jell-O in hot juices. Add remaining apricot nectar, lemon juice and salt. Chill until thickens slightly. Add almonds and pour into six individual salad molds or one small ring mold. Unmold on lettuce leaf and garnish with mayonnaise and a dash of paprika. Serves 6.

Helen Clement

Raspberry Congealed Salad

1 large or 2 small packages raspberry
  Jell-O
2 cups water
1 (10 ounce) package frozen raspberries

1 (15-1/4 ounce) can crushed
  pineapple, with juice
1/2 cup chopped pecans
Sour cream

Dissolve Jell-O in boiling water. Add frozen raspberries and stir till thawed. Add pineapple and nuts. Chill until slightly thickened. Pour into 6 cup mold or individual salad molds and chill until firm. Unmold on lettuce and serve with sour cream on top. *Easy and so good!* Serves 16.

Helen Clement

"Minted" Waldorf Salad

1 cup mayonnaise
1 cup chopped red apple, with peeling
1 cup chopped green apple, with peeling
2 cups cantaloupe chunks
1 cup celery slices

1 cup walnut halves
2 tablespoons finely chopped
  fresh mint
1/2 teaspoon ground ginger

Combine ingredients; mix lightly. Chill. Serve on lettuce leaves. *A salad with a crunchy texture.* Serves 6 to 8.

Margaret Dial Dawson

Asparagus Salad

2 envelopes unflavored gelatin
1/2 cup cold water
1 (10-1/2 ounce) can cream of
  asparagus soup
1 (8 ounce) package cream cheese

1/2 cup mayonnaise
1 (14-1/2 to 15 ounce) can cut
  asparagus, well drained
1 cup stuffed olives, chopped
1 cup celery, chopped

Soften gelatin in cold water. Heat soup to boiling. Stir in gelatin until dissolved. Cool to lukewarm, blend mayonnaise and cream cheese. Beat until smooth. Stir in gelatin mixture. Fold in asparagus and remaining ingredients. Put in ring mold. *May mix mayonnaise and Durkees and dollop on top with paprika sprinkled lightly, if desired.* Serves 6 to 8.

Betty Bell

Asparagus-Artichoke Salad

1 (10 ounce) package frozen asparagus
1 (15 ounce) can artichoke hearts,
   drained and halved
Coarse ground pepper
1/3 cup salad oil

1/4 cup fresh lemon juice
1 clove garlic, minced
1/2 teaspoon salt
4 lettuce cups
1/4 cup sliced ripe olives

Cook asparagus according to package directions. Drain. Combine asparagus and artichokes; sprinkle with a little ground pepper. Combine oil, lemon juice, garlic and salt. Whisk and pour over vegetables. Cover and chill several hours, tossing once or twice. Arrange vegetables in lettuce cups; top with ripe olive slices. *Can easily be doubled.* Serves 4.

Martha Andrews

Avocado and Sprout Salad

3-5 avocados
6-8 lettuce cups
1 small carton cottage cheese

Alfalfa sprouts
Italian dressing

Peel ripened avocados and slice; place on lettuce leaves; top with 2 to 3 heaping tablespoons of cottage cheese per serving. Sprinkle with sprouts and drizzle with Italian dressing (Good Seasons with red wine vinegar is good). *Beautiful on individual salad plates or arranged on a platter. So easy!* Serves 6.

Katherine Ramage Love

Tomato Aspic

1 (46 ounce) can tomato juice
4 envelopes Knox gelatin
1 tablespoon horseradish
Black pepper
1 tablespoon lemon juice

1 cup green onions with tops,
   chopped fine
1/2 cup sliced stuffed green
   olives
1 cup celery, chopped fine

Soften gelatin in 2 cups tomato juice. Heat until melted and add to the rest of tomato juice. Add pepper, lemon juice, chopped vegetables and horseradish. Congeal in molds. Serves 12.

Eloise Fitts

Avocado and Tomato Aspic

Avocado Layer
2 packages Knox gelatin
1/2 cup cold water
1/2 cup boiling water
3 large ripe avocados
5 tablespoons fresh lemon juice
1 tablespoon grated onion
1-1/4 teaspoons salt
4 drops of Tabasco
1/2 cup mayonnaise

Aspic Layer
2 packages Knox gelatin
3-1/2 cups tomato juice
1/2 teaspoon salt
1 teaspoon sugar
1 teaspoon Worcestershire
1/4 teaspoon Tabasco
2 tablespoons lemon juice
1 bay leaf
Onion juice to taste

Soften gelatin in cold water and then dissolve in boiling water. Cool. Puree avocado; add next 5 ingredients and mix with gelatin. Pour in sprayed mold and fill half full. Congeal. Soften gelatin in 1/2 cup of tomato juice. Heat remaining ingredients and add gelatin mixture; cool. Pour over congealed avocado layer. *This is a beautiful Christmas salad. Artichoke hearts in center of ring look wonderful!* Serves 10 to 12.

Frances Toney Hall

Beet Salad

1 (16 ounce) can beets, coarsely grated
1 (3 ounce) package lemon Jell-O
1 cup beet juice (add water to make enough)
1 tablespoon sugar
1 tablespoon vinegar
1 tablespoon horseradish
1 cup diced celery

Sauce:
1/2 cup sour cream
1/3 cup mayonnaise
1/2 teaspoon salt
1/2 cucumber, grated

Drain and grate beets saving juice. Bring juice to boil; dissolve Jell-O in it. Add rest of ingredients. Pour into 9 inch square dish. Chill until set. Serve with a dollop of cucumber sauce. Sauce: Mix all ingredients together. *Different and good!* Serves 9.

Linda Burrow VanHook

Best Ever Salad

1 (14 ounce) can French cut green beans (drained)
1 (14 ounce) can shoe peg corn (drained)
1 (14 ounce) can small green peas (drained)
1 (4 ounce) jar pimento, drained and chopped
1 cup chopped celery
1 cup chopped green bell pepper

1/4 cup chopped green onion

DRESSING:
3/4 cup vinegar)
1 cup sugar   )
1/2 cup oil   ) HEAT
Beat dressing and pour over all.
Salt and pepper to taste

Drain all canned items in colander. Add chopped vegetables. Heat dressing ingredients to boiling. Add to vegetables. *This is especially good to have on hand to go with a meat serving for a light supper or lunch. Keeps well.* Makes about 2 quarts.

Martha Halbert

Broccoli-Vegetable Salad

1 bunch broccoli
1 head cauliflower
1 medium red onion
1/2 pound bacon, crisp and crumbled
1 cup shredded cheese

Dressing
2-3 tablespoons red wine vinegar
3/4 cup Miracle Whip
1/4 cup sugar

Cut cauliflower and broccoli into bite-size pieces. Slice onion into thin slices and separate. Fry bacon crisp and crumble. Mix vegetables, bacon and cheese. Pour dressing over vegetables and let stand at least one hour. Refrigerate. *My mother's recipe.* Serves 10 to 12.

Frances Stone

Since 1867, when the women's society was organized, they have presented four honorary life memberships to women in our church: Mrs. B. J. Sloan, Mrs. W. N. Trulock, Jr., Mrs. W. Hampton Hall, and Mrs. William E. Bell.

Summer Salad

4 tomatoes, sliced
1 red onion, thinly sliced
4 ounces Mozzarella cheese, grated
1/2 cup coarsely chopped fresh basil
   or 1/3 cup dry basil
1/3 cup olive oil
1 tablespoon lemon juice
2 tablespoons red wine vinegar

1 tablespoon minced parsley
1 garlic clove, crushed
1/2 teaspoon salt
1/4 teaspoon pepper
1/2 teaspoon Dijon-style
   mustard
1/2 cup sliced pitted ripe olives
Basil sprig

Arrange 1/2 of tomatoes, 1/2 of onion and 1/2 of Mozzarella cheese, thinly sliced, in a large, shallow salad bowl. Sprinkle with 1/4 cup chopped basil. Top with remaining tomatoes, onion and cheese. In a small bowl, combine oil, lemon juice, vinegar, parsley, garlic, salt, pepper and mustard. Stir until blended. Pour over layered vegetables and cheese. Sprinkle with remaining 1/4 cup chopped basil and sliced olives. Can be made ahead. *Complete now or make ahead. Fresh basil is easy to grow and fun to have on hand.* Serves 6.

Bettye Hutt

Cucumber Salad Mold

1 (3 ounce) package Knox gelatin
1/2 cup cold water
1/2 teaspoon salt
2 (3 ounce) packages cream cheese
1 small carton cottage cheese, small curd
1 medium cucumber, grated

2 teaspoons lemon juice
3/4 cup finely chopped celery
1/2 cup mayonnaise
1/2 cup chopped pecans
1 teaspoon grated onion

Sprinkle gelatin over cold water; add salt. Cook over low heat until gelatin dissolves. Blend cream cheese and cottage cheese together; add gelatin mixture and beat well. Add all other ingredients and pour into mold. Refrigerate. To serve, unmold on lettuce leaves and top with mayonnaise. Serves 8 to 10.

Mabel Sloan Willlams

Blessed are all they that put their trust in Him.

Psalms 2:12

Perfection Salad

1 (3 ounce) package lemon Jell-O
3/4 teaspoon salt
1 cup boiling water
3/4 cup cold water
2 tablespoons vinegar
2 teaspoons grated onion
Pepper to taste

3/4 cup finely chopped cabbage
3/4 cup finely chopped celery
1/4 cup finely chopped green
   pepper
2 tablespoons diced pimento
Fresh lemon juice

Dissolve gelatin and salt in boiling water. Add cold water, vinegar, grated onion and pepper. Chill until syrupy. Fold in vegetables. Serve on lettuce leaf. Serves 6.

In memory of Eugenia Oudin Cook

Oriental Salad

1 can sliced water chestnuts
1 cup diced celery
1 small jar chopped pimento
1 large onion
1 sliced (or diced) green pepper

2 cans bean sprouts
1 large can kernel corn
1 can carrots (sliced or diced)
1 can French green beans
1 can English peas

Drain canned vegetables. Mix all the above ingredients in a large salad bowl. To make dressing, heat 1/2 cup water, 1 cup salad oil, 1 cup sugar, 1 cup cider vinegar, 2 teaspoons salt, 1 teaspoon pepper, dash of Tabasco. Pour over ingredients in bowl and refrigerate until serving. Serves 20.

Mary Wynne Perryman

When the Young Ladies Society was disbanded in 1919, they presented the church, built in 1894 at Fifth and Walnut - with the beautiful silver communion service which we still have. At the same time, they turned over to the Women's Auxilliary $1,000, which was known as the carpet fund. They also gave the pipe organ for the Fifth and Walnut church when it was built.

Caesar Salad

1 large head romaine lettuce
3/4 cup olive oil
3 tablespoons red wine vinegar
1 teaspoon Worcestershire sauce
1/2 teaspoon salt
1/4 teaspoon dry mustard
1 large clove garlic, crushed
1 egg

Dressing:
1 lemon, halved
Freshly ground pepper
1/4 cup grated Parmesan cheese
1 (2 ounce) can anchovy fillets
 (optional)
Croutons:
3 tablespoons softened butter
1/4 teaspoon garlic powder
3 (3/4" thick) slices French bread

Wash lettuce and separate leaves. Drain and refrigerate 2 hours at least. Combine olive oil, vinegar, Worcestershire sauce, salt, mustard and garlic in a blender until mixed well. Coddle egg for 3 minutes and cool. Tear leaves of romaine in bite size pieces, omitting coarse ribs. Place in large salad bowl. Break coddled egg over romaine, squeeze juice from lemon half, add ground pepper and cheese. Toss lightly. Top with croutons and anchovies, if desired. Croutons: Spread butter over both sides of bread, sprinkle with garlic powder, cut slices into 3/4 inch cubes. Bake on baking sheet at 350 degrees for 15 minutes or until crisp and dry. Cool. Serves 4 to 6.

Jo Ann Clemmons

Southwestern Caesar Salad

Dressing:
3 cloves garlic, minced
1 tablespoon chopped jalapeno chili
 peppers
1 large egg yolk
2 teaspoons anchovy paste
Juice of 1 lemon
2 tablespoons red wine vinegar
2 tablespoons Worcestershire sauce
3 tablespoons grated Parmesan cheese
1/2 teaspoon each; salt and pepper
1 cup olive oil

Cilantro Croutons:
1/2 stick unsalted butter,
 softened
1 clove minced garlic
1/3 cup grated Parmesan cheese
4 (1 inch) bias-cut slices thick
 bread
2 tablespoons fresh cilantro
Salad:
2 small heads romaine lettuce
1 (8 ounce) can shoepeg corn
Additional Parmesan cheese for
 serving

For dressing: Combine the garlic, jalapeno, egg yolk, anchovy paste, lemon juice, vinegar, Worcestershire sauce, cheese, salt and pepper in a blender or food processor. Blend at low speed, slowly adding the oil. Dressing can be made a day in advance and refrigerated. Croutons: Heat oven to 350 degrees. Mix the butter, cilantro and garlic. Spread over bread; sprinkle with cheese. Arrange on a baking sheet. Bake until golden, 8 to 10 minutes, cool. Croutons can be made in advance and stored in an airtight container. Tear romaine into pieces and mix with the corn. Add dressing to taste and toss gently. Serve on chilled plates, garnished with croutons and additional cheese. Add freshly ground pepper to taste. Makes 4 servings

Connie Mullis

Greek Salad

1 cucumber, sliced
4 small tomatoes, chopped
1 purple onion, sliced thin
1/2 cup radishes, sliced
4 ounces crumbled Feta cheese
12 Greek olives
1 tablespoon drained capers
1 head lettuce

Dressing:
1 (2 ounce) can anchovies,
  chopped
1/2 teaspoon dry mustard
1/2 cup olive oil
1 teaspoon crushed oregano
2 tablespoons wine vinegar
1/2 teaspoon salt
1/8 teaspoon cracked black pepper

Combine first eight ingredients. Mix anchovies with dry mustard and olive oil. Gently blend in remaining ingredients for dressing and serve over lettuce that has been torn in bite-size pieces. Serves 4 to 6.

Frances Toney Hall

Green Salad with Artichokes

Salad:
1 jar marinated artichoke hearts, sliced
  (reserve liquid in jar)
3 to 4 green onions, chopped
1 tomato, chopped
1/2 to 3/4 cup fresh grated Romano cheese
Red leaf or romaine lettuce
Avocado, boiled eggs, bacon, fresh mushrooms if desired

Dressing:
Reserved artichoke liquid
Olive oil
Red wine vinegar
1 medium garlic clove

Dressing: After removing artichokes from jar, add olive oil to marinade left in the jar until jar is 3/4 full. Then add red wine vinegar for the other 1/4. Then press 1 garlic clove through press into mixture. Replace top and shake. Toss with vegetables and add other ingredients. Season salad with salt and pepper. *Can easily be doubled.* Serves 4.

Nena Busby

When Mr. D. W. Richey (1868 - 1950) died, he had not missed Sunday School in 50 years. He founded Dollarway Presbyterian Church at Dew Drop and Riverside Presbyterian Church on East 2nd Avenue.

California Salad

1 medium head leaf lettuce
1 medium head red-tip lettuce
2 avocados, peeled & sliced
2 cups fresh grapefruit sections
12 large ripe olives, sliced
* 1/2 red onion, cut in rings

Dressing:
1/2 cup vegetable oil
1/4 cup red wine vinegar
1/4 cup sugar
1/2 teaspoon salt
1/2 teaspoon celery seed
1/2 teaspoon dry mustard
1/2 red onion, grated

Combine dressing ingredients and mix well. Combine salad ingredients in a large bowl. Just before serving add dressing and toss gently. * May add sliced red onion on top for garnish. Serves 8 to 10.

Susan Norton

Spinach Salad

1-1/2 pounds fresh spinach
6 green onions with tops (sliced)
Dash pepper
5 hard boiled eggs
8 slices crisp bacon, crumbled
1/2 cup sliced mushrooms

Dressing:
1 garlic clove, quartered
1/2 cup salad oil
1 teaspoon salt
1/3 teaspoon pepper
3 tablespoons fresh lemon juice
1/4 cup cider vinegar

Wash spinach and dry well. Remove stems and break into bite size pieces. Add other ingredients and refrigerate 2 hours. For dressing: Marinate garlic in oil for an hour and then combine with other ingredients; wisk together. Pour over salad and serve. Serves 8 to 10.

Gen Kennedy Wilkins

Tangy Tossed Salad

2 heads Romaine lettuce
  (1 red leaf - 1 curly leaf)
1 pint fresh strawberries, sliced
1/2 cup walnuts, lightly toasted
1 cup shredded Monterey Jack cheese

Dressing:
1 cup oil
1/2 cup red wine vinegar
3/4 cup sugar
2 cloves garlic
1/2 teaspoon each: paprika
  salt, and white pepper

Tear lettuce in bite-size pieces; add all other ingredients; whisk dressing and pour over salad. Toss and serve. *Good sweet and tart salad!* Serves 6 to 8.

Debbie Robinson

Watercress Salad

1 raw egg, beaten with fork
1 cup salad oil
1 tablespoon horseradish
2 tablespoons catsup
1 tablespoon grated onion
1-1/2 teaspoons salt
3-1/2 tablespoons vinegar

1 tablespoon paprika
1 tablespoon Worcestershire
Freshly grated pepper
6-8 slices of crisp cooked
   bacon, crumbled
6 bunches watercress

Mix all ingredients thoroughly except bacon and watercress. Wash watercress and remove tough stems. Place on individual salad plates and pour a little dressing over each serving. Top with bacon. *The piquante flavor of watercress demands a spicy dressing.* Serves 10 to 12.

Helen Claire Brooks

Catalina Salad

1 can Ranch style beans
1 cup grated Cheddar cheese
1 medium onion, chopped
2 tomatoes, chopped

3/4 bottle Catalina dressing
1/2 head shredded lettuce
1 cup crushed Fritos
2 tablespoons sliced black olives

Rinse and drain beans. Mix with cheese, onions, tomatoes, and dressing. Chill for an hour. Just before serving, add lettuce and Fritos. Top with sliced black olives. *Can use reduced fat cheese and free Catalina.* Serves 6.

LaNelle Roberts

Blender Cole Slaw

1/2 small head of cabbage, cored
   and cut into eighths
1/4 medium onion, quartered
1/4 bell pepper, quartered
1 small carrot, sliced

Dressing:
1/4 cup sour cream
1/4 cup mayonnaise
1 tablespoon lemon juice
1/2 teaspoon salt
1/8 teaspoon pepper

Mix in blender, which should be 3/4 full of vegetables. Cover with ice water. Press chop button for 5 seconds, stir and repeat twice. Drain well and mix with dressing. *So easy!* Serves 6.

Pat Lile

Twenty-Four Hour Slaw

2 medium heads cabbage, shredded
1 large onion, sliced
1/2 cup sugar

Dressing:
1 teaspoon sugar
1-1/2 teaspoons salt
1 teaspoon dry mustard
1 cup white vinegar
1/2 to 1 cup salad oil

Stir 1/2 cup sugar into cabbage and place half of this amount in large bowl. Cover with onion rings. Add remaining cabbage mixture. In medium saucepan add all dressing ingredients <u>except oil</u>. Bring to a roaring boil. Add oil. Boil again. Pour over cabbage and onion. Don't stir. Cover and refrigerate. Keeps indefinitely. *To cut down on fat I have reduced the oil without any adverse effects.*

Brenda Norsworthy

California Chicken Salad

1 stick oleo
2 cups mayonnaise
1/4 cup <u>fresh</u> minced parsley
1/2 teaspoon curry powder
1/4 teaspoon minced garlic
Pinch of marjoram
Salt and pepper to taste

4 cups diced, cooked chicken
   breasts
2 cups green seedless grapes
1/2 cup toasted, slivered
   almonds
Paprika

Melt 1 stick of oleo, cool to room temperature. Add mayonnaise, parsley, curry, garlic, marjoram, salt and pepper. Stir all together and add chicken, grapes and almonds. Toss and sprinkle paprika on top. (Try 1/4 teaspoon of curry and add according to your taste). Serves 8. *Can add up to 2 more cups of chicken to serve 10 people.*

Mabel Sloan Williams

In 1982, we opened the "church pantry" in response to needs in the community for food and clothing. Mrs. Charles Higgins was in charge.

Chicken Mousse

3 envelopes of Knox gelatin
1/2 cup cold water
4-1/2 cups seasoned chicken broth
2 teaspoons salt
1/2 teaspoon black pepper
1 cup mayonnaise
5-6 cups diced, cooked chicken

1-1/2 cups diced celery
1 teaspoon Worcestershire
1-1/2 tablespoons grated onion
1-1/2 cups chopped almonds
2 tablespoons fresh lemon
   juice
1 cup whipping cream, whipped

Soften gelatin in cold water. Heat seasoned broth, salt and pepper in saucepan and dissolve gelatin in this liquid. Cool until it begins to congeal, then blend together. Add remaining ingredients, except cream. Whip cream and add to mixture. Pour into oiled 3 quart mold. Chill until set. Serve on a lettuce leaf with garnish of mayonnaise and paprika. *Nice luncheon entree in warm weather.* Serves 16.

In memory of Mrs. Sanborn Wilkins

Cornbread Salad

1 package Hidden Valley Ranch Dressing
1 cup sour cream
1 cup mayonnaise
1 (9 ounce) pan cornbread (crumbled)
2 (16 ounce) cans pinto beans, drained
1/2 cup chopped green onions

3 large tomatoes, chopped
1/2 cup bell pepper, chopped
8 ounces shredded cheese
10 slices cooked bacon
2 (17 ounce) cans corn, drained
1 can chopped green chilies*

Mix first three ingredients together and set aside. Crumble half of cornbread in bottom of bowl. Top with half of beans. (In another bowl, combine tomato, onion and bell pepper). Use half of this mixture over beans; next layer cheese, crumbled bacon, corn and half of dressing mixture. Repeat layers, cover and chill. *For a "Tex-Mex" flavor, add green chilies to your favorite cornbread recipe. *Great with BBQ or chicken. Will keep several days.* Serves 10.

Bettye Hutt, Co-Moderator
Presbyterian Women 1991-92

Garden Pasta Salad

1/2 pound vermicelli
1 tablespoon oil
1 cup mayonnaise
2 tablespoons red wine vinegar
Salt and pepper to taste

2 finely chopped green onions
1/2 green pepper, finely
  chopped
1 small can sliced ripe olives
1 small jar chopped pimento

Cook vermicelli al dente (5 minutes) with 1 tablespoon oil. Drain; do not rinse. Stir in , while hot, mayonnaise and vinegar. Cool slightly; add salt and pepper to taste and remaining ingredients. Serves 6.

Mabel Sloan Williams

Glorious Pasta Chicken Salad

2 cups pasta (I mix Rotini and
  bow pasta)
1-1/2 cups diced celery
1/4 cup diced red onion
1/4 cup diced bell peppers
1 (11 ounce) can Mandarin oranges,
  drained

1 (8 ounce) can drained, sliced
  water chestnuts
1 cup green grapes
2 cups cooked chicken
  (chunks)
1 cup Ranch dressing

Cook pasta and drain; add remaining ingredients and gently add chicken and toss. Blend Ranch dressing in salad and toss. Cover and chill. *Shared by Dianne McGeorge.* Serves 8.

Bettye Hutt

Katibel's Pasta Delight

Rotini pasta (multi colored garden
  variety)
6 green onions, chopped
4 tomatoes, cut up
2 stalks celery, chopped

1 pound steamed, shelled
  shrimp
Garlic salt
Course ground pepper
Lawry's Caesar Salad Dressing

Cook pasta by directions on package and let cool. Add rest of ingredients. Toss gently and chill. Serves 6.

Katibel C. Perdue

Bleu-Cheese Potato Salad

5 pounds red potatoes (new)
2 tablespoons fresh parsley, chopped
3 green onions, chopped
1 cup sour cream

1/2 cup red wine vinegar
1/4 teaspoon white pepper
4 ounces bleu-cheese, crumbled
3 hard boiled eggs

Cover potatoes with water (leave peeling on) and boil till done. Drain and slice while warm. Combine remaining ingredients (except eggs) and stir in with potatoes; gently add chopped eggs (leave a few slices for garnish). Chill and serve in a large clear bowl. *Good with beef tenderloin.* Serves 10 to 12.

Alice Monroe Gage

German Potato Salad

4 medium red potatoes
1 medium white onion, sliced thin
1 teaspoon salt
1/4 teaspoon black pepper

2 tablespoons fresh parsley
2/3 cup vegetable oil
1/3 cup cider vinegar
1 tablespoon sugar

Cover potatoes with water and boil until done. Leave peeling on; drain. While potatoes are warm, peel and slice; layer potatoes and onion. Add salt, pepper and parsley on top. Bring oil, vinegar and sugar to a rolling boil. Pour warm dressing over potato mixture (do not toss) and refrigerate several hours. Cover with plastic wrap. Will keep several days. *A family favorite.* Serves 4.

In memory of Rose Cook Hutt

Mustard Potato Salad

6 cups boiled red skin potatoes
3/4 cup diced celery
1 small white onion, chopped
1/2 teaspoon salt
1/4 teaspoon pepper
Celery seed to taste
1 or 2 hard boiled eggs
1/2 cup chopped parsley

Dressing:
1 cup mayonnaise
1/4 cup Durkees
1 tablespoon mustard

Boil potatoes until just tender, then pour ice water over to cool. Cut in chunks and mix with celery and onions; stir in enough dressing to hold together. Add seasonings last and stir in hard boiled egg. Garnish with fresh chopped parsley. Serves 8 to 10.

Sally Cook

Rice-Artichoke Salad

1 (6 ounce) package Uncle Ben's long grain and wild rice - original
1 (14 ounce) can artichoke hearts, chopped and drained
1 (2 ounce) jar chopped pimento, drained
12 stuffed olives, sliced

3 green onions with tops, chopped
1 cup celery, chopped
1/2 cup mayonnaise
1 teaspoon curry powder

Cook rice according to directions leaving off butter. Cool. Add remaining ingredients and chill. *This is a great accompaniment to cold cuts: ham, turkey, etc.* Serves 6.

Leah "Pud" Harris

Pasta-Artichoke-Shrimp Salad

2 cups tripolini or small seashell macaroni
1/3 cup chopped green onion
1/2 cup chopped celery
1 (8 ounce) can artichoke hearts, quartered and drained

1-1/2 pounds shrimp, cooked and peeled
3/4 teaspoon curry powder
3/4 cup mayonnaise
1/2 cup sour cream
Capers for garnish

Cook pasta as directed. Refresh and rinse immediately in cold water. Chill. Add remaining ingredients and mix. Adjust seasoning. Chill at least 4 hours. Serve on a bed of lettuce and garnish with capers. *Best if prepared one day in advance.* Serves 8 to 10.

Jean Sanders Brown

Shrimp Salad

2 cups mayonnaise
8 ounces cream cheese, softened
Juice from 1 large or 2 medium lemons
1 onion, grated and drained
4 stalks celery, finely chopped

1/2 cup capers
Green Tabasco sauce (lots)
4 pounds shrimp, steamed (I like spicy)

Combine mayonnaise and cream cheese until smooth. Add rest of ingredients one at a time, mixing. Add shrimp last. *Wonderful served on shredded lettuce!* Serves 8.

Janie Buckley

Tuna Salad Loaf

2 (6 ounce) cans white tuna
20-24 sliced stuffed olives
3-4 stalks chopped celery
1/4 bell pepper, chopped
1 cup mayonnaise

2 envelopes of plain gelatin
6 tablespoons cold water
1/2 cup boiling water
1/4 cup fresh lemon juice

Drain tuna; place in bowl and rake with a fork. Add olives, celery, bell peppers and mayonnaise. Soften gelatin in cold water, then add boiling water to dissolve. Add lemon juice and mix together and pour into 8 or 9 inch square pan. Cover with wax paper (directly on salad) and chill until firm. Cut in squares and serve on lettuce leaf. Top with mayonnaise and a dash of paprika. *My mother served this with marinated green beans and tomatoes in the summer.* Serves 9.

Helen Clement

West Indies Salad

1 pound fresh lump crab meat
1 medium onion, chopped fine
4 ounces Wesson oil

3 ounces cider vinegar
4 ounces ice water
Salt and pepper

Divide chopped onion in half and spread 1/2 over bottom of large mixing bowl. Separate crab meat lumps and place on top of onion. Top with remaining onion. Now salt and pepper to taste. Pour over all: first the Wesson oil, next vinegar and last the ice water. Cover and place in refrigerator to marinate from 2 to 12 hours. When ready to serve, toss lightly but do not stir. Also please do not substitute for any of the ingredients as results would not be the same. *From "Bayley's" famous seafood restaurant.*

Corinne Hunter

Garlic French Dressing

1 clove garlic
1/2 teaspoon salt
1/2 teaspoon dry mustard
1/4 teaspoon paprika

1/4 teaspoon pepper
1/4 cup cider vinegar
1/2 cup salad oil

Cut garlic in quarters. Add ingredients in the order given to jar with lid. Shake well. Allow to stand at least 1 hour before serving. For best flavor, the morning you will be serving it, add 4-5 quartered cloves of garlic to dressing. Serve over salad of 1 pound fresh spinach, 1/2 pound crisp cooked bacon (crumbled), and 4 hard-cooked eggs (sliced) or your favorite green salad. *Recipe can be doubled or tripled easily.* Serves 4.

Jane G. Starling

Jacques & Suzanne's Vinaigrette

1/2 small onion, chopped
1 tablespoon Dijon mustard
1 dash Tabasco
Freshly ground pepper
* 5/8 cup tarragon vinegar
1/2 teaspoon Worcestershire

1 large clove garlic
1 raw egg
2/3 cup olive oil
1 beef bouillon cube
3 tablespoons boiling water
1-1/3 cups vegetable oil

Put first 7 ingredients in blender, add egg and blend well. Slowly add 2/3 cup olive oil. Dissolve 1 beef bouillon cube in 3 tablespoons boiling water and add. Gradually blend in 1-1/3 cup vegetable oil. Place in covered jar in refrigerator. Better if not served icy cold. Makes 3 cups.
*5/8 cup = 1/2 cup + 2 TBSP

Mayonnaise

2 whole eggs
2 tablespoons lemon juice
1-1/2 teaspoons sugar
3/4 teaspoon salt
1/8 teaspoon white pepper

1/2 teaspoon paprika
1 teaspoon dry mustard
1/2 teaspoon grated onion
(optional)
2 cups salad oil

In blender or food processor, put all ingredients <u>except</u> oil. Blend at low speed. Add <u>very</u> slowly, while blender is running, then add 2 cups of oil. Stop, stir and blend a little longer. Refrigerate. *Great on summer tomatoes or sandwiches! Worth the effort.*

Helen O'Keefe King

Poppy Seed Dressing

1-1/2 cups sugar
2 teaspoons dry mustard
2 teaspoons salt
2/3 cup vinegar
3 tablespoons onion

{ mix in blender or electric mixer

2 cups salad oil (not olive oil)
3 tablespoons poppy seeds (add slowly, beating constantly)

Store in refrigerator - do not freeze or beat or it will separate. *Terrific on any fruit, especially citrus!*

Ellen Nuckolls

Raspberry Roquefort Vinaigrette

1/2 cup plus 1 tablespoon olive oil
3 tablespoons Raspberry vinegar
Salt and pepper to taste

1/2 cup crumbled Roquefort cheese

Whisk olive oil and vinegar in a small bowl until blended. Season with salt and pepper. Mix in crumbled cheese. Variation: Add 1/4 cup dried cranberries and 1/2 cup chopped, toasted pecans or almonds to salad greens and pour dressing over all. *Very attractive!* Serves 6.

LaNelle Roberts

Roquefort Dressing

1/3 cup green onions with tops
2 cups Hellman's mayonnaise
2 cloves of garlic, chopped fine
1/2 cup chopped parsley
2 tablespoons anchovy paste

1 cup sour cream
1/4 cup vinegar
2 tablespoons fresh lemon juice
1/2 pound Roquefort cheese (or bleu cheese)

Mix mayonnaise with onions, garlic and parsley. Mix anchovy paste with sour cream and add to mayonnaise mixture. Thin with vinegar and lemon juice. Crumble cheese and stir in mixture. (If less garlic taste is desired, stick toothpick in side of whole clove and remove when desired). Keep refrigerated.

Cookbook Committee

Thousand Island Dressing

1-1/2 cups mayonnaise
1/2 cup catsup
2 tablespoons olive oil
3 tablespoons pickle relish

2 cloves crushed garlic
1 tablespoon Worcestershire
Dash of pepper

Combine together in a quart jar and mix well. Store in refrigerator . . . make a day ahead to develop flavor.

Debbie Robinson

Garlic Croutons

2 sticks butter or margarine
1/16 teaspoon garlic powder
1/2 teaspoon Italian seasoning

White or whole wheat bread
(cut in 1/2 inch cubes with
electric knife)

Arrange bread cubes on a large pan with short sides such as a jelly roll pan. Melt butter; add garlic powder and Italian seasoning. Mix well and pour over bread cubes until all are coated. Bake at 200 degrees for 45 minutes, then 300 degrees for 10 minutes until golden brown. Turn off oven and leave croutons in warm oven for an hour. Store in a plastic bag or jar. Serve with salads or soups. Can freeze.

Debbie Robinson

Honey French Dressing

1/2 cup catsup
1/4 cup vinegar
1/2 cup honey
2 tablespoons grated onion
1 teaspoon Worcestershire

Pepper to taste
1/4 teaspoon or less ground
clove
1 cup vegetable oil

Combine everything but oil in blender. Blend on/off once or twice. Gradually pour in oil while blender is running. Keep refrigerated in a jar, with lid.

Ellen Nuckolls

The blessing of the Lord, it maketh rich, and He addeth no sorrow with it.
Proverbs 10:22

Baked Apricots

2 (16 ounce) cans apricots, unpeeled
15 crushed Ritz crackers
1/2 cup brown sugar

4 tablespoons fresh lemon juice
6 tablespoons butter
Cinnamon to taste

Layer apricots, crushed crackers and brown sugar. Sprinkle with lemon juice and dot with butter. Bake uncovered at 375 degrees for 40 minutes. *Delicious as a side dish with any meat.* Serves 5 to 6.

Frances Toney Hall

Baked Orange Slices

6 oranges
1 tablespoon salt
2 cups sugar

1/2 cup light corn syrup
1/2 cup vinegar

Wash oranges. Cover with water, add salt, and boil 30 minutes. Drain, reserving 3/4 cup water. Set aside; cool. Combine sugar, corn syrup, vinegar, and reserved water. Boil 5 minutes. Cut oranges into 5 slices; remove seeds. Boil slices in syrup for 15 minutes. Arrange slices in 8x12 dish. Cover with syrup. Bake at 350 degrees for 40 minutes. Can prepare ahead and refrigerate, baking the final 40 minutes before serving. *Good and different. Great for brunch.* Serves 8 to 10.

Linda Burrow VanHook

Hot Fruit Dish

1 stick margarine
1/2 cup sugar
4 tablespoons cornstarch
1 cup sherry
1 cup fruit juice
1 (1 pound) can chunk pineapple, drained
1 (1 pound) can pears, drained

1 (1 pound) can peaches, drained
1 (1 pound) can apricots, drained
1 (1 pound) jar spiced apple rings, drained
1 can seedless grapes, drained

Melt margarine in saucepan. Add sugar, cornstarch, sherry, and juice. Stir constantly over very low heat until thick (about 5 minutes). Arrange drained fruit in a 3-quart casserole. Pour sauce over fruit. Heat in 350 degree oven for 30 minutes. This can be fixed the day before serving and be refrigerated, then reheated just before serving. Serves 10 to 15.

Betty Bell

Scalloped Apples

6 apples
1 cup sugar
1/2 teaspoon nutmeg

1/4 teaspoon cinnamon
3 cups soft bread crumbs
1/4 pound melted butter

Peel and thinly slice apples. Mix apples, sugar and spices. Pour melted butter over the bread crumbs. Put a layer of buttered crumbs in a Pyrex dish, then layer apples until all are used, ending with crumbs on top. Cover and bake for 40 minutes at 350 degrees.

Jodie Henslee

Scalloped Pineapple

6 slices day old bread
1/2 cup melted butter
1 (20 ounce) can crushed pineapple

1 cup sugar
Grated rind of 1 lemon
1 to 2 tablespoons lemon juice

Pull bread into tiny pieces. Mix with butter. Drain off 1/4 cup syrup from pineapple and discard. Mix pineapple and remaining syrup, sugar, lemon rind and juice into bread. Pour into 1-1/2 quart casserole. Bake at 350 degrees for 1 hour. *Unusual but good - great for a party.* Serves 4 to 6. *Shared by Sharlotte Hutchison.*

Mildred A. Bradley

Cranberries Amaretto

2 ounces butter
1 pound fresh cranberries
2 cups sugar
1 lemon, grated peel and juice

3 tablespoons lightly heaped
orange marmalade
1/3 cup amaretto liqueur

Melt butter, then add cranberries, sugar and lemon juice. Cook until cranberries are tender. Add lemon peel, marmalade and amaretto liqueur to mixture. Stir well. *This is a must with your Thanksgiving dinner.*

Joan B. Thompson

Hot Mustard

2 large cans dry Coleman mustard
1 cup white vinegar

1 cup sugar
3 eggs, beaten

Mix mustard and vinegar in bowl. Cover and let sit overnight. In top of double boiler, mix sugar and eggs. Stir in mustard mixture and cook until thick, 20 minutes or more. Cool. Store in refrigerator in jars.

In memory of Benijean Harness Wilkins

Mary Boellner's Cheddar Butter

8 ounces sharp Cheddar cheese,
   finely grated
1 tablespoon fresh dill (or 3/4 teaspoon dried)

4 ounces softened butter

Process all ingredients together until smooth and creamy. Wonderful on hot bread.

Janie Buckley

Hot Pepper Jelly

1/4 cup chopped or ground, red
   or green hot peppers
1-1/2 cups chopped or coarsely ground
   sweet green or red peppers

6-1/2 cups sugar
1-1/2 cups vinegar
1 bottle liquid pectin

Grind peppers on fine blade of food processor. Mix peppers, sugar, and vinegar. Bring to a boil - boil for 3 minutes. Add pectin and boil 1 minute more. Remove from heat and let set 5 minutes. Put into hot, sterilized jar and seal. *This is delicious served on top of cream cheese with crackers as an appetizer.*

Joan B. Thompson

How be it our God turned the curse into a blessing.

Nehemiah 13:2

Lillian's Strawberry Preserves

1 quart washed strawberries
4 cups sugar

Paraffin

Cover berries with boiling water and let stand 5 minutes. Drain and add 2 cups sugar and boil for 5 minutes. Add the other 2 cups sugar and boil another 5 minutes. Cool overnight. Pour into jars and seal with paraffin. *Lillian and Fred Wiese moved here from Iowa, and all that knew them were exposed to the most energetic family this church had ever known!*

Leila O'Keefe

Mother's Chili Sauce

2 quarts <u>ripe</u> tomatoes, peeled
  and chopped
3 large white onions, ground
1 bell pepper, ground
1 hot pepper, ground
3/4 cup sugar
1-1/4 pints white vinegar

1 teaspoon salt

Tie up in bag and beat:
1 tablespoon whole cloves
1 box stick cinnamon
1 teaspoon allspice
4 or 5 whole black peppercorns

Place all ingredients in large heavy pot. Cover well with water and cook slowly until thick. Remove bag of spices and pour sauce into sterile jars and seal.

In memory of Linda List Tanner

Pickled Okra

5 garlic cloves
5 heads of dill (<u>or</u> 5 teaspoons dried dill)
5 hot peppers
Whole okra pods (enough to fill 5 jars)

3 cups water
2 cups white vinegar
1/4 cup salt

Place one clove garlic, head of dill, and pepper in each sterlized jar. Wash and clean okra; pack into sterilized jars. Bring water, vinegar, and salt to boil. Pour over okra. Seal jars. (May process in water bath if needed to seal.) <u>Let stand 2 weeks before using</u>. Makes 5 pint jars.

Linda Burrow VanHook

Bread and Butter Pickles

8 onions
2 bell peppers, sliced thin
1 gallon cucumbers, sliced thin
1/2 cup salt
8 cups sugar

8 cups vinegar
3 tablespoons mustard seed
2 teaspoons turmeric
1-1/2 teaspoons ground cloves
1 teaspoon celery seed

Slice onion and peppers. Spread in layers with cucumbers and salt. Let stand 3 hours and then drain. Mix sugar, vinegar, mustard seed, turmeric, cloves, and celery seed. Scald but <u>do not</u> boil. Put cucumbers, onion and peppers in liquid and scald. Pack while hot in sterile jars.

In memory of Jane Hardy Means

Chow-Chow Pickles

1 peck green tomatoes (2 gallons)
1 dozen green bell peppers
1 dozen red bell peppers
6 hot peppers (optional or
   2 tablespoons cayenne)
1 dozen medium onions
1 large head cabbage (or 2 small)

1/2 cup salt
12 cups white vinegar
1 cup white mustard seed
   (3 boxes)
1 tablespoon celery seed
2 tablespoons allspice
2 pounds sugar

Clean, pare and grind all vegetables. Put in granite pan and sprinkle 1/2 cup salt over top. DO NOT STIR. Let stand 10 hours. Squeeze out all juice by hand. Let vinegar, sugar and spices come to a boil and pour over vegetable mixture and simmer 10-20 minutes. Ready to seal in hot sterilized jars. Makes 18 to 20 pints.

Martha Halbert

Crisp Sweet Pickles

5 cups sugar
1 cup vinegar
1/2 teaspoon celery seed

1/2 teaspoon mustard seed
2 quart jars dill pickles
Garlic

Boil sugar, vinegar, celery seed, and mustard seed. Drain dill pickles. Slice pickles into circles, about 1/4 inch thick. Place sliced pickles back into jars and pour mixture over them, and add 1 clove garlic (on toothpick) to each jar!

Anne Huff Monroe

Dill Pickles

12 dill pickles
1/2 cup olive oil
1 clove garlic
1 cup vinegar

5 cups sugar
2 tablespoons each cloves,
  cinnamon, and peppercorns

Slice pickles into 1/2 inch slices. Put into bowl and add oil and garlic. Boil vinegar, sugar, and spices 10 minutes. Add to pickles and let stand 4 days, stirring every day. Then pack, heat brine and pour over.

In memory of Mrs. H. K. Toney

Frozen Bread and Butter Pickles

16 cups sliced cucumbers, unpeeled
2/3 cup salt
2 onions, chopped
2 bell peppers, chopped
3 cups apple cider vinegar

4-1/2 cups sugar
3 teaspoons celery seed
2 teaspoons mustard seed
2 teaspoons turmeric

Cover first 4 ingredients with water and let stand overnight. Next morning drain, but do not wash. Pack in any kind of jar or carton you can freeze in. Heat next 5 ingredients and pour liquid over pickles. Put in freezer. When you are ready to eat, put jar in refrigerator for 2 days, then they are ready.

Frances Toney Hall

Hot & Spicy Pickles

1 gallon hamburger dills
5 pounds granulated sugar
1 bottle Tabasco (regular size)

1/2 of 2 ounce jar minced
  garlic
Juice from pickles

Drain pickles overnight; reserve juice. In large bowl mix sugar, Tabasco, garlic and reserved juice; stir to mix well. Alternate layers of pickles and sugar mixture in the gallon jug that the pickles came in. Turn for 5 days then store in smaller containers; refrigerate. Also, can store in smaller, sterilized containers. Refrigerate. Can be processed in a water bath to seal. Makes 7 pints.

Ann Bartlett Benton

COOKING LIGHTLY

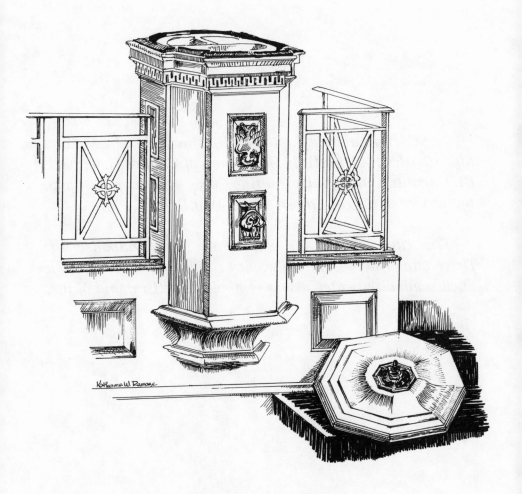

Katherine W. Ramage

The Carrara marble Baptismal Font was given by Mr. and Mrs. Charles H. Triplett, Jr. in memory of Charles H. Triplett, III, Captain, United States Marine Corps, who gave his life in the service of his country in World War II.

The carvings on the Baptismal Font symbolize the Descending Dove — The Holy Spirit coming from heaven. The Shell symbolizes water, also a symbol of baptism, and of life.

Mexicorn Dip

1 (11 ounce) can Mexicorn
1 (4.5 ounce) can chopped green chilies
1 jalapeno pepper, minced

8 ounces no-fat sour cream
1/2 teaspoon salt

Mix. Serve with baked tortilla chips.

Linda Burrow VanHook,
Co-Moderator, Presbyterian Women 1995-96

Buttermilk Corn Muffins

1 cup yellow corn meal
1 cup flour
2 teaspoons baking powder
1/4 teaspoon soda
1/4 teaspoon salt

1-1/2 cups nonfat buttermilk
1/4 cup frozen egg substitute,
 thawed
1 tablespoon vegetable oil

Combine dry ingredients in a large bowl, making a well in the center of the mixture. Combine liquid ingredients. Add to the cornmeal mixture, stirring just until dry ingredients are moistened. Grease muffin pans with vegetable spray and fill three-fourths full. Bake at 425 degrees approximately 20 minutes. Remove from pan immediately and cool on wire racks. Makes 12.

Margaret Dial Dawson

Gazpacho

1 clove garlic, split
4 ripe tomatoes
1-1/2 cucumbers
1/2 cup minced onion
1 (4 ounce) jar minced pimentos

2-1/4 cups tomato juice
3 tablespoons lemon juice
Dash of Tabasco
Salt and pepper to taste

Rub a glass bowl with garlic clove. Peel and finely chop tomatoes and cucumbers. Add onion, pimentos, tomato juice, and lemon juice. Add Tabasco, salt and pepper. Chill. Serves 6.

MarJo Dill

Chicken Soup Supreme

3 skinless chicken breasts
3 chicken bouillon cubes
8 cups water
1/4 cup fresh oregano
  (or 1 tablespoon dry oregano)
1/8 cup fresh lemon basil
  (or 1 teaspoon dry basil)
1/8 cup fresh thyme
  (or 1 teaspoon dry thyme)
1/8 cup fresh marjoram
  (or 1/2 teaspoon dry marjoram)

2 tablespoons coarsely chopped
  chives
2 garlic buds, minced
1 onion, chopped
3 ears corn (cut off cob and
  scrape cob)
4 tomatoes, peeled & chopped
1/2 teaspoon sugar
2 ribs celery, sliced thin
2 carrots, sliced thin
1/2 cup macaroni

Combine chicken with water and bouillon cubes in large, heavy pot and cook over medium heat approximately 30 minutes. Remove chicken and set aside. Prepare herbs and vegetables while chicken is cooking. When tomatoes are chopped, sprinkle sugar on them. Add all to the broth and cook slowly for 30 minutes. Tear chicken into bite-size pieces and add to soup. Cover pot and cook very slowly for 30 minutes. To serve, sprinkle with lemon pepper and Parmesan cheese to taste. Serves 16.

Ruth Anne Mathews

Low-Fat Turkey Chili

3 pounds ground turkey
2 onions, diced
1 red bell pepper, diced
1 (8 ounce) can tomato sauce
1 (8 ounce) can Ro-Tel tomatoes
2 cans kidney beans
2 cans stewed tomatoes
2 cups water
1 (8 ounce) can mushrooms (optional)

2 tablespoons garlic
1 package taco seasoning
3 tablespoons chili powder
1 teaspoon cumin
2 teaspoons salt
1/2 teaspoon pepper
Tabasco to taste
Worcestershire sauce to taste
Shredded lite cheddar cheese

Brown turkey, onion, and red bell pepper in large pan. Add other ingredients. Cook approximately 2 hours over low heat, stirring occasionally. To serve, sprinkle with shredded cheese (optional). Better if made a day ahead. Can use ground round in place of turkey, if desired. Serves 12.

Ann Brown Turner

Shrimp and Black Bean Chili

1 large onion, chopped
1 tablespoon oil
1 green bell pepper, chopped
1 yellow bell pepper, chopped
1 red bell pepper, chopped
1 cup chicken broth
1 (28 ounce) can whole tomatoes
with juice

2 (16 ounce) cans black beans
1/2 cup picante sauce (hot or
medium)
1 teaspoon cumin
1/2 teaspoon basil
2 pounds raw medium shrimp,
peeled

Saute onions in oil; add peppers and cook until soft. Add remaining ingredients, except shrimp; cook till hot. Just before serving, add shrimp and cook until done. (Shrimp turns pink when done). *Good served over basmati rice with Caesar salad and Mexican cornbread.* Serves 6 to 8.

Ann Rogers

Light Pasta Primavera

1 (12 ounce) package spaghetti or
linguine
1/2 bunch broccoli, cut into 1 inch
pieces (about 2 cups)
2 tablespoons olive oil
1 (12 ounce) package mushrooms,
each cut in half
1 small onion, minced
1 small carrot, cut into matchstick-thin
strips
1 small red pepper, cut into 1/4 inch strips (optional)

1 (12 ounce) can evaporated
skim milk
2 teaspoons instant chicken
bouillon
1-1/4 teaspoons cornstarch
1/2 teaspoon salt
1 medium tomato, diced
2 tablespoons Parmesan cheese
2 tablespoons minced parsley

Cook spaghetti according to label directions; drain. Keep warm. In 1 inch boiling water, bring broccoli pieces to boiling. Cover and simmer 2 to 3 minutes till tender-crisp. Drain. While broccoli is cooking, heat olive oil in 12 inch skillet over high heat. Add mushrooms, onion, carrot, and red pepper (if desired), stirring frequently until vegetables are golden and tender-crisp. Mix evaporated skim milk, chicken bouillon, cornstarch, and salt. Stir into vegetable mixture. Heat to boiling. Boil 1 minute. Add diced tomato, Parmesan cheese, parsley, broccoli, and spaghetti, tossing well to coat. Heat through. Serves 6.

Sue Deneke

Yogurt Cheese

16 ounces plain yogurt

Place yogurt in strainer lined with several coffee filters. Balance the strainer on top of a small bowl and cover with plastic wrap. Place in refrigerator for 2 days. The liquid will drain from the yogurt into the bottom of the bowl. Pour off. The remaining Yogurt Cheese will keep several weeks in covered bowl in the refrigerator. Use in place of sour cream or cream cheese. Spread on bagels, muffins, or crackers.

Diane Fisk

Summer Pasta Salad

1/4 cup vegetable oil
1 tablespoon sugar
3 tablespoons dry white wine
2 tablespoons lemon juice
1 teaspoon basil
1 teaspoon salt
1/4 teaspoon pepper
Several dashes Tabasco sauce

4 medium tomatoes, peeled and diced
1 medium cucumber, peeled and diced
1 small green pepper, chopped
1 small onion, diced
1/4 cup chopped parsley
1 package spinach fettuccini
Feta cheese

Dressing: Mix oil with sugar, wine, lemon juice, basil, salt, pepper, and Tabasco. Combine with vegetables. Chill. Cook pasta according to package directions. Rinse with cold water until chilled. Serve marinated vegetables over pasta. Crumble feta cheese over all. Serves 3 to 4.

Linda Burrow VanHook

Strawberry-Nut Salad

2 (3 ounce) packages sugar-free
  strawberry gelatin
1 cup boiling water
1 (16 ounce) package frozen
  whole strawberries, thawed,
  halved, and drained
1 (20 ounce) can crushed pineapple, drained

1 cup chopped pecans
3 medium bananas
8 ounces nonfat sour cream
1/4 cup fat-free mayonnaise
1/2 teaspoon grated orange
  rind

Dissolve gelatin in boiling water. Stir in strawberries, pineapple, and pecans. Set aside. Place bananas in blender and pulse 3 times or until finely chopped, but not mashed. Stir into gelatin mixture. Spoon half of mixture into a lightly greased 11x7 baking dish. Refrigerate until almost set. Do not refrigerate the remaining strawberry mixture. Combine sour cream, mayonnaise, and orange rind. Spread over congealed strawberry layer. Top with remaining strawberry mixture. Cover and chill 8 hours. Serves 10.

Margaret Dial Dawson

Authentic Chili Beans

2 cups dried pinto beans,
  soaked overnight
1-1/2 quarts water
1/2 large onion, chopped
1 clove garlic
1 bay leaf
2 tablespoons oil
2-1/2 tablespoons flour

2-3 teaspoons chili powder
1-2 teaspoons cumin
1 onion, chopped
Salt and pepper to taste
4 cups cooked rice, brown or white
1/2 pound Monterey Jack or Cheddar
  cheese, shredded (optional)

Simmer beans, 1/2 onion, garlic, and bay leaf in water or stock for 2 hours. In separate pan, heat oil and add flour, chili powder, and cumin to make a roux paste, cooking for 5 minutes and stirring constantly over low heat. Do Not Burn the Roux! Add roux and onion to beans and cook for another hour until the beans are soft and the chili is thickened. Adjust seasonings and serve over rice. Sprinkle with cheese, if desired. Serves 6 to 8.

Cynthia Barefield Williams

Low-Fat Mashed Potatoes

10-12 medium potatoes
2-3 tablespoons Molly McButter
1/2 cup minced onion

1/2 cup skim milk (approx.)
Salt and pepper to taste

Peel potatoes; cook; mash. Add Molly McButter and onion. Beat with mixer and add milk until desired consistency. 8 to 10 servings.

Ann Brown Turner

Oven Fries

4 medium potatoes
1 tablespoon oil
1/8 teaspoon garlic powder
1/8 teaspoon onion powder

1-1/2 teaspoons paprika
1/4 teaspoon salt
1/4 teaspoon fresh ground
  black pepper

Wash potatoes well and slice lengthwise into strips, leaving skins on. Line a shallow baking pan with foil. Place all the ingredients in the pan, tossing well to coat the potatoes with oil and seasonings. Bake at 425 degrees for about 35 minutes, stirring often until potatoes are tender. Serves 4.

Sue Deneke

Potatoes with Parsley

1/4 cup water
1 chicken bouillon cube
4 medium red potatoes

1/2 teaspoon lemon pepper
1 cup fresh parsley, chopped

In heavy stainless or water-less cookware, heat water and dissolve bouillon cube. Add quartered potatoes and lemon pepper. Cover and cook over medium low heat 20 minutes. Add parsley. Cover and cook 10 minutes longer over low heat. Stir occasionally during cooking and add water if needed to keep from sticking to pan. Serves 4.

Ruth Anne Mathews

Twice-Baked Potatoes

4 baking potatoes
2 ounces lowfat cream cheese, cubed
 and softened
2 tablespoons snipped chives
1/4 teaspoon dried basil, crushed

1/8 teaspoon salt
Dash pepper
3-4 tablespoons skim milk
Paprika

Bake potatoes until tender. Cool slightly and cut in half lengthwise. Gently scoop out pulp, leaving a thin shell. Set shells aside. Beat pulp, cream cheese, chives, basil, salt, and pepper until smooth adding milk one tablespoon at a time until fluffy. Spoon potato mixture back into shells and sprinkle with paprika. Loosely cover with foil. Bake at 375 degrees for 10 minutes. Remove foil and continue baking 10 additional minutes. Serves 4.

Sue Deneke

Baked Stuffed Tomatoes

4 medium tomatoes
2 cloves garlic, minced
1 tablespoon margarine
1 tablespoon fresh basil, or
 1 teaspoon dried basil, crushed

1/2 cup chopped green pepper
3/4 cup croutons
2 tablespoons snipped fresh
 parsley

Cut 1/2 inch from top of each tomato and discard. Scoop out pulp; coarsely chop and set aside. Saute garlic in margarine for 30 seconds. Stir in tomato pulp, green pepper, and basil. Cook 2 minutes. Stir in croutons and parsley. Spoon mixture into tomatoes and arrange stuffed tomatoes in a 9 inch pie plate. Bake, uncovered, for 10-15 minutes at 350 degrees. Serves 4.

Sue Deneke

Creole Zucchini

3 medium zucchini squash, sliced
1 (14-1/2 ounce) can tomatoes,
    cut up and drained
1 chopped onion
6 cloves garlic, crushed

1 tablespoon salsa
1/2 teaspoon Creole seasoning
18 green olives, sliced
Salt and pepper to taste

Saute onion and garlic in tomato juice until clear. Add zucchini, tomatoes, olives, salsa and spices. Cover and cook till tender. *Good as vegetable or can be served over pasta or rice. (Less than 1 gram fat per serving).* Serves 4 to 6.

Jimmie Don Norsworthy

Caribbean Pork Tenderloin

2 lean pork tenderloins, about
    1/2 pound each
1 teaspoon grated orange peel
1/2 cup orange juice
2 tablespoons lime juice
2 tablespoons chopped fresh cilantro
1/2 teaspoon cracked black pepper

2 cloves garlic, cut in half
1 teaspoon cornstarch
1/4 teaspoon salt
1 teaspoon vegetable oil
1 large ripe plantain, cut in
    1/4 inch slices

Trim fat from tenderloin and cut across grain into 1/8 inch slices. Mix orange peel, orange juice, lime juice, cilantro, pepper, and garlic in large glass or plastic bowl. Stir in pork. Cover and refrigerate 30 minutes. Remove pork from marinade and drain. Stir conrstarch and salt into marinade; reserve. Heat oil in skillet over medium-high heat. Saute pork in oil about 4 minutes or until no longer pink. Stir in plantain; saute until brown. Stir in marinade mixture. Heat to boiling, stirring constantly. Boil and stir 1 minute. Serves 4.

Sue Deneke

For two weeks during the flood of 1927, the women of the church served food and provided clothes for the flood refugees, keeping the church open day and night.

Meat Loaf

3/4 pound extra lean ground beef
3/4 pound ground turkey
1/2 cup regular oats
1/2 cup tomato puree
1/4 cup chopped onion

2 tablespoons fresh parsley, chopped
1/2 teaspoon Italian seasoning
1/2 teaspoon salt
1/4 teaspoon pepper
1 clove garlic, finely chopped

Mix all ingredients thoroughly. Place mixture in ungreased loaf pan, or shape into loaf in ungreased rectangular pan. Bake, uncovered, in pre-heated 350 degree oven for 1-1/4 to 1-1/2 hours or until center is no longer pink.
MICROWAVE DIRECTIONS: Place mixture in ungreased microwavable loaf dish. Cover with waxed paper. Microwave at medium-high (70%) for 18 to 20 minutes, rotating dish 1/2 turn after 9 minutes. When center is no longer pink, remove from dish to serving platter. Cover and let stand 5 minutes before serving. Serves 8.

Sue Deneke

Chinese Chicken

2 cups water
2 tablespoons chicken instant bouillon
2 tablespoons cornstarch
1-1/2 tablespoons soy sauce
1 tablespoon sugar
2 cups diced, cooked chicken breast
(skin removed)
1 medium green pepper, thinly sliced

1 medium onion, thinly sliced
1 cup diagonally cut carrots
1 cup diagonally cut celery
8 ounces fresh mushrooms,
thinly sliced
1 (8 ounce) can sliced water
chestnuts, optional
Cooked rice or chow mein noodles

In large skillet, combine water, bouillon, cornstarch, soy sauce, and sugar. Cook over low heat until dissolved and slightly thick. Add chicken and vegetables. Simmer, uncovered, until tender. Serve over rice or chow mein noodles. Serves 6.

Debbie Johnson

Portraits of our ministers were painted by Miss Adele Hudson, Barbara Delle Gregory, and Betty Dortch Russell.

Low-Fat Chicken Spread

4 skinless chicken breasts
1/2 teaspoon Jane's "Crazy Pepper"
1 onion
4 stalks celery
1/4 teaspoon garlic powder

1 teaspoon Cavender's seasoning
2 teaspoons lemon juice
1/2 teaspoon salt
Fat-free mayonnaise to desired consistency

Cook chicken breasts in water seasoned with "Crazy Pepper" till done. Cool. Process onions and celery in food processor till finely ground. Process chicken till finely ground. Mix. Add spices, lemon juice, and just enough mayonnaise to moisten and stick together. Serve on bread or with fat-free crackers or pretzel chips.

Ann Brown Turner

Orange Stir-Fried Chicken

4 boneless, skinless chicken breast
  halves (about 1 pound)
1 tablespoon low-sodium soy sauce
1 teaspoon cornstarch
1 teaspoon grated ginger root, <u>or</u>
  1/2 teaspoon ground ginger
1 clove garlic, finely chopped
1/2 cup orange juice

2 teaspoons cornstarch
2 teaspoons vegetable oil
3 cups thinly sliced mushrooms
  (about 8 ounces)
1/2 cup coarsely shredded
  carrot (about 1 medium)
2 cups cooked rice

Trim fat from chicken and cut in 1/4 inch strips. Mix soy sauce, 1 teaspoon cornstarch, ginger, and garlic in a glass or plastic bowl. Stir in chicken. Cover and refrigerate 30 minutes. Mix orange juice and 2 teaspoons cornstarch until dissolved. Heat 1 teaspoon oil in 10 inch skillet over high heat. Add chicken mixture, stir-frying until chicken turns white. Remove chicken from skillet. Add remaining oil to skillet, and stir-fry mushrooms and carrots about 3 minutes till tender. Stir in chicken and orange juice mixture. Heat to boiling, stirring constantly. Cook and stir 30 seconds, or until thickened. Serve over hot rice. Serves 4.

Sue Deneke

Skillet Chicken Paella

1-1/4 pounds skinless, boneless chicken
   breasts, cut into bite-size strips
1 tablespoon olive or cooking oil
1 medium onion, chopped
2 cloves garlic, minced
2-1/4 cups chicken broth
1 cup long-grain rice, uncooked
1 teaspoon dried oregano, crushed
1/2 teaspoon paprika

1/4 teaspoon salt
1/4 teaspoon pepper
1/8 teaspoon saffron or turmeric
1 (14.5 ounce) can stewed
   tomatoes, diced
1 medium red bell pepper, cut
   into strips
3/4 cup frozen peas

Rinse chicken and pat dry with paper towels. Heat oil in 10 inch skillet; cook chicken strips, half at a time, for 2 - 3 minutes or until no longer pink. Remove chicken from the skillet. Add onion and garlic to skillet; cook till tender, but not brown. Remove skillet from heat. Add broth, uncooked rice, oregano, paprika, salt, pepper, and saffron or turmeric. Bring to a boil; reduce heat, cover, and simmer about 15 minutes. Add undrained tomatoes, red pepper, and frozen peas. Cover and cook additional 5 minutes or until rice is tender. Stir in chicken. Cook and stir about 1 minute more or until heated through. Serves 4 to 6.

Ann Benton

Angel Pie

20 lowfat Ritz crackers
1/2 cup chopped pecans
1/2 cup sugar

3 egg whites
1/2 cup sugar
1 teaspoon vanilla
Light Cool Whip or Dream Whip

Crush crackers. Mix crumbs with pecans and 1/2 cup sugar. Beat egg whites till very stiff, gradually adding 1/2 cup sugar and vanilla. Fold cracker mixture into egg whites. Spread in a pan sprayed with Pam, and bake at 350 degrees for 25 minutes. Cool. Top with Cool Whip to serve. Serves 6 to 8.

Corinne Hunter,
President, Women of the Church 1970-72

Banana Split Pie *(Sugar-Free)*

8 (2-1/2 inch) square graham crackers,
   crushed
8 teaspoons diet margarine
2 packages Equal
1 (3 ounce) package instant sugar-free
   vanilla pudding

2 cups skim milk
1 medium banana
1 cup crushed pineapple, well
   drained
1 cup Cool Whip

Mix crackers, margarine, and sweetener. Pat into 8 inch pie pan. (May bake if desired). Mix pudding with milk. Slice banana over crust. Pour pudding over banana. Top with well-drained pineapple; then top with Cool Whip. Serves 6.

MarJo Dill

Featherweight Cheesecake

Crust:
1 cup graham cracker crumbs
3 tablespoons sugar
3 tablespoons light margarine, melted
Filling:
2 (8 ounce) packages light cream cheese, softened
1/2 cup sugar
1 tablespoon lemon juice
1 teaspoon grated lemon rind
1/2 teaspoon vanilla
2 eggs, separated

Topping:
1 cup light sour cream
2 tablespoons sugar
1 teaspoon vanilla

Crust: Combine crumbs, sugar, and margarine. Press into bottom of 9 inch springform pan. Bake for 8 minutes at 325 degrees.

Filling: Combine cream cheese, sugar, lemon juice, lemon rind, and vanilla, mixing at medium speed with electric mixer until well blended. Add egg yolks, one at a time, mixing well. Fold in stiffly beaten egg whites. Pour over crust and bake 45 minutes at 300 degrees.

Topping: Combine sour cream, sugar, and vanilla. Carefully spread over cheesecake. Continue baking for an additional 10 minutes. Loosen cake from rim of pan; cool before removing rim. Chill.

May top with sugar-free strawberry preserves, if desired. Serves 12.

Dana Dawson McLellan

No-Fat Chocolate Sauce

3/4 cup sugar
1/4 cup cocoa
1 tablespoon + 1 teaspoon cornstarch

3/4 cup evaporated skim milk
1 teaspoon vanilla

Mix dry ingredients in saucepan. Slowly add milk. Cook until thick. Cook and stir additional 2 minutes. Remove from heat. Add vanilla. Refrigerate. Doubles easily. Will keep in refrigerator for several weeks. Makes approximately 1 cup.

Ann Benton

Low-Fat Margarita Cheesecake

Crust:
1-1/4 cups fat-free pretzel crumbs
  or gingersnap crumbs
1/4 cup unsalted butter, melted
Filling:
3 (8 ounce) packages fat-free cream
  cheese, softened
1-1/4 cups fat-free sour cream
3/4 cup plus 2 tablespoons sugar
3 tablespoons Triple Sec (or other orange liqueur)
3 tablespoons tequila
5 tablespoons fresh lime juice
4 eggs

Topping:
3/4 cup fat-free sour cream
2 tablespoons fresh lime juice
1 tablespoon tequila
1 tablespoon sugar

Very thin lime slices for garnish

Crust: Spray 9 inch springform pan well with vegetable spray. Mix crumbs with butter until well blended. Press over bottom and up sides of prepared pan. Refrigerate.

Filling: Using electric mixer, beat cheese till fluffy. Add sour cream, sugar, Triple Sec, tequila, and lime juice. Beat in eggs. Pour into crust. Bake in 350 degree pre-heated oven until outside 2 inches are set, approximately 50 minutes. Remove from oven and turn oven off.

Topping: Blend sour cream, lime juice, tequila, and sugar. Spread over cheese-cake. Return to hot oven. Let stand 45 minutes. (Cheesecake will look very soft, but will set up when chilled). Refrigerate until well chilled, up to 1 day. Serves 12.

Ann Rogers

The first wedding in our new sanctuary was when Marilyn Hearne McGeorge married Hugh David Young on May 30, 1974.

VEGETABLES

Katherine W. Ramage

The communion table was a gift of Mrs. Adam B. Robinson, Sr., Mr. and Mrs. T. Walker Lewis, Jr., and Mr. and Mrs. Adam B. Robinson, Jr. in memory of her husband and their father, Mr. Adam B. Robinson, Sr.

The silver chalice was given in memory of Zaphney Orto Humphreys, Lieutenant Colonel, United States Marine Corps, by his family.

Artichokes with Flair

1 (8 ounce) can artichoke hearts, drained
2 (10 ounce) packages frozen chopped
  spinach, cooked and drained
1 (8 ounce) package cream cheese

1 stick butter
1/2 pound bacon, cooked and
  crumbled
Parmesan cheese

Quarter drained artichoke hearts and spread over bottom of an 8x8 casserole. Spoon spinach over artichokes. Melt butter and cream cheese in a small saucepan (cream cheese will be lumpy). Pour and spread over spinach. Sprinkle crumbled bacon over cream cheese mixture. Sprinkle well with Parmesan cheese. Bake at 350 degrees for 30 minutes. *An easy and elegant side dish with beef.* Serves 6.

Joan B. Thompson

Asparagus Soufflé

1 tablespoon flour
1/4 teaspoon salt
1/8 teaspoon sugar
Dash pepper
1 cup milk

3 eggs, separated and beaten
  well, separately
1 cup sharp Cheddar, grated
4 whole saltines, crumbled
1 can asparagus, cut up & drained

Mix together dry ingredients with a little milk. Add remaining milk and well-beaten egg yolks. Cook in double boiler until slightly thickened. Add grated cheese and crumbled crackers and asparagus. Fold in stiffly beaten whites. Bake at 350 degrees until golden brown. Serve immediately. Serves 4.

Marion Ryland Love

Creamed Asparagus

Dressing:
2 tablespoons butter
1 tablespoon flour
1 cup sweet milk or cream

Fresh asparagus
Boiling water
Salt

Dressing: Melt butter in double boiler. Stir in flour and add sweet milk or cream. Cook until smooth. Set aside.
Asparagus: Wash fresh asparagus well; break off tough ends. Plunge asparagus into 6 quarts boiling water, seasoned with 1-1/2 teaspoons salt. Boil rapidly for a few minutes, just until fork tender, but crisp. Do not overcook. Asparagus will continue cooking when removed from liquid. Serve with dressing. *Mrs. Crawford was responsible for raising the money to build the first Davis Hospital at 11th & Cherry Streets. Oak trees from 34th & Cherry Street to the Pine Bluff Country Club (lining both sides) were planted some years later in her honor.*

In memory of Mrs. J. W. Crawford

Barbecue Beans

2 pounds ground beef
1 large onion, chopped
1 large green pepper, chopped
Salt and pepper

1/2 large bottle (1 pound, 2
ounce) Kraft barbecue sauce
3 (12 ounce) cans pork and
beans

Brown the ground beef, onion and green pepper together, adding salt and pepper to taste. Add barbecue sauce and simmer 5 minutes. Add pork and beans and bake in a covered dish one hour at 250 degrees. Serves 10.

Sue Norton Smith

Bean Hot-Dish

1/2 pound bacon, cut up fine, cooked
and drained
1/2 pound ground beef, browned and
drained
1 small onion, chopped, cooked with beef
1 (No. 2 can) kidney beans, drained
1 large can pork and beans
1 (No. 2 can) lima beans, drained

1 (No. 2 can) butter beans,
drained
1 cup catsup
1/2 cup brown sugar
1/2 teaspoon prepared mustard
2 tablespoons vinegar
1 tablespoon Worcestershire
sauce

Mix all the ingredients; bake one hour at 350 degrees. (You may also add one fourth pound cubed Velveeta cheese). Serves 10 to 12.

Liana Seigfried

Doris's Bean Casserole

1 package frozen French green beans
1 package frozen baby limas
1 package frozen tiny English peas
1/2 cup mayonnaise

2/3 cup whipping cream,
whipped
1-1/2 ounces Parmesan cheese

Cook vegetables according to package directions. Place in large mixing bowl. Add mayonnaise, whipping cream and Parmesan. Pour into buttered casserole. Bake 45 minutes at 350 degrees. Serves 8.

Ellen Nuckolls

Green Beans Oriental

2 (5 ounce) cans sliced water chestnuts
4 tablespoons oil
4 tablespoons soy sauce
2 (10 ounce) packages frozen French style green beans

2 teaspoons sugar
Salt and pepper to taste

Saute water chestnuts in oil until golden brown. Add soy sauce, beans and sugar. Season. Cook on low heat until beans are just tender-crisp and still bright green, separating them with a fork as they defrost. Add salt and pepper to taste. Serves six.

Karen Needler

Red Bean Rave

3/4 cup celery, chopped
1/2 cup green bell pepper, chopped
1 small onion, chopped
1 (10 ounce) can diced tomatoes
1 large jalapeno pepper, diced
1 pound dried red beans, rinsed

1 pound smoked sausage, sliced
1 tablespoon Fajita seasoning
1-1/2 teaspoons Creole seasoning
4 cups water
2 cups cooked rice

Wash vegetables; chop and put into crockpot. Add tomatoes and jalapeno pepper. Rinse beans and put into pot. Brown sliced sausage and place sausage, and all other ingredients into crockpot. Cook overnight on low heat or cook on top of stove in a Dutch oven until beans are tender. Add more water if needed. Serve over cooked rice. Serves 6 to 8.

Robin Banks Dawson

The greatest tribute ever paid to a Pine Bluff citizen was paid to our minister, Dr. Joseph I. Norris, when he died. The Arkansas Power and Light Company arranged for dimming all electric power over the entire system out of Pine Bluff for one minute at 3:00 p.m., the time of his funeral. All street cars in the city remained idle for three minutes from 3:00 until 3:03 as a tribute. The Arkansas Short Leaf Lumber Company shut down its entire plant for five minutes beginning at 3:00 and all the stores in Pine Bluff closed during Dr. Norris' funeral. His body laid in state at the church and the elders and deacons served as a 24 hour honor guard. The beautiful stone cross at the entrance of Graceland cemetery was erected in memory of Dr. J. I. Norris by church members and his friends in Pine Bluff.

Broccoli Puff

1/3 stick margarine
1 onion, finely chopped
2 packages frozen chopped broccoli,
  thawed

1 can cream of celery soup
1 (6 ounce) roll garlic cheese
1/3 cup sliced almonds
1/2 cup fine bread crumbs

Slightly saute onion in margarine. Place with thawed broccoli, soup, cheese and almonds in buttered casserole. Top with bread crumbs. Bake at 350 degrees for 25 minutes. Serves 6 to 8. Freezes well.

In memory of Shirley McLellan

Broccoli Ring

5 frozen boxes chopped broccoli
1 cup chopped onion
1 pound sausage
1/2 cup bread crumbs

6 tablespoons cream
6 eggs, well beaten
1/2 teaspoon nutmeg
Salt to taste

Fry onion and sausage; drain. Cook broccoli according to directions on box, and drain. Combine cream, bread crumbs, onion, nutmeg and beaten eggs, mix with all other ingredients. Put in greased mold or casserole and place in pan of water to bake at 350 degrees for 1 hour, or until firm. Fills one large ring mold or two 1-1/2 quart casseroles. Serves 12 to 14. Freezes well.

Sis Bellingrath

Broccoli Casserole

2 packages chopped, frozen broccoli
1 stick butter
1 can cream of chicken soup
1 can cream of mushroom soup

1 can water chestnuts, drained
1 (8 ounce) package herb-
  seasoned stuffing mix

Cook the broccoli with the butter by package directions. Save the juice. Add the chicken soup, mushroom soup and the water chestnuts. Add the herb seasoned stuffing mix. Bake at 350 degrees for 40 minutes.

In memory of Laurie Tatman

Brussels Sprouts in Vinaigrette

4 cups Brussels sprouts
4 tablespoons sherry vinegar
4 tablespoons pure maple syrup
1 tablespoon Dijon mustard
1/2 cup walnut oil

Pinch freshly grated nutmeg
Salt and freshly ground pepper
to taste
1 cup chopped walnuts

Cut an "X" in bottom of each sprout. Steam until tender but firm (may substitute frozen). Whisk together the vinegar, syrup and mustard. Gradually add oil and whisk. Season with nutmeg, salt and pepper. Toss Brussels sprouts with walnuts and vinaigrette. May prepare ahead and warm slightly in microwave. Serves 6 to 8.

Bettye Hutt

Carrot Soufflé

2 cups - one pound cooked mashed
carrots - pureed in food processor
1 cup milk
1 stick butter, softened
2 tablespoons grated onion
1 teaspoon salt

1/8 teaspoon white pepper
1/8 teaspoon cayenne pepper
1 cup cornflake crumbs
3/4 cup grated sharp Cheddar
cheese
3 eggs, slightly beaten

Combine carrots, milk, butter, onion and seasonings. Add cornflake crumbs and cheese. Fold eggs into mixture and put in 1-1/2 quart casserole that has been sprayed with Pam. Bake at 350 degrees for 40-45 minutes. May be prepared without baking and put in refrigerator or freezer to be baked later. If using from frozen state, allow one hour for cooking. Serves 8 to 10.

Gail Bellingrath

Blessed are the meek; for they shall inherit the earth.

Matthew 5:5

Carrots with Seedless Green Grapes

3/4 cup butter
1 teaspoon dried chervil
1/8 teaspoon garlic powder
Pinch of celery salt
18 carrots or 2 pounds carrots

2 teaspoons dried basil
3 cups seedless green grapes
2 tablespoons lemon juice
Salt and pepper to taste

Melt butter in pan and add the chervil, garlic powder, and a good pinch of celery salt. Let stand. Scrape carrots and cut into strips 3 inches long. Cook until crisp-tender in boiling salted water with basil. Remove from heat; add the grapes. Let stand 3 minutes - no longer. Drain water, add lemon juice and butter mixture. Shake the pan. Salt and pepper, stir gently. *Fabulous and pretty.*

Pat Lile

Cauliflower with Mushroom Cheese Sauce

1 medium head cauliflower, washed
1-1/2 cups mushrooms, sliced & washed
2 tablespoons butter
2 tablespoons flour
1/4 teaspoon salt
1/8 teaspoon white pepper

1 cup milk
1 cup sharp cheese, grated
1 teaspoon prepared mustard
1 tablespoon parsley, snipped
2 hard-cooked eggs, sieved

Steam whole head of cauliflower in basket for 15 minutes, until crisp-tender. Cook fresh mushrooms in butter just until tender. Blend flour, salt and white pepper into butter. Add milk; cook, stirring constantly, until thickened. Stir in cheese and mustard. Heat until cheese melts (low heat). Place cauliflower on platter; spoon sauce over it. Sprinkle sieved eggs and parsley over the cauliflower. Serves 6.

In memory of Laura Dawson Chamberlin

Miss May Triplett and Mr. John Armer Perdue were the first couple married in the Fifth and Walnut Church on February 19, 1895.

Jiffy Corn Casserole

1 small onion, chopped
1/2 cup butter
1 (15 ounce) can cream style corn
1 (15 ounce) can whole kernel corn

3 eggs, beaten
1 package Jiffy cornbread mix
1 cup grated Cheddar cheese

Saute chopped onion in butter. Set aside. Mix the two corns, eggs, cornbread mix and onions. Put in buttered 2-1/2 quart casserole. Bake 30 minutes at 350 degrees. Top with cheese. Bake an additional 15 minutes at 350 degrees. Do not overcook! Should be moist.

Linda Burrow VanHook

Pan De Elote Casserole

1 (1 pound) can cream style corn
1 cup biscuit mix
1 egg, beaten
2 tablespoons melted butter
1 tablespoon sugar

1/2 cup milk
1 (4 ounce) can green chilies, chopped
1/2 pound Monterey Jack cheese, sliced thin

Combine first six ingredients. Pour one-half of batter into a greased glass baking dish (8x8 inch). Cover with chilies and cheese. Cover cheese with remaining batter. Bake at 400 degrees for 20 minutes. Serves 6.

Ann Bartlett Benton

Santa Fe Corn

2 cans yellow kernel corn, drained
2 small cans green chilies, chopped
1 (8 ounce) package cream cheese

4 tablespoons butter
3-4 bacon slices, cooked and drained

Drain corn; add to green chilies. Soften cream cheese with butter; add to corn and chilies. Put in casserole and cover with crumbled, cooked bacon. Cook at 350 degrees until bubbly - about 30 minutes. Serves 6 to 8.

Maxine Alexander

Eggplant and Oysters

1 eggplant, medium size
4 tablespoons finely chopped onions
1/4 cup butter
1/2 cup dry bread crumbs

1/2 teaspoon salt
1 pint oysters
1/2 cup light cream

Peel the eggplant and cut in 1/2 inch cubes. Cook in boiling salted water until soft. <u>Drain</u>. Saute the onion in butter until yellow and add bread crumbs and salt. Heat oysters slowly in own liquid just until edges curl. Drain. Layer eggplant in buttered casserole, sprinkle with crumbs and onions, then oysters, then repeat, until the casserole is filled, with crumbs on top. Cover with light cream. Add cream carefully - do not let it get soupy. Bake at 350 degrees until brown on top.

Frances Toney Hall

Stuffed Eggplant

2 large eggplants
3 slices white bread, crumbed
1/4 cup milk
3 eggs, beaten

1 medium onion, chopped
1-1/2 tablespoons butter
Salt to taste
Pepper to taste

Wash eggplant; cut in half lengthwise and scoop out meat. Boil meat until tender in small amount of water. Soak bread in milk and squeeze almost dry. Saute onion in butter; season. Add all ingredients and mix well. Stuff shells. Top with bread crumbs and bake at 350 degrees until brown, about 25 minutes. *Mrs. Eddins was a long time member of First Presbyterian. She was Jane Stone's grandmother.* Serves 4.

In memory of Annie Martin Eddins

Hominy Casserole

2 (16 ounce) cans white hominy,
  drained
1 small can chopped chilies
1 small grated onion
1 cup sour cream

1 cup grated Mozzarella cheese
1/2 teaspoon salt
1 tablespoon juice from chilies
Paprika or parsley flakes

Mix well and bake in covered dish at 350 degrees for 30 minutes. Before serving sprinkle top with paprika or parsley flakes. *Try it - you'll like it!* Serves 4 to 5.

Mildred Everett

Sherried Mushrooms

1 pound mushrooms
6 tablespoons butter, divided
1/4 cup green onions, minced
1/8 teaspoon salt
1/8 teaspoon white pepper

Sauce:
1 tablespoon flour
1 cup Half and Half
1 tablespoon sherry
1/8 teaspoon garlic powder
Paprika

Rinse, pat dry and slice mushrooms. Heat 4 tablespoons butter in a medium pan. Saute mushrooms and onions until mushrooms are slightly browned; stir occasionally. Stir in salt and pepper. Set aside and keep warm. Melt remaining 2 tablespoons butter in a small pan. Ad flour and cook stirring over low heat until lightly browned. Gradually add cream; stir constantly. Add sherry and garlic powder, mushrooms and onion. Serve over toasted patty shells or over cooked chicken breasts or on top of a filet, or as a side dish. Serves 4.

Dana Dawson McLellan

Creamed Onions

6 white onions, sliced
1/4 teaspoon salt
Water to cover onions
White Sauce:
2 tablespoons flour

1 cup milk
Salt and pepper
1 tablespoon sugar
Home-made buttered bread
crumbs

Boil onions in salted water until clear. Do not overcook! Drain well. Make a white sauce with flour, milk, salt and pepper to taste and sugar. Put in casserole and top with crumbs. Bake at 350 degrees until bubbly. *Good with steak!* Serves 4.

Annie L. Tatman Williams

Easy Onions

3 cans small whole onions, drained
1 small jar pimento
1 can cream of mushroom soup

1 cup sharp cheese, grated
1 cup slivered almonds

Mix together and bake until bubbly in oven in casserole. Can be heated on top of stove and served in vegetable dish. Be sure to carefully mix and keep onions whole. Serves 6 to 8.

Frances Toney Hall

Hoppin' John Casserole

2 tablespoons shortening
1 medium onion, chopped
1/2 cup celery
1 (16 ounce) can tomatoes
1/2 teaspoon salt
1/4 teaspoon black pepper

2 bay leaves
1 (15 ounce) can black-eyed
  peas, drained
2 cups coarsely chopped ham
1-1/2 cups cooked rice
1-1/2 cups grated cheese

Add onions and celery to shortening. Cook until done. Add tomatoes, salt, pepper, bay leaves and simmer 15 minutes. Remove bay leaves. Combine ham, peas, rice and tomato mixture in 2 quart casserole. Bake at 325 degrees for 20 minutes. Cover with cheese and return to oven until cheese is melted. Serves 4 to 5.

Betty Perryman

Spicy Black-Eyed Peas

3 strips bacon, cooked
1 onion, chopped
1/2 green pepper, chopped

3 cans black-eyed peas
1 can Ro-Tel
Salt and pepper

In large saucepan fry bacon until crisp. Saute onion and green pepper until soft, in pan with bacon. Add peas and Ro-Tel. Cook until hot. Season to taste. Serves eight.

LaNelle Roberts

Stuffed Green Peppers

1 (6 ounce) Uncle Ben's long grain
  and wild rice, cooked
1/4 pint sour cream
1 egg, beaten
2 tablespoons butter

2 tablespoons milk
2 (2-1/2 ounce) jars sliced
  mushrooms, drained
4-5 green peppers

Cook rice according to package directions. Combine with remaining ingredients, except green peppers. Prepare green peppers - core and wash. Place mixture in peppers. Place stuffed peppers in greased baking dish. Add enough water to fill to 1 inch depth. Cover an bake in 350 degree oven for 35 minutes. Remove cover and bake 10 minutes longer. Serves 4.

Mrs. Peter Ahlgrim

Boursin Potato Gratin

2 cups heavy cream
2/3 cup Boursin cheese (see recipe)
2 tablespoons green onion, minced
1 clove garlic, minced
2-1/2 pounds red new potatoes,
  scrubbed and sliced 1/4" thick

Salt and pepper to taste
2 tablespoons fresh parsley or
  2 teaspoons dried parsley
1 tablespoon chives

In a 1-1/2 quart saucepan, heat cream, Boursin cheese, onions and garlic over medium heat. Stir until cheese melts. Generously butter a 9x13x2 inch baking dish. Arrange half of the sliced potatoes in the dish, in slightly overlapping rows. Season with salt and pepper. Pour half of the cheese mixture over potatoes. Sprinkle with chives. Repeat layers. Bake in 400 degree oven about 45 minutes or until potatoes are tender and the top is golden brown. Serves 6.

Grace Hoffman

Boursin Cheese with Black Pepper

3 cloves garlic, minced
1/2 tablespoon salt
1 (8 ounce) package cream cheese
1/4 cup butter

2 tablespoons fresh parsley,
  finely chopped, or 2 tablespoons dried parsley flakes
1-2 tablespoons coarsely ground
  black pepper

In a small bowl, make a paste with the garlic and salt. Beat cream cheese, butter, parsley, pepper and garlic mixture with electric mixer until smooth. Serve with Potatoes Gratin (above), or as an appetizer with crackers.

Grace Hoffman

Creamy Potato Casserole

6 large red potatoes
2/3 cup milk
1 stick butter or margarine, softened
8 ounces cream cheese, softened
8 ounces sour cream

Salt and pepper to taste
1 clove garlic, minced
1/4 cup chopped green onion
1 cup medium or sharp
  Cheddar cheese, grated

Peel and cube potatoes. Cook in a small amount of boiling, salted water, covered, for 20-25 minutes or until tender. Drain. Place in a large bowl. Beat with electric mixer on low speed. Add milk and butter; beat until fluffy. Add cream cheese, sour cream, salt, pepper, and garlic to potato mixture and beat. Stir in onion. Transfer to a 2-quart round casserole. Top with cheese. Bake at 350 degrees about 30 minutes or until bubbly. Serves 8 to 10.

Grace Hoffman

Presbyterian Potatoes

1 (10 ounce) package frozen, chopped
 spinach
4 cups boiling water
1 stick butter
1/2 cup whole milk or Half and Half
2 teaspoons salt
1/4 teaspoon black pepper

1 teaspoon sugar
5 cups Hungry Jack instant
 potatoes
1 (8 ounce) carton sour cream
1-1/2 teaspoons dried dill weed
4 tablespoons frozen chives

Cook spinach according to instructions on package and drain very well. Combine boiling water, butter, milk, salt, pepper and sugar. Stir in instant potatoes until moistened. Add sour cream, dill weed and chives. Stir well. Blend in the spinach. Bake in a greased 2 quart dish at 350 degrees until hot and bubbly. Serves 8.

Pat Lile

Roasted New Potatoes

30 new potatoes
Olive oil

Salt and pepper
Garlic powder

Wash potatoes; make single peel around middle; coat with olive oil and place on cookie sheet. Sprinkle with seasonings. Bake at 375 degrees for 30 minutes then turn, re-season and continue baking for 30 more minutes. *May be roasted ahead and served at room temperature.* Serves 6 to 8.

Gail Morschheimer

Sweet Potato Puffs

2 cups cooked, mashed sweet potatoes
1/4 teaspoon salt
1 egg, well beaten

1 tablespoon melted butter
8 large marshmallows
Crushed cornflakes

Combine potatoes, salt, butter and egg. Mix well; shape into balls, with marshmallows in center. Roll balls in cornflake crumbs. Bake in a lightly buttered 2 quart baking dish at 325 degrees for 15-20 minutes or until good and hot. Serves 8. *Mrs. Dawson was a long-time member of our church.*

In memory of Allie Banks Dawson

Sweet Potato Soufflé

2 large sweet potatoes (2-1/2 pounds)
1 cup sugar
1/2 cup evaporated milk
1/3 cup butter, softened
2 large eggs
1 tablespoon orange juice concentrate,
   thawed

1/4 teaspoon salt
1 cup firmly packed brown
   sugar
1 cup chopped pecans
1/3 cup all-purpose flour
1/3 cup butter, melted

Wash and cook sweet potatoes in boiling water for 30 minutes or until tender. Let cool to touch; peel and mash potatoes. Combine potatoes and next 6 ingredients, and spoon evenly into 2 lightly buttered 9-inch pie plates or one larger baking dish. Combine brown sugar, pecans and flour; sprinkle evenly over potato mixture. Drizzle evenly with 1/3 cup melted butter. Bake at 350 degrees for 25 minutes. *My mother's recipe - a favorite of ours.* Serves 6 to 8.

Margaret Dial Dawson

Spinach and Artichoke Casserole

2 (10 ounce) packages frozen, chopped
   spinach, cooked and well drained
1/2 cup finely chopped onion
1 stick butter
1 (16 ounce) can artichokes, quartered

1 pint sour cream
1/2 cup Parmesan, grated
1 teaspoon salt
1/4 teaspoon pepper
1 teaspoon lemon juice

Cook spinach and drain; saute onion in butter. Mix with artichokes using 1/4 cup Parmesan and pour in buttered 2-1/2 quart casserole. Top with remaining 1/4 cup Parmesan. Bake at 350 degrees for 20-30 minutes. Can be doubled. May be frozen - thaw before cooking *A family favorite!* Serves 6.

Bettye Hutt

Mr. and Mrs. J. Harvey Means and Mrs. W. M. Toney started the Sunday School at Riverside which later became Riverside Church. Mr. Means was on the school board and secured Riverside School to have Sunday School in every Sunday. Miss Elizabeth Simmons (now Mrs. Virginius Barnett) also taught there. In 1932 they had 48 pupils and 4 teachers. Mrs. Toney taught the boys' class.

Ritzy Spinach

3 (10 ounce) packages frozen, chopped
   spinach, thawed and well drained
3 tablespoons butter, melted
1 garlic clove, minced

1 can cream of mushroom soup
1 (6 ounce) roll Kraft jalapeno
   cheese, grated
1/4 cup Ritz crackers, crushed

Slightly cook spinach to thaw. Squeeze all liquid from the spinach. Add butter and garlic. Stir in soup and cheese. (Mixture can be microwaved to melt). Pour in casserole dish. Bake at 350 degrees for 20 minutes. Top with crackers the last 5 minutes of cooking time. Serves 8.

Jo Neal

Acorn Squash with Ginger

2 large acorn squash
3 tablespoons butter
2 tablespoons honey
1 tablespoon lime juice

1 teaspoon ground ginger
Cayenne to taste
Salt

Wash squash. Pierce squash several places with a fork; place on paper towel in microwave oven and cook uncovered 4 minutes on high. Turn squash over and cook 4-6 minutes or until surface gives under pressure. In glass measuring cup combine butter, honey, lime juice and ginger. Cook uncovered 1-1/2 minutes or until bubbly. Cut squash in half lengthwise and scoop out, discarding seeds and membrane. Place, cut side up, in shallow dish. Spoon butter mixture over squash and sprinkle lightly with cayenne. Cook 1 to 2 minutes in microwave basting once with remaining butter. Serves 2.

Nancy Ryland Williamson

Brenda's Posh Squash

2 pounds yellow squash, sliced
1 small onion, chopped
1 cup mayonnaise
1 cup Parmesan
2 eggs, slightly beaten

1/2 teaspoon salt
1/4 teaspoon pepper
Topping:
1/2 cup cracker crumbs
1 tablespoon butter, melted

Wash and prepare vegetables. Cook vegetables together and drain. Add other ingredients in food processor and blend till fluffy. Spray casserole with Pam. Fill and add topping. Bake at 350 degrees for 30 minutes. Serves 6 to 8.

Bettye Hutt

Roasted Squash

6 yellow squash ⎱ cut into 2-3"
6 zucchini ⎰ long wedges
2 onions
1/4-1/2 cup best quality olive oil

1-2 teaspoons crushed garlic
1-2 teaspoons seasoning
   (Cavenders or salt, pepper
   and any herb)

Shake vegetables in big baggie with oil and seasonings. Put in single layer in shallow baking pan. Roast in 375 degree oven until tender - a little bit browned and shriveled. Serve warm or at room temperature. Also works for eggplant, new potatoes, etc. Cooking times may vary for each vegetable. Serves 8.

Ellen Nuckolls

Skillet Zucchini

1 pound zucchini, sliced
1/2 cup butter or oleo
1/4 teaspoon garlic salt

Pepper to taste
2 tablespoons water
Parmesan cheese

Wash and slice unpeeled zucchini. Toss in melted butter. Add seasonings and water. Cover and simmer over low heat 10 minutes or until tender. Drain. Sprinkle with Parmesan cheese and return lid until melted. Serves 4.

Nena Busby

Baked Green Tomatoes

Green tomato slices
Onion slices

Salt and pepper
Grated sharp Cheddar cheese

Layer tomatoes and onion, seasoning each layer. Top with cheese. Bake at 350 degrees until bubbly, about 30 minutes. *This is a Cordon Bleu recipe given to me by Kay Salyer.*

Sally Cook,
Moderator, Presbyterian Women
1996-97

Fried Green Tomatoes

4 large green tomatoes (about 2 pounds), washed
3/4 cup all-purpose flour or cornmeal
1 teaspoon salt

1/8 teaspoon pepper
3 tablespoons bacon drippings
6 tablespoons vegetable oil

Remove and discard a very thin slice from tops and bottoms of tomatoes; cut tomatoes into 1/4 inch thick slices. Combine flour, salt and pepper in a shallow dish; dredge tomato slices on each side in mixture. Heat bacon drippings and oil in a large cast iron skillet over medium heat until hot; add 1/3 of the slices. Cook 2 minutes on each side. Drain on paper towels. Repeat. Serve immediately. *Can also be used to fry okra or eggplant.* Serves 4 to 6.

Janie Buckley

Scalloped Tomatoes

1-1/2 cups bread cubes
1/3 cup melted butter
1 (14 ounce) can tomatoes, chunk style

1/3 cup brown sugar
1/4 teaspoon salt
1/4 teaspoon basil

Place bread in a 1 quart baking dish. Pour butter over bread and coat well. Mix tomatoes with brown sugar, salt and basil. Pour over bread and mix gently. Bake at 425 degrees for 25-30 minutes. Serves 4.

Bobbye Nixon

Tomatoes with Spinach

12 thick tomato slices
2 (10 ounce) packages frozen spinach, cooked and well drained
1 cup seasoned bread crumbs
1 cup green onions, finely chopped
6 eggs, slightly beaten

3/4 cup melted butter
1/2 cup grated Parmesan cheese
1 teaspoon thyme
3/4 teaspoon salt
1/2 teaspoon garlic

Wash and slice tomatoes. Place tomatoes in a 13x9 buttered baking dish. Squeeze excess water from spinach and combine with other ingredients. Mound mixture on top of tomato slices. Bake at 350 degrees for 15 minutes or until spinach is set. Do not overcook. *Henry Martin Dial, my father, requested this at Christmas time!* Serves 12.

Margaret Dial Dawson

Vegetables with Zesty Sauce

6 tablespoons butter, melted
3 tablespoon sugar
2 tablespoons prepared mustard
2 tablespoons vinegar
2 tablespoons lemon juice

3 packages frozen broccoli (or)
2 cans whole green beans,
drained
Crumbled cooked bacon, if
desired

Prepare sauce from butter, sugar, mustard, vinegar and lemon juice. Heat and pour over cooked vegetables. Sprinkle bacon over top. Serves 8.

Mrs. Collins Andrews, Jr.

Emma's Sauce

3/4 cup mayonnaise
1 tablespoon lemon juice
Dash of Tabasco
1/4 teaspoon Lawry's seasoning

2 hard cooked eggs, diced
1 teaspoon Worcestershire
sauce
1 teaspoon grated onion

Mix all ingredients; mashing the eggs. Season to your taste with Tabasco and Lawry's seasoning. *This is a great vegetable sauce for fresh or cooked vegetables, etc. green beans, drained.*

In memory of Emma Mae Brown

Parmesan Cheese Sauce

1 cup butter
2 cups Hellman's mayonnaise
1 cup Parmesan cheese, grated

1/2 cup onion, grated
1 teaspoon Worcestershire
sauce

Melt butter and cool. Add rest of ingredients and mix thoroughly. If too thin ,add more cheese. *Wonderful over fresh cooked asparagus.*

Connie Mullis

Blessed are ye that weep now; for ye shall laugh.

Matthew 6:21

120

Emerald Rice Medley

1 onion, chopped
1 bell pepper, chopped
1 stick margarine
2 cans cream of celery soup
1 large jar Jalapeno Cheese Whiz

2 (10 ounce) boxes frozen,
   chopped broccoli, cooked
   and drained
2 cups cooked rice

Saute onion and bell pepper in melted margarine on low heat for 4 or 5 minutes, stirring frequently. Combine all ingredients and bake in covered, buttered 2 quart casserole. Bake at 350 degrees for 15 minutes. Serves 12.

Mary Snavely

Green Rice Casserole

1-1/4 cups (5 ounces) shredded
   Monterey Jack or Swiss cheese
1 cup ricotta cheese
1 cup mayonnaise
1/2 teaspoon garlic salt
1/4 teaspoon pepper

3 cups cooked rice
1 (10 ounce) package frozen,
   chopped broccoli, thawed
   and drained
1 cup frozen green peas, thawed
1/4 cup diced green onions
   (optional)

Combine 1 cup Monterey Jack cheese and next 4 ingredients in a large bowl; stir in rice, broccoli, and peas. Spoon rice mixture lightly into a buttered 2 quart casserole. Bake, uncovered, at 375 degrees for 20 minutes. Sprinkle casserole with remaining cheese, and bake 5 additional minutes. Serves 6 to 8.

Margaret Dial Dawson

Monterey Rice

1 cup uncooked long grain rice
2 (10 ounce) cans diced Ro-Tel tomatoes
   undrained
1 cup water
1 teaspoon salt
2/3 cup pimento-stuffed olives, sliced

1/4 cup vegetable oil
1/2 cup chopped onion
1 cup (4 ounces) Monterey
   Jack cheese, grated

Combine all ingredients in a flat 2 quart casserole. Cook covered with foil at 350 degrees for 45 minutes. Stir and bake uncovered 15 more minutes or until rice is done. *Good with a Mexican dinner.* Serves 8.

Mrs. John Ingram

Oriental Rice

1 package Uncle Ben's white-wild
  rice mixture
1 cup chopped celery
1 cup chopped onion
3 tablespoons butter
2 tablespoons soy sauce

1 (3 ounce) can broiled
  mushrooms in butter
1 (5 ounce) can sliced water
  chestnuts
1/3 cup sliced almonds

Cook rice according to directions, using the enclosed seasoning in package. Saute celery and onion in butter and add all ingredients to rice. Put in casserole. Bake at 350 degrees for 20 to 25 minutes. Serves 6.

Frances Toney Hall

Pecan Rice

1 (14-1/2 ounce) can chicken broth
1 tablespoon dry sherry
Water
1 cup uncooked long grain rice, rinsed
2 tablespoons margarine or butter
1 cup sliced fresh mushrooms

1/2 cup green onions, sliced
  with some tops
1 teaspoon minced garlic
1/2 cup toasted pecans,
  coarsely chopped
1 tablespoon grated orange peel
  (zest)

In saucepan combine broth, sherry and enough water to equal 2 cups; bring to a boil. Stir in rice; reduce heat to simmer. Cook covered until tender (about 20 minutes). Drain any remaining liquid. In small skillet melt margarine; saute mushrooms and onions and garlic until tender. Place in microwaveable casserole. May microwave on high for 7 minutes, stirring twice. Stir in pecans and orange peel. Bake in 350 degrees oven until hot, about 15 minutes. Serves 6.

Ann Peterson

Sausage Almond Rice

1 pound sausage
1/2 cup onion, chopped
1/2 cup celery, chopped
1-1/2 cups raw rice

2 cans chicken broth
1/2 cup slivered almonds,
  toasted
1 tablespoon soy sauce

Cook sausage, onion and celery until done. Drain and place into a 3 quart casserole. Add rice, broth, almonds, and soy sauce. Bake at 375 degrees for 45 minutes to 1 hour. May be prepared ahead, refrigerated and baked before serving. Serves 6.

Liana Siegfried

SEAFOODS

The interior of the chapel and the furnishings were gifts of Mr. and Mrs. Miles Stanley Cook, Sr.

The full-length carving of the Savior is footed by the four Evangelists: St. Matthew (Man) - symbolizing Christ's humanity; St. Mark (Lion) - Christ's royalty; St. Luke (Ox) - Christ's sacrifice; and St. John (Eagle) - Christ's divinity.

The four doors symbolize the four Evangelists. The blue carvings in the doors represent the Greek letter Chi and the red carvings represent the Greek letter Rho. Together they form a monogram of our Lord Jesus Christ.

The carved IHS monogram (meaning Jesus) is centered in the raised nimbus window above the descending dove, representing the Holy Spirit.

Crabmeat and Artichokes

8 tablespoons butter, divided use
4 tablespoons flour
1 cup strong chicken broth
1 cup heavy cream
1/2 teaspoon salt
   (omit if broth is salty)
1/2 teaspoon cayenne pepper

2 tablespoons sherry
6 ounces grated Parmesan
   cheese
1 (15-1/2 ounce) can artichoke
   hearts, drained and quartered
1 pound lump crabmeat
1 cup fine bread crumbs

Prepare cream sauce with 4 tablespoons of the butter, flour, chicken broth and cream. Add salt if needed, and red pepper and sherry. Return to low heat and cook alcohol off sherry. Remove and add cheese and artichoke hearts; mix well. Add crabmeat and mix gently. Saute crumbs in remaining 4 tablespoons butter. Put crabmeat mixture in buttered shells or ramekins. Top with crumbs. Bake in 350 degree oven until hot and bubbling. Serves 6.

In memory of Irma Jeter Wilkins,
President Women's Auxiliary 1920-21

Crabmeat Au Gratin

1 large onion
3/4 cup minced celery
2 cloves garlic
1/4 cup minced bell pepper
1 stick butter
1/2 cup flour
12 ounces evaporated milk
3 egg yolks, beaten
1 teaspoon salt
1/2 teaspoon black pepper

1/4 teaspoon Tabasco sauce
1/2 cup grated Swiss cheese
3 tablespoons diced pimento
Chopped fresh parsley
2 tablespoons chopped green
   onion
2 cups lump white crabmeat
1/2 pound grated sharp
   Cheddar

In a large saucepan, saute onion, celery, garlic and bell pepper in butter until vegetables are wilted (about 5-6 minutes). Blend in flour. Add milk and blend well. Remove from heat and add egg yolks and seasonings. Cook over low heat for 5 minutes, stirring. Remove and add Swiss cheese, pimento, parsley and onions. Carefully add crabmeat. Pour into buttered individual au gratin dishes and cover with Cheddar cheese. Bake in 375 degree oven 15-20 minutes. Serve hot. Serves 8.

Lil Quinn

Crab Quiche

2 tablespoons white or green onion,
  minced
1 tablespoon butter
1 cup mushrooms, sliced
1 cup lump crabmeat, drained
1 tablespoon flour
1-1/2 cups Swiss cheese, grated
9 inch pastry shell, partially baked

3 eggs
1 cup Half and Half
1/2 teaspoon salt
Dash white pepper
Dash nutmeg
Dash Tabasco sauce
Minced parsley

Saute onion and mushrooms in butter until tender. Mix with crabmeat and flour and set aside. Sprinkle half of cheese in pastry shell; then spread that with crab mixture; then sprinkle remaining cheese on top. Beat eggs, cream, salt, pepper, nutmeg and Tabasco until well mixed but not frothy, using a wire whisk. Pour into shell and bake at 350 degrees for 30-40 minutes or until set and lightly browned. Sprinkle with parsley. For crabmeat, you can substitute a mixture of 1/2 cup shrimp and scallops, cooked and well drained, and 1/2 cup crabmeat. Serves 6 to 7.

Mildred Andrews Bradley

Crabmeat and Spaghetti

8 ounces thin spaghetti
1 can mushroom soup
1/4 pound oleo, melted
1/2 pint light cream
1/2 teaspoon salt
2 cups grated Cheddar cheese
1/2 cup chopped onion

1 tablespoon chopped green
  pepper
1 small jar chopped pimento
3 hard boiled eggs, chopped
1 pound crabmeat or
2 (7 ounce) cans crabmeat

Cook spaghetti. While it is cooking, heat soup until smooth and add oleo, cream, salt, cheese, onion, green pepper and pimento. Add eggs, reserving some to garnish top. Add crabmeat and stir gently. Add to drained spaghetti and put in buttered casserole. Bake in 350 degree oven until it bubbles. Serves 8.

Mary Sue Neblett

Blessed are ye that hunger now; for ye shall be filled.

Luke 6:21

Deviled Crab

2 cans crabmeat
1 cup milk
1 stick butter
2 tablespoons Worcestershire sauce
Salt and pepper to taste
1 to 1-1/2 cups cracker crumbs
4 ounces white wine

2 hard boiled eggs, grated
Juice of 1/2 lemon
Extra cracker crumbs
1 stick butter
Finely chopped parsley
Lemon slices

Cook first 5 ingredients in double boiler. Then add cracker crumbs. Add wine, eggs, and lemon juice. Put in crab shells or ramekins. Sprinkle with cracker crumbs and dot with butter. Bake at 400 degrees until hot. Garnish with parsley and lemon slices. Serves 4 to 6.

In memory of Julia Wagner List

Microwave Crabmeat Mornay

1/2 cup butter
1/2 pound fresh or 1 (8 ounce) can
  mushrooms, cut in half
Small bunch green onions, with tops,
  chopped fine
1/2 cup parsley, chopped
2 tablespoons flour
1-1/2 cups light cream, or 1 can evaporated milk

1/2 pound Swiss cheese, grated
1 tablespoon white wine
1 teaspoon salt
1/2 teaspoon cayenne pepper
1 pound white lump crabmeat
Seasoned bread crumbs

Microwave butter 1 minute in 2 quart measuring cup or dish. Saute mushrooms, onion and parsley on high 5 minutes. Blend in flour and cream. Cook on high 3 minutes or until it thickens. Stir in cheese and cook on high 1 minute or until melted. Add wine, salt and red pepper and gently fold in crabmeat. Spoon into shells or ramekins (or casserole), sprinkling with crumbs. Place 3 or 4 filled shells at a time in microwave on high 1-1/2 minutes or until heated through. Cooking time may vary according to the strength of the microwave. Serves 6.

Nancy Ryland Williamson

The mission churches which have been established from the First Presbyterian Church are S.C. Alexander Memorial (now Central Presbyterian), Second Presbyterian, Dollarway Presbyterian, Riverside Presbyterian, Faith Presbyterian, Presbyterian Church in Stuttgart, Arkansas.

South Carolina Crabmeat

1/4 cup butter
1/4 cup flour
1 cup light cream
1 teaspoon salt
1/8 teaspoon pepper
1/8 teaspoon red pepper

1/4 cup sherry
1 pound crabmeat or
1 pound shrimp or
1/2 pound of each, shelled
3/4 cup grated sharp Cheddar
cheese

Make a cream sauce using the first 7 ingredients. Add crabmeat or shrimp. Put into 4 to 6 shells or ramekins. Sprinkle cheese on top. Bake at 425 degrees about 10 minutes. Serves 4 to 6.

Annie Laurie Tatman Williams

Crawfish Boulettes

1 medium onion, chopped fine
1 cup celery, chopped fine
3 tablespoons margarine
1 pound crab claw meat, drained
1 pound crawfish tails,
shelled and ground

1/4 cup green onion tops,
chopped fine
1 egg, beaten
Bread crumbs
Salt and pepper to taste
A few teaspoons lemon juice
Oil for deep frying

Saute onion and celery in margarine until brown. Drain. To this, add crabmeat, crawfish, and onion tops. Stir in egg. Add bread crumbs until mixture is meat-ball consistency. Add salt, pepper and lemon juice. Shape in small balls. Fry until brown in deep fat. Cook very fast. Servings: 50 cocktail size balls.

Lil Quinn

Alexander Memorial Church on the corner of Sixteenth & Poplar was built in the summer of 1910 through the efforts of our church. The largest contributors were Mr. Sam Alexander and Mrs. Mary C. Taylor. It was named for Dr. S. C. Alexander, Pine Bluff Presbytery's Evangelist. We furnished founding members and financial support for many years. The name was later changed to Central Presbyterian.

Crawfish or Shrimp Étouffée

2 teaspoons salt
1/2 teaspoon red pepper
1/2 teaspoon black pepper
1 teaspoon dried basil leaves
1/2 teaspoon dried thyme leaves
7 tablespoons peanut oil
3/4 cup flour
1 onion, chopped
1/2 cup chopped celery

1 tablespoon garlic, minced
1 cup chopped green onions
3 cups chicken broth
1 tablespoon lemon juice
1/2 cup butter
2 pounds of crawfish or
  2 pounds of shrimp or
  1 pound of each, shelled
4 cups cooked rice

Mix all dry seasonings together. Heat peanut oil, add flour and make a dark brown roux. Add vegetables and garlic. Saute a few minutes over lower heat. Add seasonings, lemon juice and heated chicken broth (one cup at a time). Stir with wire whisk until thick. Set aside. Melt butter and saute shellfish about one minute, stirring constantly. Add to sauce. Heat and serve over hot rice. *This is very spicy. Reduce red and black pepper to 1/4 teaspoon if you don't like food hot.* Serves 8.

Janie Buckley

Crawfish Fettuccine

1-1/2 cups margarine
3 medium onions, chopped
2 medium bell peppers, chopped
1/4 cup flour
4 tablespoons parsley flakes
3 pounds shelled crawfish tails
1 pint Half and Half

1 pound Velveeta cheese, cubed
2 teaspoons jalapeno relish
3 tablespoons minced garlic
Salt, red and black pepper,
  to taste
1 pound fettuccine, cooked
Parmesan cheese for topping

Melt margarine. Saute onion and bell peppers until tender. Add flour. Cover and cook 15 minutes, stirring often to prevent sticking. Add parsley and crawfish. Cook 15 minutes covered. Add cream, cheese, relish, garlic, salt and pepper. Cover and cook 20 minutes. Remove from heat. Cook noodles until done. Mix drained noodles and crawfish mixture together. Pour into 3 quart greased casserole and bake at 350 degree for 15-20 minutes. Shrimp can be substituted for crawfish. Serves 10.

Ann Brown Turner

Baked Salmon Croquettes

1 large can salmon	1/4 teaspoon salt
1/4 cup butter	3/4 teaspoon Tabasco sauce
2 tablespoons minced onion	1 tablespoon lemon juice
1/3 cup flour	2 cups corn flake crumbs

Drain salmon and reserve juice. Melt butter and saute onion. Add flour and cook for a minute or two. Add juice from salmon and stir until smooth. Add next three ingredients. Add 1/2 cup corn flake crumbs. Chill. Make into patties and roll in more corn flake crumbs. Bake on greased cookie sheet at 400 degrees for 20 minutes or so. Can make patties hours ahead. Good served with tartar sauce. Serves 4 to 6.

Annie Laurie Tatman Williams

Salmon Croquettes

1 large can salmon	Pepper to taste
1/4 cup juice, drained from salmon	1/2 cup chopped green onions
1 heaping teaspoon baking powder	1/2 teaspoon Worcestershire
1 egg	sauce
1/2 cup flour	Oil for deep frying

Drain salmon, saving 1/4 cup of juice. Add baking powder to juice and beat with a fork until it foams. Mix salmon and egg with a fork. Add flour and stir. Add pepper, onion and Worcestershire. Add salmon juice mixture and mix well. Drop by small spoonfuls into hot oil and fry. This must be cooked within 15 minutes of preparing. Serves 4.

Jane Gillespie Starling,
President Women of the Church 1983-84

A service of thanksgiving for victory and cessation of combat in World War Two was held in the church auditorium at 7:30 p.m., August 8th, 1945. Three brave young men, children of this congregation, surrendered their lives in service to their country. Lieutenant Sterling Moore Clark, Eventon, N.C., May 22, 1944; Captain Charles H. Triplett, III, Saipan, June 15, 1944; 2nd Lieutenant Carl D. Rutledge, Jr., Holland, October 26, 1944, Infantry.

God knows the way, He holds the key,
He guides us with unerring hand,
Sometime up there we'll understand.

Salmon Loaf with Creamy Dill Sauce

2 tablespoons salad oil
3/4 cup finely chopped celery
1/2 cup chopped onion
1 small (7-3/4 ounce) can salmon
1 egg
1 (5-1/2 ounce) can evaporated milk
1 cup fresh bread crumbs
1 teaspoon salt
1/4 teaspoon pepper

SAUCE:
1/2 cup mayonnaise
1/4 cup sour cream
1 tablespoon salmon juice
1 tablespoon milk
1/2 teaspoon salt
1/2 teaspoon sugar
1/8 teaspoon pepper
2 teaspoons finely chopped fresh
dill or 1 teaspoon dried dill

In a 2 quart saucepan over medium-high heat saute in oil the celery and onion. Remove from heat. Add salmon and its juice and remaining ingredients. Mix well with fork. Pour into greased 6" by 3-1/2" loaf pan or 2-cup oven dish. Bake at 350 degrees about 50 minutes. Dill Sauce: Combine ingredients and stir with wire whisk. Refrigerate. Serve as an accompaniment to loaf. The loaf may be prepared one day before baking. Easy to double or triple recipe. Serves 2.

Mrs. Peter Ahlgrim

Salmon Loaf

1 large can salmon, drained
3 ounces cream cheese, softened
4 heaping tablespoons mayonnaise
6 green onions, finely chopped

2 tablespoons grated onion
Juice of 1/2 lemon
Salt and pepper to taste
1 scant cup cracker crumbs

Drain salmon and flake with fork. Mix cream cheese and mayonnaise. Add green onions, onion, lemon juice and seasonings. Add salmon and cracker crumbs. Bake in a greased loaf pan in a 350 degree oven for 45 minutes or until hot through. Serves 4.

In memory of Julia McAlmont Noel

Mrs. Noel was a pioneer member of the First Presbyterian Church at Fourth & Chestnut. We are indebted to her for the memoirs she wrote about the church which she joined as a child.

Barbecued Shrimp

1 pound raw shrimp in shells
1/2 cup salad oil
1/4 cup melted butter (no substitute)
2 tablespoons fresh lemon juice
2 tablespoons dry white wine
1 tablespoon Worcestershire
1 tablespoon parsley flakes
1 teaspoon cracked pepper

1 teaspoon fresh garlic, minced
1/2 teaspoon salt
1/2 teaspoon Knorr Swiss Arormat Seasoning for Meat
1/2 teaspoon Lowry's lemon pepper
2 shakes Tabasco sauce

Rinse and drain shrimp and place in bottom of a baking dish. Combine all other ingredients and pour over shrimp. Bake in 400 degree oven for about 20 minutes, turning once or twice. Serve in bowls with sauce and crusty French bread to dip in sauce. Serves 2 to 4.

Gen Kennedy Wilkins

Bud's Shrimp

5 pounds jumbo shrimp
1 large bottle Italian dressing
1/2 cup lemon juice
1 pound margarine

Worcestershire sauce
Tabasco sauce
Garlic salt

Place unpeeled shrimp in a large baking pan. Pour dressing and lemon juice over shrimp. Cut margarine into small pieces, scattering it over shrimp. Sprinkle mixture with seasonings. When melted, this mixture will nearly cover the shrimp. Bake at 300 degrees for about 45 minutes, turning often. Serves 6 to 8.

Margaret Dial Dawson

Herbed Shrimp and Feta Casserole

2 large eggs
1 cup evaporated milk
1 cup plain yogurt
8 ounces Feta cheese, crumbled
1/3 pound Swiss cheese, shredded
1/3 cup fresh parsley, chopped
1 teaspoon dried basil
1 teaspoon dried oregano
4 cloves garlic, minced

1/2 pound angel hair pasta, cooked
1 (16 ounce) jar mild, chunky salsa
1 pound medium shrimp, uncooked, peeled
1/2 pound Mozzarella cheese, shredded

Preheat oven to 350 degrees. Coat bottom and sides of an 8x12 inch baking dish with cooking spray. In separate bowl, blend eggs, milk, yogurt, Feta and Swiss cheeses, parsley, basil, oregano and garlic. Spread half of pasta over bottom of baking dish. Cover with salsa. Add half of the shrimp. Spread remaining pasta over shrimp. Pour and spread egg mixture over pasta. Add remaining shrimp and top with Mozzarella cheese. Bake 30 minutes. Remove from oven and let stand 10 minutes before serving. Serves 10 to 12.

In memory of Mollie Haley Grober

Margie's Shrimp Victoria

1 pound medium raw shrimp, peeled
  and deveined
1/4 cup minced onion
4 tablespoons butter
1/2 pound mushrooms, quartered

1 tablespoon butter
1 tablespoon all-purpose flour
Salt and freshly ground black
  pepper to taste
1 cup sour cream

In a skillet, saute shrimp and onion in 4 tablespoons butter until shrimp are pink. Add mushrooms and cook 5 minutes. Stir in remaining butter, flour, salt and pepper. Cook 1 minute. Slowly stir in sour cream, blending until hot and smooth. This is good with a simple lemon rice, made by adding lemon peel and lemon juice to rice while cooking. *Given to me by Margie Sturdivant.* Serves 4-6.

Janie Buckley

Seafood Mornay in Shells

1/2 cup butter
1/2 pound fresh mushrooms <u>or</u>
  1 (8 ounce) can mushrooms
1 small bunch green onions,
  finely chopped
2 tablespoons fresh parsley <u>or</u>
  1-1/2 teaspoons dried parsley
2 tablespoons flour

1/2 pound Swiss cheese, grated
1 tablespoon white wine
1 teaspoon salt
1/2 teaspoon cayenne pepper
Seasoned pepper
3/4 pound crab meat, cooked
1/4 pound shrimp, cooked
8 pastry shells

1-1/2 cups light cream <u>or</u> 1 (13 ounce) can evaporated milk

Microwave butter in 2 quart measuring cup for 1 minute. Saute mushrooms, onions, and parsley on high for 5 minutes. Blend in flour and cream. Cook on high for 3 minutes or until mixture thickens. Stir in cheese and cook on high for 1 minute or until cheese is melted. Add wine, salt, and peppers and gently fold in the seafoods. Spoon hot mixture into pastry shells. Serves 8.

In memory of Cherry Higgins

Shrimp Creole

5 tablespoons oil
4 tablespoons flour
1 large onion, chopped
1/4 cup green pepper, chopped
6-8 green onions with tops, chopped
1/2 cup parsley, chopped
1/2 cup celery, chopped
1 small clove garlic, minced

1 (8 ounce) can tomato sauce
1 can water
1 tablespoon Worcestershire
  sauce
1/4 teaspoon Tabasco sauce
Salt, red & black pepper, to taste
1 bay leaf
2-3 pounds shrimp, raw, peeled

Make a roux of oil and flour. Add onions, green pepper, green onions, parsley, celery and garlic. Mix well. Add tomato sauce and water. Add Worcestershire sauce, Tabasco sauce, salt, peppers and bay leaf. Simmer for one hour. Add shrimp. Cook just until shrimp is done. Serve over rice. Serves 4 to 6.

Joan B. Thompson

Shrimp Creole

4 slices bacon
1/2 cup chopped onions
1/2 cup chopped celery
1/2 cup chopped bell peppers
2 cups tomatoes
1/2 cup chili sauce

1/4 teaspoon black pepper
1 teaspoon salt
Tabasco to taste
1 pound peeled boiled shrimp
  (reserve water)

Fry bacon and remove from pan. In drippings, brown slightly the onion, celery and bell peppers. Add tomatoes and other ingredients and cook slowly until thickened, stirring occasionally. Add shrimp 30 minutes before serving. Crumble bacon and add last. If the sauce gets too thick, add water from shrimp boiling to thin it a little. Serve over rice. Serves 4.

Jodie Henslee

From: Memorial Volume of Board of World Missions -
"The expenses of Dr. and Mrs. William F. Bull, missionaries to Korea, were borne by our church from 1899 until they returned in 1941". We had our own missionaries in Korea for 42 years. In 1899 our church only had 310 members. We feel very blessed with God's help to have been able to do this.

Shrimp Florentine

2 pounds shrimp, peeled
8 ounces fresh mushrooms
1/2 pound cooked bacon,
  cut in bite size pieces
4 green onions, chopped
1 stick butter
2 packages frozen spinach
4 tablespoons butter
4 tablespoons flour

1 cup milk
Salt and pepper
Nutmeg
Garlic
1 cup plain bread crumbs
1/2 pound Cheddar cheese, grated
1/2 pound Mozzarella cheese,
  grated
2 cups mayonnaise

Saute first 4 ingredients in butter and set aside. Cook spinach and drain well. Melt butter. Add flour, stirring. Add milk gradually, and stir until thickened. Mix shrimp mixture with spinach and season to taste with salt, pepper, nutmeg and garlic. Place in oblong Pyrex dish. Pour white sauce over shrimp and spinach and top with bread crumbs. Mix cheeses and mayonnaise and place on crumbs. Bake at 350 degrees for 20 minutes. This can be made one day before baking. Serves 8.

Gail Morschheimer

Shrimp and Rice Casserole

1 box long grain and wild rice
4 tablespoons butter
4 tablespoons chopped onion
4 tablespoons lemon juice
2 cups cream of mushroom soup,
  undiluted

Dash Worcestershire sauce
Dash pepper
1 cup grated Cheddar cheese
2 pounds shrimp, boiled and
  peeled
1 can fried onion rings

Prepare rice according to directions on box. Melt butter and saute onions. Add lemon juice, soup, Worcestershire sauce, pepper and cheese. When cheese is melted, add rice and mix well. Put in large casserole. This can be done ahead. Prior to serving, let warm to room temperature and heat in 300 degree oven until heated through. About 15 minutes before serving, add shrimp and mix. Top with onion rings. Serves 8.

Anne Huff Monroe

Shrimp Jambalaya

1-1/2 pounds smoked sausage
3 tablespoons bacon drippings
3 tablespoons flour
2 medium onions, chopped
1 bunch green onions, chopped
2 tablespoons parsley, chopped

2 cloves garlic, minced
2-1/2 cups water
2 cups rice
2 teaspoons salt
3/4 teaspoon red pepper
1/2 pound cooked shrimp

Brown sausage in bacon drippings. Remove sausage and add flour. Brown flour to a dark roux. Add onions, parsley and garlic. Cook until soft. Add water, rice, salt, pepper and browned sausage. When it comes to a boil, lower heat to lowest point and cook for about 1 hour, covered tightly, or until rice is done. Stir and check occasionally. Add shrimp. Serves 5 to 6.

Debbie Robinson and Gail Bellingrath

Steamed Shrimp

4 cups water
2 cups white wine or 6 cups beer
2 tablespoons crushed red pepper

3 tablespoons salt
1/4 cup olive oil
4 pounds shrimp in shells

Combine all ingredients except shrimp Use either wine and water combination or all beer. Simmer covered a few minutes and then let it set until time to boil shrimp. Can do this several hours ahead. Bring back to a boil, add shrimp, cover and boil 3 minutes. Remove from heat. Let set covered at least 10 minutes. Serve warm with cocktail sauce or cold with remoulade sauce. Serves 4 to 8.

Janie Buckley

Cocktail Sauce

1 bottle chili sauce
2/3 cup catsup
1/3 cup prepared horseradish (or more)

2 teaspoons Worcestershire
1/2 teaspoon salt
1 tablespoon fresh lemon juice

Mix well and serve with boiled shrimp or crab claws.

Leila Wilkins O'Keefe

Pickwick Shrimp Sauce

1 bottle Heinz Chili Sauce
3/4 cup Hellman's Mayonnaise
2 teaspoons anchovy paste

2 tablespoons tarragon vinegar
2 tablespoons Worcestershire
1/2 teaspoon Tabasco

Mix above and store in refrigerator. *Wonderful on shrimp. This recipe came from a friend in Montgomery, Alabama.*

Cathy Kennedy

Remoulade Sauce

2 cups mayonnaise
1 tablespoon green pepper,
  finely chopped
1 tablespoon onion, finely chopped
1/2 teaspoon chopped fresh parsley
2 tablespoons capers, drained and
  mashed (optional)

1 teaspoon anchovy paste
Lemon juice to taste
2 tablespoons Creole mustard
Boiled shrimp, deveined
Lettuce
Hard boiled eggs, quartered

Mix well all ingredients except shrimp, lettuce and eggs. Serve over boiled shrimp on bed of lettuce. Garnish with quarters of boiled eggs.

In memory of Juanita Atkins Bohnert

Sunday Night One Pot Boil

Large pot of water
3 lemons
2 bags shrimp boil
1 small bottle shrimp boil

Small new potatoes
Corn on the cob
Shrimp (5 pounds)
Salt to taste

Bring water to boil. Add lemons, cut in quarters, and all the shrimp boil seasoning. Boil for a few minutes. Add potatoes and corn and cook until done. Add shrimp and boil for 5 minutes. Drain and serve.

Don A. Eilbott

Fried Oysters

Oysters
Salted milk
Flour
Salt and pepper

Beaten eggs
Cracker crumbs
Vegetable oil

Soak oysters in salted milk at least 10 minutes. Drop in seasoned flour, shake and drop in beaten eggs. Roll in cracker crumbs. Chill at least 1 hour. Fry oysters in oil over medium heat as soon as you remove them from refrigerator. Drain on paper towels.

Lara Hutt

Roy's Fried Oysters

Raw oysters
Yellow corn meal

Crisco shortening (not oil)

All commercial oysters are washed and, as a result, they lose their natural salty taste and firmness. As soon as you get them, pour off most of the excess water and add salt to the remaining oysters and water until the raw oysters have a natural salty taste. Add generous amount of salt and black pepper to more yellow corn meal than you think you will use. Heat shortening until hot, check temperature by dropping a little cornmeal into shortening to see if it browns. Meal oysters quickly and immediately put them individually into shortening. Turn once. Cook until lightly brown for "soft" oysters or brown for "hard" oysters.

Roy Hunter

Oyster Meuniére

1-1/2 sticks butter
6 cloves garlic, finely minced
1 tablespoon minced parsley

4 dozen fried oysters
(use Roy's Fried Oyster recipe)

Melt butter. Add garlic and cook over high heat, shaking pan constantly, until butter is foamy and light brown. Add parsley. Drizzle over oysters which have been placed on individual serving plates. Serves 6.

Janie Buckley

Oysters Bienville

3 tablespoons butter
1/4 cup minced green onion
1 clove garlic, minced
1/4 cup flour
3/4 cup boiled shrimp, finely diced
(reserve broth)
3/4 cup chopped canned mushrooms,
drained (reserve juice)
3/4 cup combined liquid from
shrimp and mushrooms

3 tablespoons white wine
Salt to taste
Dash red pepper
2 beaten egg yolks
1 teaspoon Worcestershire sauce
2 teaspoons chopped parsley
1 dozen oyster shells
Rock salt
1 dozen oysters, well drained
Buttered bread crumbs & paprika

In butter, saute onion and garlic until tender. Blend in flour and cook slowly for about 5 minutes, stirring constantly. Don't brown. Remove from heat and blend in shrimp-mushroom liquid, white wine, salt and red pepper. Blend egg yolks into mixture and cook slowly for about 15 minutes, adding shrimp, mushrooms, Worcestershire sauce and parsley while it cooks. When ready to bake, place 2 pie pans filled with rock salt in 350 degree oven to preheat salt. Place well drained oysters on oiled oyster shells; place on top of rock salt. Cover each with sauce. Sprinkle with bread crumbs and paprika. Bake in 350 degree oven for 15 minutes. Can increase recipe. Serves 2.

Lil Quinn,
President Women of the Church 1986-88

Oysters Johnny Reb

2 quarts oysters, drained
1/2 cup finely chopped parsley
1 cup finely chopped green onion
2 tablespoons lemon juice
1 tablespoon Worcestershire
Tabasco

Salt and pepper
2 cups fine cracker crumbs
3/4 cup melted butter
Paprika
3/4 cup Half and Half

Put layer of oysters in bottom of greased shallow 2 quart baking dish. Sprinkle with half of next 8 ingredients. Repeat. Sprinkle with paprika. Just before baking, pour cream into evenly spaced holes, being careful not to moisten crumb topping. Bake at 375 degrees for 30 minutes or until firm. Serves 12 to 15.

Ann Porter Price Clark

Oysters Rockefeller

4 stalks celery
4 bunches green onions, chopped
2 boxes frozen spinach (don't cook,
  but thaw and squeeze)
4 tablespoons parsley
3 tablespoons catsup
1/2 lemon, squeezed
1/2 teaspoon cayenne
3 tablespoons Worcestershire

1 tablespoon salt
1 (2 ounce) can anchovies
3 large cloves garlic, pressed
1-1/2 level teaspoons powdered
  anise (not seed)
2-1/2 sticks butter
Fresh oysters (1 pint or more)
Bread crumbs

Combine all ingredients except oysters and bread crumbs in food processor. Process until almost smooth. This sauce can be made ahead or frozen and thawed before used. Poach oysters 1 minute or until they curl. Drain well. Put oysters in greased baking dish and cover with sauce. sprinkle bread on top just before baking. Bake at 350 degrees for 20 minutes or until brown on top. This sauce can also be used on oysters in greased, individual shells. *Shared by my friends, Mr. and Mrs. Robert J. Whann.*

Sally Cook

Baked Catfish

4 catfish fillets, fresh or frozen
1 cup bread crumbs, cracker crumbs
  or cornflake crumbs
1/2 cup grated Parmesan cheese
1 tablespoon chopped parsley

1/4 cup sesame seeds
1/8 teaspoon red pepper
1/8 teaspoon black pepper
1/2 teaspoon salt
1 cup milk

Thaw fish if frozen. Line baking sheet with aluminum foil. Combine next 7 ingredients. Dip fillets in milk and roll in crumb mixture. Bake at 400 degrees for 20-25 minutes or until fish is golden brown. Serves 4.

Gail Bellingrath

At the end of World War I, late in the evening on November 11, 1918, whistles blew, church bells rang and all porch lights went on. Everyone congregated in the streets. The Presbyterians and many others, led by Dr. Norris, marched down Walnut Street to the Presbyterian Church, where they gathered for prayers and hymns of thanksgiving.

Baked Fish Fillets

1-1/2 to 2 pounds fish fillets (any kind)
Cayenne pepper
1 tablespoon lemon juice
1/8 teaspoon paprika
2 tablespoons butter

2 tablespoons flour
1 teaspoon salt
1 cup milk
1/4 cup bread crumbs
1 tablespoon chopped parsley

Season fish with pepper and place in flat microwave-safe baking dish. Top with lemon juice and paprika. In 4-cup measuring cup, melt butter on high in microwave 1 minute. Add flour and salt. Stir in milk slowly. Cook on high 2 or 3 minutes until thick. Pour sauce over fish. Sprinkle with bread crumbs and parsley. Microwave on medium 15 minutes, rotating dish at 7 minutes. Cooking time: 19 minutes. Serves 4.

Nancy Ryland Williamson

Bass Fillets

10 medium size bass fillets
Salt and pepper to taste
1/4 cup flour
1 egg

1/4 cup sweet milk
2-1/2 cups cracker crumbs
Oil for deep frying

Wash and drain fillets. Mix salt, pepper and flour together. Roll the fillets in this mixture. Beat egg. Add milk and mix well. Dip fillets in this mixture. Then roll in cracker crumbs. Fry in deep fat (375 degrees) until crispy and brown, approximately 10 to 12 minutes. Serve while hot with tartar sauce. Serves 8 to 10.

In memory of Mrs. Rufus A. Martin (Helen)

In 1964-1965 when Frances Hall was president we had 16 day circles, 2 night circles, a home circle (each circle had 30 members) and one Business Women's circle. Average attendance at circles: 20. Monday afternoons were reserved for church, the first for board meeting, the second for auxiliary meeting, the third for Circle meeting, the fourth for visitation.

Blackened Fish

1 tablespoon paprika
2-1/2 teaspoons salt
1 teaspoon each:
  onion powder
  garlic powder
1/2 teaspoon cayenne pepper
  (more if you like it extra hot)
3/4 teaspoon each:
  white pepper
  black pepper

1/2 teaspoon each:
  dried thyme
  oregano
1 cup unsalted butter, melted
6 fish fillets cut 1/2 inch thick
  (use a firm flesh fish such as
  redfish or red snapper)

Combine all dry ingredients. Heat a large cast iron skillet over very high heat for 10 minutes. Dip each fillet in melted butter so that both sides are well coated. Then sprinkle seasoning mix generously and evenly on both sides of the fillets, patting it in by hand. Place fillets in hot skillet and pour 1 teaspoon melted butter on top of each one. Cook, uncovered, on same high heat for 2 minutes until underside is charred. Turn fish over, add 1 teaspoon melted butter on top and cook another 2 minutes. Serve with a lemon butter sauce if desired. *This will make smoke so open the windows!* Serves 6.

Helen Claire Brooks

Bronzed Catfish
with Mushroom Crawfish Sauce

8 catfish fillets
2 tablespoons bronzing mix
  or Creole seasoning
4 tablespoons mayonnaise
1 cup fresh mushrooms, sliced
1/2 cup sliced shallots or
  green onions
1/4 cup minced parsley

2 tablespoons garlic, crushed
1/2 pound peeled, cleaned
  crawfish tails, fresh or frozen
4 tablespoons butter
2 cans cream of mushroom soup
2 tablespoons sherry
Salt and pepper (white, black
  and cayenne) to taste

Rub the bronzing or seasoning mix on both sides of fillets. Then spread a thin layer of mayonnaise on both sides and let sit for 15 minutes. Saute mushrooms, shallots, parsley, garlic and crawfish tails in 2 tablespoons of butter for 3-5 minutes. Add soup and sherry and stir until smooth. Add salt and peppers to taste. In a skillet (high heat) bronze the fillets about 3 minutes per side. Pour sauce over fillets in a casserole dish and bake uncovered for 20 minutes at 350 degrees. Serves 8.

Ann Brown Turner

Margie's Orange Roughy Parmesan

2 pounds orange roughy
 (or Dover sole)
2 tablespoons fresh lemon juice
1/2 cup freshly grated Parmesan cheese
4 tablespoons butter, softened
3 tablespoons mayonnaise

3 tablespoons chopped green
 onion
1/4 teaspoon salt
Freshly ground pepper to taste
Dash Tabasco sauce

In a buttered baking dish, place fillets in a single layer. Brush with lemon juice. Let stand for 10 minutes. In a small bowl, combine rest of ingredients. Broil fillets 3 to 4 inches under preheated broiler for 5 minutes. Spread with cheese mixture and broil for an additional 2 to 3 minutes. Watch closely! *Given to me by Margie Sturdivant.* Serves 4.

Janie Buckley

Portuguese Paella

1 lobster
2 pound shrimp
1/2 pound crawfish tails, cooked
 (optional)
1 pound lump crabmeat (optional)
8 Poblano or banana peppers
1/2 cup olive oil, divided use
1-1/2 cups rice
6 garlic buds, minced
6 cups chicken broth

Juice of 1 lemon
8 ounces clam juice
1 cup whole, pitted or stuffed
 green olives
1 (3-1/4 ounce) can pitted
 black olives
Small jar chopped pimento
1 bunch green onions, chopped
Finely chopped parsley

I have the lobster and shrimp steamed (very spicy) at the store; or you can steam them yourself. Peel shrimp and remove meat from lobster tail and claws. Cut in 1 inch pieces. I save the lobster body to use for garnish. Set all seafood aside. Cut peppers in half, remove seeds and place on cookie sheet. Drizzle with 2-4 tablespoons olive oil and roast in a 350 degree oven until soft. Saute rice and garlic in remaining olive oil for 3-4 minutes over medium heat. Add chicken broth, lemon juice and clam juice. Bring to a boil, cover, reduce heat to low and cook 20 minutes or until tender. This should be real juicy, not dry, fluffy rice. Add next 4 ingredients and roasted peppers. Can be cooked to this point a few hours ahead. Add seafood and stir gently. Put in fairly deep casserole, not a traditional flat paella dish. Bake in 350 degree oven until hot. To garnish, cover top with parsley; put the lobster body shell on top. Serves 6 to 8.

Janie Buckley

MEATS

The bells were given to the church in 1973 by Mr. and Mrs. Fred J. Ingram.

The three bells are made of bronze and weigh approximately 1,600 pounds each and were made in Holland. The carillon plays recordings of selected hymns and sacred music.

Aunt Florence's Brisket

Beef brisket, 3-5 pounds
Salt, pepper, garlic powder
1 can beef consommé

3/4 cup lemon juice
1/2 bottle soy sauce

Rub salt, pepper and garlic powder into both sides of brisket. Place fat side up in a foil lined pan. Mix together the next three ingredients and pour over meat. Seal foil tightly around brisket. Refrigerate overnight or for a few hours for best flavor. Bake covered in slow oven - 300 degrees for 5 hours. *Let stand on serving platter for about 20 minutes before slicing.* Serves 8 to 10.

Ann Clark

Barbecued Brisket

7-9 pound beef brisket
1 generous teaspoon minced garlic
1 teaspoon celery seeds
3 tablespoons freshly ground pepper
1 teaspoon ground ginger (optional)
4 large bay leaves, crumbed

1 (12 ounce) can tomato paste
1/2 cup Worcestershire sauce
1 cup dark soy sauce
1 cup packed brown sugar
2 medium onions, thinly sliced

Preheat oven to 350 degrees. Rub all sides of brisket with garlic. Place on heavy-duty foil. Combine celery seeds, pepper, ginger and crushed bay leaf. Sprinkle on all sides of meat. Mix tomato paste, Worcestershire sauce, soy sauce and brown sugar; rub on meat. Score the fat side of brisket and place onions on top. Wrap in the foil and seal tightly, placing fat side up. Cook in foil for 4 hours. Open the foil to expose onions and cook for another hour. Sauce - degrease the sauce. Place drippings into saucepan. Add a little water (1/2 - 1 cup), beer or wine. *This is delicious served over sliced meat.*

Debbie Robinson

Beef with Green Pepper

1 pound round steak cut 1/2 inch thick
1 clove garlic, crushed, with
  1 teaspoon salt
2 cups beef bouillon
2 tablespoons water

2 tablespoons soy sauce
2 tablespoons cornstarch
1 large green pepper, cut in
  thin strips
1/4 teaspoon ginger

Cut meat into thin strips, about 1/4 inch wide. Brown meat quickly in hot drippings or oil. Add garlic, salt, and bouillon. Cover pan tightly and cook slowly about 30 minutes, or until tender. Blend cornstarch, soy sauce and water. Stir into meat. Cook, stirring constantly, until thick. Add green pepper and ginger; heat through. Green pepper should retain color and crispness. Serve over hot rice or flat noodles. *This doubles easily. I have used Chinese pea pods in place of green onion. Partially frozen steak easier to slice.* Serves 4 to 6.

Mrs. Peter Ahlgrim

Beef Tenderloin

1 whole beef tenderloin
1/2 cup olive oil

1 bottle Wishbone Italian
Dressing

Marinate beef tenderloin in Italian Dressing for at least 12 hours, turning often and basting. Preheat oven to 400 degrees. Sear meat 5 minutes on each side in open pan on rack. Turn oven to 350 degrees. Cook 10 minutes per pound for rare, 15 minutes for medium. *Easy!*

Nancy Ryland Williamson,
President, Women of the Church 1961-62

"Birdwell" Casserole

2 pounds ground beef or turkey
3 chopped onions
1 cup chopped celery
Salt and pepper to taste
3 cans cream of mushroom soup
1-1/2 cans water
1 small can chopped ripe olives

1-1/2 pounds grated cheese
1 small can English peas,
drained
1 (4 ounce) jar chopped
pimiento
1 (16 ounce) package noodles
Parmesan cheese

Saute meat, onions, celery. Add salt and pepper to taste. Heat soup, water, olives and cheese. Add peas and pimiento. When hot, mix with meat mixture. Cook noodles according to package directions. In 2 large (9x13) casseroles, layer noodles and meat mixture twice, ending with meat. Sprinkle with Parmesan cheese. Bake at 350 degrees for 30 minutes. Freezes very well. *I found this recipe in a Texas cookbook. Since Birdwell is my maiden name, I decided to try it.* Serves 22 to 24.

Jackie Quinn
Moderator, Presbyterian Women 1988-89

Blessed is the man that endureth temptation; for when he is tried, he shall receive the crown of life, which the Lord hath promised to them that love Him.

James 1:12

Bubble and Squeak

1/2 to 1 pound Polish sausage
1 large onion
4 or 5 potatoes, cut in chunks
Cabbage, cut in chunks

Salt
Pepper
1/4 to 1/2 cup water

Brown sausage and onion till onion is clear and the bottom of the pan is <u>good and brown</u>. (You may need to add a small amount of margarine if pan is too dry.) Add raw cabbage and potatoes (may leave peel on if desired). Reduce heat. Add water. Simmer, covered, until potatoes and cabbage are done, about 30 minutes. *Because of the name, children are tempted to try eating cabbage. This recipe came from England and is called Bubble & Squeak because of the sounds made by the cabbage and the dish as it simmers.*

Brenda Norsworthy

Easy Beef Stroganoff

1-1/2 pounds round steak
1 envelope onion soup mix
1 can cream of mushroom soup

1 can cream of celery soup
1 cup sour cream
1 package egg noodles

Cut steak into small strips or pieces. Put steak, soup mix and soups in crockpot and cook for 6 to 8 hours. Fold in sour cream just before serving. Serve over egg noodles cooked per package instructions. Serves 4.

Claudette Dixon

Enchilada Casserole

2 pounds ground chuck
1 large onion, chopped
2 tablespoons chili powder
2 tablespoons cumin, ground
1 teaspoon salt
1 can Ranch Style Beans

6 corn tortillas, thawed
1-1/2 cups Monterey Jack, grated
1/2 cup Cheddar cheese, grated
1 (16 ounce) jar thick salsa
1 (10 -1/2ounce) can cream of
    mushroom soup

Cook meat and onions in large skillet until brown and tender. Drain. Add chili powder, cumin and salt. Stir well. Cook mixture over low heat for 10 minutes. Spoon into a 13x9 inch pan sprayed with Pam. Layer beans, tortillas, and both cheeses over meat mixture. Pour 1 cup of thick salsa over cheese. Spread soup over top of casserole to seal it. Cover and refrigerate overnight. Bake, uncovered, at 350 degrees for 1 hour. Serve with chopped fresh tomato and crisp lettuce and top with a dollop of remaining salsa. Serves 6.

Eleanor B. Joerden

Evelyn's Scout Spaghetti

1 cup Wesson oil
2 cups chopped onion
5 pounds ground beef
8 minced garlic buds
24 ounces canned sliced mushrooms
1 cup snipped fresh parsley
2 cups salad olives (large jar), drained
32 ounces tomato sauce

4 (14-1/2 ounce) cans tomatoes,
chopped
2 tablespoon salt
2 teaspoons pepper
1 tablespoon sugar
12-14 ounces thin spaghetti
16 ounces grated cheese

In hot oil simmer onion 5 minutes. Add ground beef and garlic and cook until brown. Add undrained mushrooms, parsley, drained olives, tomato sauce and tomatoes, salt and pepper and sugar. Simmer covered 1 hour, then uncovered 2-1/2 to 3 hours. Cook and drain spaghetti. Place spaghetti on plate, sprinkle with cheese, cover with sauce. You may sprinkle a little Parmesan cheese on top, if desired. *Evelyn Edington fed this to Scouts in Troop 100 at the church at Fifth and Walnut. They loved it!* Serves 16.

Virginia Edington

Firecracker Enchilada Casserole

2 pounds ground beef
1 large onion, chopped
2 tablespoons chili powder
2-3 teaspoons cumin
1 teaspoon salt
1 (15 ounce) can Ranch Style Beans
6 corn tortillas

6 ounces shredded Monterey
Jack cheese
6 ounces shredded sharp
Cheddar cheese
1 can Ro-Tel
1 can cream of mushroom
soup, undiluted

Cook beef and onion in a large skillet until brown and onion is tender, discarding pan drippings. Add seasonings, stir well and cook mixture over low heat 10 minutes. Spoon meat mixture into a 9x13 casserole. Drain beans, saving juice and layer over beef. Tear tortillas and layer over beans. Spread cheese over all. Combine bean juice, Ro-Tel and soup. Spread over casserole. Cover and refrigerate overnight. Uncover and bake at 350 degrees for 1 hour. *Enjoy! I blend the Ro-Tel as I want a smooth sauce.* Serves 8 to 10 generously.

Jane G. Starling

French Beef Casserole

6 slices bacon
1 pound lean beef, cut into
   1-1/2 inch cubes
1/2 cup flour
1 teaspoon salt
1 cup red wine
2 tablespoons parsley
1/2 garlic clove
1/2 teaspoon thyme

1 (10-1/2 ounce) can beef broth
6 medium potatoes, peeled and
   quartered
12 small white onions (use
   canned onions)
3 carrots, sliced lengthwise
1 (4 ounce) can mushrooms
Parsley for garnish

Cook bacon until crisp; drain on paper towels and set aside; reserve drippings. Shake beef cubes, a few at a time, in a paper bag containing the flour and salt. Brown beef cubes in bacon drippings and remove to a 2 quart casserole. Pour wine into an electric blender. Add parsley, garlic, thyme and beef broth; blend until well pureed. Pour over meat in casserole. Cover and bake at 350 degrees for 1 hour. Stir in potatoes, onions and carrots into casserole. Replace cover and bake 1 hour longer or until vegetables are done. Stir in mushrooms. Crumble bacon on top and sprinkle with additional parsley. *Just add a green salad and hot buttered French bread.* Serves 5 to 6.

Bobbye Nixon

Ham Loaf

3/4 pound fresh ground pork
3/4 pound cooked ham
1 beaten egg
1/2 cup milk
1/2 cup moist bread crumbs
Salt and pepper
Pineapple rings

Sauce:
1 cup brown sugar
1/2 teaspoon dry mustard
1/4 cup water
1/4 cup vinegar

Combine ground pork and cooked ham, mixing well. Add beaten egg, 1/2 cup milk, 1/2 cup moist bread crumbs, and salt & pepper. Mix and form into one large or two smaller loaves. Place canned pineapple rings on top. To make sauce, put brown sugar, dry mustard, water, and vinegar in small saucepan and heat until sugar is dissolved. Then pour over loaf before placing in oven. Bake 1 hour and 10 minutes at 375 degrees. If all the sauce is absorbed in cooking, make and heat another sauce recipe to serve on side as gravy. *This was my mother Doris M. Murray's recipe.* Serves 10 to 12.

Jo Ann Clemmons

Hot Tamales

2 pounds ground beef
1 medium onion, chopped
3 garlic cloves, minced
1 teaspoon salt
1/2 cup yellow cornmeal
1 scant teaspoon red pepper
1/2 cup water
1 teaspoon black pepper
8 ounces tomato sauce

4 teaspoons chili powder
2 teaspoons cumin
*Meal mixture

} Broth mixture to cook tamales
8 to 10 cans chicken broth
2 teaspoons chili powder
1 teaspoon salt
1 (8 ounce) can tomato sauce
Box of coffee filters

Mix first 11 ingredients together. Form into little weiners. Roll in the following meal mixture: *2 cups yellow cornmeal, 2-1/2 teaspoons salt, scant 1/2 teaspoon red pepper, 1 teaspoon cumin. Place formed meat on coffee filter. Sprinkle with an additional 2 teaspoons cornmeal mixture. Roll tightly in filter folding in ends of paper. Pack tightly in deep pan, seam side down. Cover with the above broth mixture and weight down. Simmer for 1 hour. May be frozen and should be packed with broth to keep moist. Makes 25-30 tamales.

Martha Halbert

Husband's Delight

4 ounces cream cheese
1 (8 ounce) carton sour cream
1 small onion, chopped
1 pound ground chuck
1 tablespoon butter
1 (8 ounce) can tomato sauce

1/2 teaspoon sugar
1/2 teaspoon salt
Dash pepper
1 (5 ounce) package narrow
 egg noodles
Grated Cheddar cheese

Mix cream cheese, sour cream and onion. Brown meat in butter. Add seasonings and tomato sauce. Cook noodles as directed on package. Layer noodles, beef mixture and cream cheese mixture into 2-quart casserole. Top with grated Cheddar cheese. Bake at 350 degrees for 30 minutes. Serves 4 to 6.

Susan Norton

> *Blessed are they which do hunger and thirst after righteousness; for they shall be filled.*
>
> Matthew 5:6

Judy's Swiss Steak

1-1/2 to 2 pounds tenderized round
   steak
Salt and pepper
Vegetable oil

1 (#2) can tomatoes, undrained
3/4 to 1 cup flour
1/4 cup chopped onions

Place steak in one piece on waxed paper. Sprinkle salt and pepper on steak. Roll in flour, pounding flour into meat. Heat oil in heavy skillet; brown meat. Bring the tomatoes and chopped onions to a boil. Place browned steak in greased casserole and cover with hot tomatoes and onions. Bake in covered casserole at 350 degrees for 1-1/2 to 2 hours. Tomato gravy can be served over steak. *Easy to prepare - good served with mashed potatoes. Easy meat recipe for teens and men to prepare.* Serves 4 to 6.

Mary Snavely

Lamb Chops Dijon

4 lamb chops (about 1-1/2 pounds)
1 lemon, cut in half
Garlic pepper

1 cup chopped fresh parsley
1/2 cup Dijon mustard
2 tablespoons bread crumbs

Trim fat from chops. Rub both sides with lemon; sprinkle garlic pepper. Combine next 3 ingredients, mix well and press on both sides of chops. Place in 12x8x2 inch baking pan coated with cooking spray. Bake, uncovered, at 500 degrees for 4 minutes. Reduce heat to 350 degrees and bake 15 minutes. Serves 4.

Cookbook Committee

PRAYER FOR SERVICEMEN

Mighty Father, everlasting God, in whom we live and beyond whose care we cannot drift, we commit to Thee our soldiers, sailors, marines, and airmen, in all their places, unknown perhaps, to us, but always known to Thee. Guide and protect them by Thy Spirit's presence. Bring them in victory back to us, if it be Thy will. Make them worthy of their country, their cause, and their God, and make us worthy of them. In Jesus' name. Amen. *This prayer was prayed every Sunday morning during World War II.*

Mom's Meatloaf

1 pound ground beef
3 slices bread
1/2 cup milk
1 egg, beaten
1 medium onion, chopped
1 tablespoon Worcestershire
1 teaspoon salt
1/4 teaspoon pepper

Sauce:
2 tablespoons tomato paste
2 (14-1/2 ounce) cans tomatoes,
  and juice
2 tablespoons brown sugar
1/2 medium onion, chopped
1/2 teaspoon salt
1/4 teaspoon pepper

Tear bread into bite size pieces and cover with milk to soak. Add beaten egg to ground meat. Add bread and milk mixture. Add chopped onion and seasonings. Make a big round patty. Brown patty on both sides in a small amount of bacon drippings or shortening. (I use an iron skillet for this - but any oven skillet will do). Mix tomato sauce ingredients and pour over meatloaf. Bake at 350 degrees for 45 minutes to 1 hour. Serves 6 to 8.

Bobbye Nixon

Mother's Italian Spaghetti

1-1/2 pounds stew meat
Flour, to dust meat
1/2 cup oil
2 tablespoons flour
2 (14-1/2 ounce) cans tomatoes
1 can water
1-1/2 teaspoons chili powder

3 large bay leaves
1 large onion
2 garlic buttons
1 pound fresh mushrooms
1 pound sharp Cheddar cheese
1 (16 ounce) package spaghetti
Salt and pepper to taste

Salt, pepper and flour stew meat on all sides. Brown in 1/2 cup oil. Remove meat from skillet. Add 2 tablespoons flour to grease in skillet and brown. Add tomatoes which have been mashed. Add 1 can of water and stir till smooth. Add chili powder and bay leaves. While mixture is simmering, grind meat, onion and garlic and add to sauce. Saute mushrooms in 1 tablespoon butter and add to meat mixture. Place in pot; cover and place in oven for 2 hours, stirring occasionally. Remove from oven and add 1 cup grated cheese. Stir until cheese melts. Cook spaghetti according to package directions. Serve on warm plates, ladle sauce on top of spaghetti and sprinkle with cheese on top. *A completely different kind of "Italian" spaghetti. This has been in the family since before my grandmother's time, but I have never had it anywhere else!* Serves 10.

In memory of Joe Howell Smith

Mother's Never-Fail Beef Tenderloin

2-3 pounds beef tenderloin
2 ounces oil
Lemon pepper marinade
Worcestershire sauce

Other seasonings to taste
2 ounces butter
Heavy duty foil

Rub foil with oil. Sprinkle lemon pepper, seasonings and Worcestershire sauce over tenderloin. Put butter pats on top of filet. Pre-heat oven to 400 degrees. Seal foil tightly and place steak in large pan. Bake for 30 minutes at 400 degrees. Open foil and roll back from filet. Bake for 15 minutes. It will be rare in the center and pink on the outside. *The timing must be followed exactly.* Serves 6.

Jane G. Starling

No Peek Stew

1 pound beef stew meat
1 package dry onion soup
1/2 cup red wine

1 can mushroom soup
Rice or noodles

Mix meat with onion soup and wine. Cover tightly. Bake 2 to 3 hours at 300 degrees. Add mushroom soup. Pour over rice or noodles cooked your way. *Prepare this easy one before going to soccer field or ball park. Your family will call you a genius.* Serves 4 to 5.

In memory of Tippie (Mrs. T. W.) Puddephatt

Oven Beef Stew

1 pound very lean stew meat
1 package frozen stew vegetables
1/4 cup frozen chopped bell pepper
1 (8 ounce) can tomato sauce
1 tablespoon Worcestershire

1/8 cup soy sauce
1 tablespoon brown sugar
1/2 teaspoon salt
1/2 cup water

Mix all ingredients in oven pan. Cover and bake at 250 to 300 degrees. Cook until meat is fork tender, or about 2 hours. *I put in crockpot instead of oven. Very easy and good.*

Frances Toney Hall

Poor Boy Filets

1 pound lean ground beef
Lemon pepper
Salt
1/4 cup grated Parmesan cheese
3 ounces mushrooms, canned or fresh
2 tablespoons onion, finely chopped

2 tablespoons green pepper,
  finely chopped (optional)
Worcestershire sauce to taste
  (optional)
5 slices bacon

Mix ground beef, lemon pepper, salt and Parmesan cheese. In a separate bowl, mix mushrooms, onions, Worcestershire sauce and green peppers. Add to ground beef mixture. Mix well with hands. Place on piece of waxed paper and shape into roll. Refrigerate for about 30 minutes to make it easier to cut. Cut into desired thickness; wrap with a strip of bacon around outer edge of each steak; secure with toothpick. *These are wonderful grilled outside or broiled in an oven. Good for summer cookouts!* Serves 5.

Sue Deneke

Pork Tenderloin with Apricot Glaze

Two 1 pound pork tenderloins
4-6 garlic cloves, cut into thin slices
2 teaspoons canola oil
1/2 teaspoon salt
1/2 teaspoon pepper

2 teaspoons dried rosemary,
  crumbled
2/3 cup apricot pourable
  All Fruit
Fresh rosemary sprigs

Heat oven to 425 degrees. Cut 1/2 inch deep slits on surface of pork tenderloins; insert garlic. Combine oil, salt, pepper and rosemary. Place tenderloins on rack in roasting pan, tucking tails under to make uniform in thickness. Rub with oil-seasoning mixture. Brush with apricot pourable fruit. Roast until instant-read thermometer reaches 155 degrees (20-25 minutes). Remove from oven, cover with foil and allow to stand 5 minutes before slicing. Garnish with rosemary. *Naturally-sweetened pourable fruit provides a complimentary glaze for lean and tender pork tenderloins which have been seasoned with garlic and rosemary.* Serves 6.

Ann Peterson

And they shall put my name upon the children of Israel; and I will bless them.

Numbers 7:27

Pork Chops with Soy-Orange Sauce

3/4 cup fresh orange juice
2 tablespoons soy sauce
1 teaspoon sugar
1 clove garlic, peeled and crushed
1/4 teaspoon freshly ground black pepper

8 sprigs fresh thyme or
  1/4 teaspoon dried
2 tablespoons (1/4 stick) butter
2 tablespoons safflower oil
8 lean (1/2" thick) loin pork chops

Combine orange juice with the soy sauce, sugar, garlic, pepper, and thyme sprigs. Set aside. With a very sharp knife, score the pork chops 1/8 inch deep in a crisscross pattern on each side. Place in a glass dish in a single layer. Pour marinade over chops and let sit at least 30 minutes. Drain and reserve marinade. Heat the butter and oil in a large skillet until hot. Add the chops in a single layer and saute' over medium high heat for 3 minutes on each side, browning them well. Reduce heat to low and pour reserved marinade over chops. Cook until done, about 8 to 10 minutes longer. Reduce the marinade in the skillet to 1/3 cup. Pour over the cooked chops and serve immediately. Pork chops may be grilled. Reduce the marinade separately in a saucepan and pour over the chops after removing from grill.

Gail Bellingrath

Pork Loin Roast

4-5 pound pork roast
Salt and pepper
Garlic powder
Dijon mustard

Honey Glaze:
2 tablespoons butter
1/2 cup honey
1/2 cup catsup
2 tablespoons lemon juice
2 tablespoons brown sugar
1 clove garlic
Combine and simmer 5 minutes

Sprinkle roast with salt and pepper and generously with garlic powder. Brush top with Dijon mustard. Bake at 325 degrees for 2 hours. Brush with honey glaze 15 minutes after you put the roast in oven. This is to give the mustard time to set on the roast. Brush glaze about every 15-20 minutes. *This is a family favorite.* Serves 8.

Joan B. Thompson

Pork Tenderloin Roast

Two 1-1/2 pound pork tenderloins
4 bacon slices
Marinade:
2 cloves garlic, crushed
1/2 cup soy sauce
2 tablespoons minced onion
1/4 teaspoon pepper
2 tablespoons vinegar
1/2 cup water

Mustard Sauce:
1/4 cup sour cream
1/2 cup mayonnaise
3 tablespoons brown mustard
1 tablespoon minced onion
1 teaspoon vinegar
Salt and pepper to taste

Marinate tenderloins for 4 to 6 hours. Place bacon slices on tenderloins and bake in 325 degree oven, uncovered, for 1-1/2 hours. Baste frequently with marinade. Serve with mustard sauce. Serves 8.

Grace Hoffman

Quickie Hash

3 tablespoons bacon drippings <u>or</u>
    butter
1 medium onion, diced
1 stalk celery, diced
3-4 cups leftover roast
2 medium potatoes, cubed

4 carrots, diced
Salt and pepper
Beef juice from roast <u>or</u>
    bouillon <u>or</u> consomme
    (about 3 cups)

Heat bacon drippings or butter. Add onions and celery, cooking until clear. Add meat and cook a few minutes. Add potatoes, carrots, seasonings, and beef juice or bouillon. Simmer until gravy is thickened and vegetables are done, approximately 25-30 minutes. Serves 10 to 12.

Mary Snavely

When we received the news that the Allied troops had landed in France on D Day, June 6, 1944, Dr. Newton opened the church at Fifth and Walnut, staying all day and until late that night. People from all over town came by to pray for our troops. Some stayed all day - some would come and go back to work. Everyone prayed together.

Beef Spaghetti Pie

1 pound lean ground beef
1 teaspoon garlic powder
1/2 teaspoon ground oregano
1/2 teaspoon ground cumin
1/2 teaspoon salt
1 (10 ounce) can diced tomatoes
   with green chilies, undrained
1 cup sour cream
1-1/2 cups shredded Monterey Jack cheese

Pasta Shell:
1 (7 ounce) package spaghetti,
   uncooked
1 cup shredded Monterey Jack
   cheese
1 egg
1/2 teaspoon salt
1/4 teaspoon garlic powder

Cook spaghetti according to package directions; drain. Process together cheese, egg, salt and garlic powder. Add spaghetti and toss. Arrange in 9 inch pie dish, pressing to form a shell. Heat large skillet over medium heat until hot. Add ground beef, brown 5 minutes; pour off drippings. Add garlic powder, oregano, cumin and salt. Stir in tomatoes. Bring to a boil; cook 5 minutes, stirring occasionally. Reserve 3 tablespoons beef mixture for garnish. Stir sour cream into other beef; spoon into pasta shell. Place one cup cheese in center. Spoon reserved beef mixture onto center of cheese; bake 15 minutes at 350 degrees. Serves 4.

Margaret Ann Dial Dawson

Ribs and Kraut

Bacon
1-2 large jars kraut
Ribs, cut apart

Onion
Salt
Pepper

Line Pyrex casserole with strips of bacon. Cover with slices of onion. Drain kraut, and sprinkle over the onions. Lay one layer of ribs over this. Salt and pepper to taste. Bake 1 hour and 45 minutes at 350 degrees. *Great!* Serves 6.

Pat Lile

Roast Beef

5 pounds good quality roast beef, i.e.
   rib eye, standing rib

Salt and freshly ground pepper
4 tablespoons butter, softened

At least 2 hours before you intend to roast the beef, remove from refrigerator. Turn oven to 500 degrees for 20 minutes before proceeding. Rub roast with salt and pepper and spread it with softened butter. Put roast on a rack in a roasting pan and put in oven. Roast 5 minutes per pound and then, without opening oven door, turn off heat and leave roast in oven for 2 hours. <u>Do not open door.</u> After 2 hours, open door and touch roast. If it is hot, it's ready to serve. If luke-warm, cook at 500 degrees for another 10 minutes. Serve with pan juices, Bearnaise or Madeira sauce. *This will turn out a medium rare serving. If you want medium, increase cooking time to 6-7 minutes per pound.* Serves 8.

Helen Claire Brooks

J. G.'s Roast and Red Gravy

3 tablespoons cooking oil
4 pound roast (rump or shoulder)
4 tablespoons flour
2 to 2-1/2 cups water
Salt and pepper to taste

1 heaping teaspoon chili powder
1 heaping teaspoon paprika
1 tablespoon vinegar
2 garlic buttons

Brown roast in oil and place in roaster. Add flour to remaining oil and brown to a rich milk chocolate color. (May add Kitchen Bouquet). Add water, salt and pepper and stir until smooth. Add remaining ingredients and pour over roast. Cover and cook at least 40 minutes per pound. Be sure to stir occasionally, adding water if necessary. Correct seasonings and serve. *Gravy should be a dark reddish brown in color.* Serves 8.

Joanne Smith

In the late 1800's, Mrs. W. H. Langford was organist and director of the choir, serving without pay and furnishing the music. The Langfords built the house later known as the Simmons home. The church had a paid choir until 1948. Mrs. J. W. Wilkins was the chairman of the music committee and Mrs. Jesse Core was the paid choir director. Some of the members of the choir were Mr. Dolph Kastor, Mr. Ray West (who served without pay), Mr. George Heister, Mr. Andrew Quattlebaum, Mr. John Gillespie, Mr. Ernest Alexander, Mrs. John Hohman, Miss Betty O'Keefe, and Mr. Victor Howell.

Spiced Beef Brisket

1 (3 to 4 pound) beef brisket
1 large clove garlic, halved
Paprika
1 tablespoon cooking oil
1/2 cup vinegar
1/2 cup chili sauce

3 tablespoons brown sugar
1/2 teaspoon seasoned salt
1 cup chopped celery leaves
2 medium onions, sliced and
  separated into rings
6 large carrots cut into sticks

Rub beef with garlic and sprinkle with paprika; discard garlic. In Dutch oven, brown beef on all sides in hot oil. Drain fat and transfer beef to pan. Stir together the vinegar, chili sauce, brown sugar and seasoned salt. Pour over beef and refrigerate overnight, turning frequently. Return beef and marinade to Dutch oven; add celery and onions; bring to boil. Reduce heat, cover and simmer 2 hours, basting often. Add carrots and cook 30 minutes more; remove beef and vegetables; boil juices 5 minutes or until reduced to 1 cup. *A real hit at family night suppers. Shared by Betty Brown.*

Ann Benton

Spaghetti Carbonara á la Seawell

6 to 8 tablespoons butter, creamed
2 to 3 eggs, beaten
1 to 1-1/2 cups Parmesan cheese, grated
4 slices bacon or 3 slices ham,
  cooked and chopped
1/4 pound mild Italian pork sausage,
  cooked and crumbled

1 cup heavy cream
1 pound spaghetti
1 tablespoon parsley
1 teaspoon dried red pepper
  flakes
Salt and pepper
Extra grated cheese

Have butter, eggs and cheese set aside in separate bowls at room temperature. Mix cooked meats and cream. Heat to simmer and keep warm. Cook spaghetti according to package directions. Drain. Put in heated serving bowl. Stir in butter, parsley, pepper flakes and cheese. Stir in meat and cream mixture. Stir in eggs. Season with salt and pepper. Serve with extra cheese. *You can cook the meats ahead of time and keep in refrigerator. Given to me by my brother's wife.* Serves 6 to 8.

Anne Seawell Robinson

Spaghetti with Meatballs

3/4 pound ground chuck
1/4 pound ground pork
1 cup bread crumbs
1/2 cup grated Parmesan cheese
1 tablespoon minced parsley
2 small cloves garlic, cut fine
1/2 cup milk
2 eggs, beaten
1-1/2 teaspoons salt
1/8 teaspoon pepper
1 cup minced onion

2 tablespoons flour
5 cups tomatoes
6 tablespoons minced parsley
6 tablespoons minced green
  pepper
2-1/2 teaspoons salt
1/4 teaspoon pepper
3 teaspoons sugar
2 bay leaves, crumbled
1 teaspoon Worcestershire sauce
1 (8 ounce) package spaghetti

Use first 10 ingredients to form meatballs. Pan fry in a small amount of fat; remove. Saute minced onion in fat. Drain grease, blend in flour. In a large pot, add remaining ingredients. Simmer about one hour, uncovered, stirring occasionally. Serve hot over cooked, drained spaghetti. Sprinkle with grated sharp cheese. *This sounds like it contains everything but the kitchen sink, but once assembled, it's worth it. From a 1950 Betty Crocker Cookbook.* Serves 6 to 8.

Lucille Fey

Surprise Cornbread

1 cup cornmeal
3/4 teaspoon salt
2 eggs, well beaten
1 cup milk
2 tablespoons oil
1/2 teaspoon soda
1 (16 ounce) can cream style corn

1 pound ground beef
1 large onion, chopped
1 (4-1/2 ounces) can chopped
  green chili peppers
2 cups Cheddar cheese, grated

Combine first 7 ingredients, blending well; set aside. Brown ground beef and onions; drain. Stir in chili peppers. Spoon 1/2 of cornmeal mixture in a 9x13x2 baking pan sprayed with Pam. Sprinkle with cheese. Spread meat mixture over cheese. Spoon remaining batter over meat. Bake at 350 degrees for 45 to 50 minutes. Cut in square to serve. Serves 4 to 6.

Diane Fisk

Sweet and Sour Meatballs

1 pound ground beef
3/4 cup rolled oats
1/2 cup milk
1/4 cup finely chopped water chestnuts
1 teaspoon Worcestershire sauce
1/2 teaspoon onion salt
1/2 teaspoon garlic salt
Few drops hot pepper sauce
2 tablespoons oleo

Sauce:
1 cup sugar
3/4 cup vinegar
3/4 cup water
1 teaspoon paprika
1/2 teaspoon salt
2 tablespoons cornstarch
1 tablespoon water

Combine all ingredients except oleo. Mix thoroughly. Shape into bite-sized balls. Brown in oleo and drain on paper towels. Sauce: Combine sugar, vinegar, water, paprika and salt in large skillet. Heat. Blend cornstarch and water and add to hot mix. Add meatballs. Serve. *This is a must for the Christmas holidays. Freezes well.* Makes 36 meatballs.

Joan B. Thompson

Tallerine

1-1/2 pounds ground chuck
1 onion, chopped
2 buttons garlic, chopped
1 green pepper, chopped
1 tablespoon chili powder
1 tablespoon salt

1 can tomatoes
1 can Mexicorn
1 cup grated cheese
1 (5 ounce) package broad noodles
1 can sliced ripe olives

Saute onion, garlic, bell pepper and ground chuck. Add salt, then chili powder. Add tomatoes and corn; cook 30 minutes. Fold in cheese, noodles and olives. Better made a day ahead. *Freezes well!* Serves 4 to 6.

Teryl's Favorite Pot Roast

4 pound boneless roast (rump, round or sirloin tip)
6 tablespoons cooking oil
Salt and pepper and flour

5 cups chopped onions
1 cup hot water
1 tablespoon Worcestershire sauce

Sprinkle salt and pepper over roast and pat in. Then roll in flour. Put oil in heavy iron pot and brown meat on all sides. Add chopped onions and saute until very brown. This takes about 20 minutes. Add 1 cup hot water and 1 tablespoon Worcestershire. Return roast to pot and cook slowly for about 2 hours on top of stove or in a 325 degree oven. *In 1957, my mother-in-law, Lil Quinn, assured me that this recipe would keep my new husband happy forever.* Serves 6.

Helen Claire Brooks

Apricot-Jalapeno Sauce

4 ounces dried apricots, diced
3/4 cup bourbon
1 (16 ounce) can apricot halves, drained
4 jalapeno peppers, seeded and very
  finely diced

1/2 teaspoon ground cumin
1/4 teaspoon dried red pepper
  flakes
Zest and juice of 1 lime

In a saucepan, combine dried apricots, canned apricots and bourbon. Bring to a boil, then reduce to lowest heat and simmer uncovered for 30 minutes. Remove from heat, cover and cool. Transfer mixture to a food processor and pulse 6 times, or puree coarsely in a blender. Remove to a bowl and stir in jalapenos, cumin, red pepper flakes, lime juice and zest. *Great with pork, chicken or duck!* Makes 2 cups.

Ann Rogers

Barbecue Sauce

1 pint water
1/4 cup vinegar
3 tablespoons sugar
1 tablespoon chili powder

1 teaspoon lemon juice
1 teaspoon Worcestershire
1 teaspoon salt

Bring to a boil. Use to baste ribs or chicken. Any sauce left over can be refrigerated for later use.

Lucille Fey

Mrs. Harper's Barbecue Sauce

1/2 cup sugar
1 bottle catsup
1 lemon, cut in half
1 small pod garlic, whole

1 pint vinegar
1 cup yellow mustard
1 can tomato paste
2 teaspoons salt

To taste: Black pepper (approximately 2 tablespoons)
           Cayenne pepper (approximately 2 tablespoons)
Chili powder (if you want to use this, add with the vinegar)

Bring to a boil and then add: 1 pint Wesson oil. DON'T PANIC - Sauce separates - but it is supposed to do that!!! Keep warm over low flame. Do not boil again. Freezes very well.

Ann Rogers

Bearnaise Sauce

2 tablespoons white wine vinegar
2 tablespoons dry white wine
1 tablespoon chopped shallots
1 tablespoon chopped fresh tarragon
  leaves or 1 teaspoon dried tarragon

8 tablespoons (1 stick) unsalted
  butter
3 egg yolks
Salt & freshly ground black
  pepper, to taste

Combine vinegar, wine, shallots, and tarragon in a small saucepan. Place over high heat and boil until reduced by half, about 1 minute. Remove the pan from the heat and allow to cool to room temperature. Melt the butter. Combine the egg yolks and the reserved shallot mixture in the top of a double boiler. Beat yolks and shallot mixture until light colored. Gradually whisk in the melted butter over low heat. Continue whisking until the sauce has thickened. Season to taste with salt and pepper. Serve immediately *Delicious with beef, artichokes, asparagus, poached eggs, and fish. Makes 1-1/2 cups.*

Ann Rogers

Heavenly Cranberry Sauce

2 pounds cranberries
2 cups walnuts, chopped
3 cups sugar

Juice and grated rind of
  2 lemons
2 cups orange marmalade

Wash and drain cranberries well. Place in shallow baking dish and cover with chopped walnuts, sugar, juice and grated rind of lemons, and orange marmalade. Cover tightly and bake for 45 minutes at 350 degrees. Makes 2 quarts. Can be halved. Serve with turkey.

Frances Toney Hall

Horseradish Sauce

2 cups sour cream
1 tablespoon horseradish
2 teaspoons lemon juice
1/4 teaspoon lemon-pepper seasoning

Salt to taste
1 tablespoon chopped chives or
  1 teaspoon dill seed
Paprika

Mix together all ingredients and spoon into bowl. Sprinkle with paprika. Serve with roast beef. Makes 2 cups sauce.

Joan B. Thompson

Hot Wine Sauce

1 tablespoon butter
1/2 jar red currant jelly
1 tablespoon lemon juice
Pinch of cayenne

1/2 cup port wine
3 cloves
1/2 to 1 teaspoon salt

Simmer all ingredients, except wine, for 5 minutes. Strain. Add wine. Thicken sauce with cornstarch mixture (1 tablespoon cornstarch dissolved in 1/2 cup water). Keeps well in refrigerator. Serve warm with pork or poultry. *Particularly good with pork tenderloin.*

Grace Hoffman

Jezebel Sauce

1 (18 ounce) jar pineapple preserves
1 (18 ounce) jar apple jelly
1 small can dry mustard

1 small jar of horseradish
1 tablespoon cracked pepper

Combine all ingredients; blend well. Put in jelly jars and refrigerate. This will keep indefinitely. *A delicious condiment with pork, ham, or roast beef.*

Joan B. Thompson

Meat Marinade for Beef Tenderloin

1/2 cup soy sauce
1/4 cup brown sugar
1/2 teaspoon ginger

4 cloves garlic
2 tablespoons olive oil
1/2 teaspoon cracked pepper

Combine all the above ingredients. Place meat in a heavy plastic bag or plastic covered bowl. Pour mixture over meat and marinate for up to 3 days, turning often. Cook meat 20 minutes per pound at 450 degrees or over hot coals for 20 minutes.

Bart Mullis

Plum Sauce

3 cups plum jam
3 tablespoons mustard

3 tablespoons horseradish
1 tablespoon lemon juice

Mix all together. Serve with ham or pork roast.

Cookbook Committee

Quick Barbecue Sauce

4 tablespoons catsup
3 tablespoons Worcestershire

Juice of 1 lemon
1 stick of butter or margarine

Melt butter and add other ingredients. Blend and bring to a boil.

Mrs. Ferd Bellingrath,
President, Women of the Church 1966-68

Sally's Shish Kabob Marinade

1/2 cup catsup
1 teaspoon salt
2 tablespoons steak sauce
2 tablespoons sugar

2 tablespoons vinegar
2 tablespoons Worcestershire
1/4 cup water
2 tablespoons oil

Bring ingredients to a boil and pour over cubed round steak or sirloin. Seal in Ziploc bag, turning periodically. Baste kabobs with sauce while grilling. Enough for 2 pound roast. Serves 4.

Jane G. Starling

May 27, 1928 - The Session unanimously requested Dr. Fry to repeat the sermon on "Hell" preached May 20, 1928.

POULTRY and WILD GAME

LUX LUCET IN TENEBRIS

CHURCH SEAL

The Dove: *Represents the Holy Spirit descending from heaven.*

(John 1:32)

The Star: *Represents Christ Himself.*

(Num. 24:17; Rev. 22;16)

The Lamp: *Represents the Witnessing Church.*

(Matt. 5:15 and 16)

The Burning Bush: *Represents the Indestructible Church.*

(Exodus 3:1-11)

The Laurel Wreath: *Represents Victory and the Church Triumphant.*

The Scroll (at the bottom): *Carries the Latin inscription which means "The light shineth in the darkness".*

Best Ever Chicken Strips

2-1/2 pounds chicken breasts
   (or turkey), cut in strips
1/2 cup fresh lemon juice
1 tablespoon seasoned salt
1 tablespoon lemon pepper

2 cups flour
1 tablespoon seasoned salt
2 tablespoons lemon pepper
1 stick melted oleo

Mix chicken, lemon juice, seasoned salt and lemon pepper. Cover and marinate at least 10 minutes or up to overnight. Shake in a bag with flour and additional seasoned salt and lemon pepper. Fry in oleo until golden brown on both sides; then bake at 400 degrees for about 10 to 12 minutes or until done. Serves 5 to 6.

Pat Lile

Bridge Day Casserole

6 chicken breasts, cooked and cut up
2 cans artichoke hearts, drained
   and halved
1 bunch green onions, chopped
2 cans cream of chicken soup
1 cup mayonnaise
1/2 teaspoon curry powder
2 to 3 teaspoons fresh lemon juice

1 cup grated Swiss cheese
1 (8 ounce) can sliced
   mushrooms, drained
Ritz cracker crumbs
Frozen spinach, (optional)
   cooked and drained

Combine chicken, artichokes and green onion and place in 9x13 casserole dish. Mix well: soup, mayonnaise, curry powder, lemon juice, Swiss cheese, and mushrooms. Top with Ritz cracker crumbs. Bake at 350 degrees for 30 to 40 minutes. May be served on bed of spinach. Serves 8.

Ellen Nuckolls

In 1952, the Women of the Church presented Dr. McColgan a new study completely furnished "worthy of our worthy pastor".

Cheesy Chicken Spaghetti

1 fryer and 2 chicken breasts <u>or</u>
  6 chicken breasts
Seasoned salt
Garlic
Celery stalks
1/2 cup chopped onion
1 cup chopped celery   *bell peppers*

2 cans cream of chicken soup
1 (12 ounce) package
  vermicelli
1 pound Velveeta cheese
1 to 2 cups mild Cheddar
  cheese

Simmer chicken in about 8-10 cups water seasoned with seasoned salt, garlic and celery stalks. When tender, remove chicken from bone and cut into bite size pieces. Skim or strain broth and cook onion and celery in broth until tender. Mix in 2 cans of soup until smooth. Add vermicelli and cook 5 to 7 minutes. Add Velveeta and stir until melted. Top with grated Cheddar cheese and bake in oven until bubbly, about 15 to 20 minutes at 350 degrees. Serves 12.

Grace Hoffman

Chicken á la King

1/2 cup butter
1/4 cup sifted flour
1/2 pint cream
1 pint milk
Salt and cayenne pepper to taste

1 chicken or 4 breasts, cut up
1 cup celery, chopped
2 tablespoons green pepper,
  chopped
2 tablespoons chopped pimento

Cream together the butter and flour over low heat. When it bubbles, slowly add cream and milk, whisking constantly, until it boils. Simmer slowly for 5 minutes. Add salt and cayenne pepper. Mix in other ingredients and keep warm in a double boiler. Serve in patty shells or toast cups. Serves 4 to 6.

In memory of Annie B. Brown

Chicken á la Orange

8 chicken breasts, skinned & deboned
2 tablespoons flour
1/2 teaspoon salt
1/2 teaspoon pepper
1/2 teaspoon paprika

3 tablespoons shortening
1 can cream of chicken soup
1/2 soup can of orange juice
Generous dash of ginger
Generous dash of nutmeg

Dust chicken with flour, seasoned with salt, pepper and paprika. In heavy pan, brown chicken in shortening. Place chicken in baking dish. Add soup, orange juice, ginger, and nutmeg. Cover with foil. Bake at 325 degrees for 45 minutes. Serves 8.

Joan B. Thompson

Chicken and Artichoke Crepes

16 Entree Crepes (see recipe below)
5 tablespoons butter
1/2 cup minced onion
1/4 pound fresh mushrooms, sliced
3 tablespoons flour
2/3 cup chicken broth
1/2 cup Half and Half

2-1/2 cups diced cooked chicken
1 can quartered artichoke
  hearts, drained
1/3 cup grated Parmesan cheese
1/2 teaspoon crushed rosemary
1/2 teaspoon salt
1 cup shredded Swiss cheese

Set crepes aside. Saute onion and mushroom slices in 2 tablespoons butter. Stir until cooked. Add remaining butter and flour stirring until bubbly. Gradually add broth and cream stirring until mixture thickens. Remove from heat. Stir in chicken, artichokes, Parmesan, rosemary, and salt. Divide evenly among crepes. Roll up and place seam side down in greased shallow baking dish. May be covered and refrigerated for several hours at this point. Bake uncovered at 350 degrees 20 minutes or until hot. Sprinkle cheese on top last 5 minutes. Serves 8 or 16.

Helen O'Keefe King

Entree Crepes

1 cup plain flour
3/4 cup water
3/4 cup milk
3 eggs

2 tablespoons melted butter,
  cooled
1/4 teaspoon salt

Use blender, mixer or whisk, and mix all ingredients until smooth. Refrigerate at least one hour. Batter should be thick like heavy cream. Cook in crepe pan until bubbles break. Crepes may be stored in refrigerator for several days or frozen. Place paper towel between each crepe and wrap well to store. Makes 16 crepes.

Helen O'Keefe King

The bride's room in the new church was given in memory of Mrs. Alexander M. Barrow, by her children, Mr. and Mrs. Wylie M. Barrow and her granddaughter, Ann Barrow Trulock Taylor (Mrs. Ewing Taylor).

Chicken and Dumplings

1 (3-1/2 pound) chicken
1 stalk celery
1 small onion, quartered
Salt and pepper to taste

2 cups flour
1 egg, beaten
Canned broth (if needed)

Boil chicken (in enough water to cover) with onion, celery, salt, and pepper. When very tender, remove chicken and strain, reserving broth. Skin and debone chicken. Place 1 cup flour in a bowl and make a well in the center. Add beaten egg to the well, and work in flour with a fork until just mixed. Bring broth back to a rolling boil. Add 1 cup of the broth to the flour/egg mixture and mix quickly. Note: Broth must be boiling. Add remaining 1 cup of flour and stir until well mixed, adding more flour if necessary to make a stiff dough. Turn out onto a floured board and roll very thin (1/8 inch). Cut in strips and drop, one at a time, into boiling broth. Simmer on low heat about 1 hour, stirring often. Serves 4 to 6.

Cynthia Barefield Williams

Chicken and Noodles

1 chicken or 3 breasts
1 (8 ounce) package egg noodles
1 large bell pepper, chopped
1 large onion, chopped
1 (4 ounce) jar diced pimento, drained

1 can cream of mushroom soup
8 ounces grated Cheddar cheese
Salt and pepper to taste

Cook chicken in well seasoned broth. Cool and cut up, reserving broth. (Cook broth a little longer to reduce quantity if needed). Cook noodles, onion and bell peppers in broth. Drain and add pimentos, soup and chicken. Put in greased casserole and bake at 350 degrees for about 25 minutes or until bubbly. Top with cheese during last 10 minutes. Serves 6 to 8.

In memory of Annie Martin Eddins

Chicken and Rice Casserole

1 chicken, cooked and diced,
  reserving broth
1 cup rice
1/2 teaspoon salt
1 cup celery, chopped
1 cup onion, chopped
1 cup bell pepper, chopped

1/2 cup butter
1 (4 ounce) can sliced
  mushrooms
1 (6 ounce) can sliced water
  chestnuts
Salt and pepper
8 ounces grated Cheddar cheese

Cook the rice in 2-1/2 cups of chicken broth, with 1/2 teaspoon salt, for 15 minutes. In skillet, saute celery, onion, and bell pepper in butter. Add mushrooms and water chestnuts and cook in skillet 2 or 3 minutes longer. Mix with chicken and 1/2 to 1 cup of broth. Salt and pepper to taste. Add 1/2 of cheese and mix. Pour into large buttered casserole dish and cover with remaining cheese. Bake at 350 degrees for 30 minutes. Serves 8.

Eleanor B. Joerden

Chicken and Rice Casserole

3 thin strips bacon
1 box long grain and wild rice mixed
1/4 cup regular rice
1 can mushrooms

1 can cream of chicken soup
1 can Swanson's chicken broth
6 chicken breasts
1 package dry onion soup mix

Lay bacon in bottom of casserole. Sprinkle the rices over bacon.Sprinkle with seasoning packet from wild rice. Add mushrooms. Mix broth and soup. Pour over mushrooms and rice. Lay chicken breasts on top and sprinkle with 2 to 3 tablespoons dry soup mix. Cover and bake 1-1/2 hours at 325 degrees. Remove foil last few minutes and let brown. Serves 6.

Frances Toney Hall

Chicken and Shrimp Enchiladas

2 tablespoons butter
1 small onion, diced
1 can cream of chicken soup
1 small can evaporated milk
1 teaspoon chili powder
1/2 teaspoon cumin
1 can diced Ro-Tel tomatoes,
    partially drained

2 cups shredded Cheddar or
    Velveeta, divided
3 chicken breasts, cooked and
    cut into bite size pieces
1/2 pound cooked shrimp,
    peeled
6 or 8 flour tortillas

In a skillet over medium-high heat, cook onion in butter for 1 or 2 minutes. Add soup, milk, chili powder, cumin, Ro-Tel, and 1-1/2 cups cheese. Bring to a boil. Reduce heat. Add chicken and shrimp and simmer a few minutes. Wrap tortillas in plastic wrap and microwave for 30 seconds to soften. Spoon 2 to 3 tablespoons sauce on each tortilla. Roll up and place seam side down in a casserole. Pour remaining sauce over enchiladas and sprinkle with 1/2 cup of cheese. Bake 10 to 15 minutes in 350 degree oven. *Serve with guacamole, sour cream, and sliced ripe olives.* Serves 4 to 6.

Grace Hoffman

Presidential Enchiladas

2 tablespoons cooking oil
2 (4 ounce) cans green chilies, chopped
1 large clove garlic, minced
1 (28 ounce) can tomatoes, diced
2 cups chopped onion
2 teaspoons salt

1/2 teaspoon oregano
3 cups shredded cooked chicken
2 cups sour cream
2 cups grated Cheddar cheese
1/3 cup oil
12 corn tortillas

Saute in skillet green chilies and garlic in oil. Drain tomatoes, reserving 1/2 cup liquid. Add tomatoes, onion, 1 teaspoon salt, oregano, and reserved liquid to chilies and garlic. Simmer uncovered until thick (about 20 minutes). Set aside. Combine chicken, sour cream, cheese, and remaining salt. Heat 1/3 cup oil in skillet and soften tortillas. Drain on paper towels. Fill with chicken mixture and roll. Place seam side down in a 9x13 Pyrex pan. Cover with sauce and bake at 325 degrees until thoroughly heated. Serves 12.

Margaret Dial Dawson

Chicken Divan Parisienne

2 cups cooked and sliced chicken
2 packages frozen broccoli spears, cooked
1 package onion soup mix

1 pint sour cream
1 cup heavy cream, whipped
1 tablespoon Parmesan cheese

Add soup mix to sour cream and beat until well blended. Arrange broccoli spears in bottom of sprayed shallow 9x13 Pyrex pan. Spoon half of sauce over broccoli. Cover with chicken slices. Fold whipped cream into sour cream mixture and pour over chicken. Bake at 350 degrees for 20 to 25 minutes. Sprinkle Parmesan and brown slightly at very last. *Agnes and her husband, "Dr. Pete", were missionaries to China for many years. He served as our Associate Minister from 1961 until 1966.*

In memory of Agnes Richardson

Chicken Pot Pie

6 tablespoons butter
5 tablespoons flour
2 cups chicken broth
Salt and pepper to taste
1 cup milk

3 to 4 chicken breasts, cooked
2 cups cooked potatoes
3/4 cup cooked carrots
1 can tiny English peas
6-8 biscuits, homemade preferred

Melt butter in skillet. Add flour and brown. Pour in broth and milk. Add generous amount of salt and pepper to taste. Cook until mixture begins to thicken. Place chopped cooked chicken, potatoes, carrots and peas in 9x13 or large casserole dish. Pour broth mixture over chicken and vegetables. Place biscuits on top of mixture and brown in oven for 20 to 30 minutes at 375 degrees. May substitute turkey for chicken.

Melissa Cook

Chicken Reuben

4 chicken breasts, uncooked
1/4 teaspoon salt
1/8 teaspoon pepper
1 (15-1/2 ounce) can sauerkraut,
    drained <u>well</u>

4 slices Swiss cheese
1-1/4 cups Thousand Island
    salad dressing
1 tablespoon parsley, chopped

In sprayed oblong Pyrex pan, place chicken and sprinkle with salt and pepper. Pour sauerkraut over chicken and top with cheese slices. Pour salad dressing over cheese. Cover and bake at 325 degrees for 1-1/2 hours. Sprinkle with chopped parsley before serving. Serves 4.

Angela Ross

Chicken Saute á la Maribor

2-1/2 pounds chicken pieces or
   4 chicken breasts
3 ounces butter
Salt and pepper
1 tablespoon chopped onion
1 clove garlic, sliced

2 teaspoons flour
8 ounces dry white wine
12 to 15 pitted black olives
1/2 pound fresh mushrooms,
   sliced

Heat butter in pan until it turns brown. Add chicken, salt and pepper. Cook until brown on all sides. Add onion and garlic and cook until transparent but not brown. Stir in flour and add wine, olives and mushrooms. Cook slowly 25 to 30 minutes (or until done) on top of stove. Garnish with parsley, chopped or sprigs. Serves 4.

Gerry Leslie

Chicken Seafood Artichoke Casserole

4 cans artichokes, drained
4 pounds shrimp, cooked and cleaned
12 to 14 chicken breasts, cooked & diced
3 pounds fresh mushrooms
3 tablespoons butter
6 cups thick white sauce
2 tablespoons Worcestershire
Salt and pepper

1 cup sherry
1/2 cup Parmesan cheese
Paprika and chopped parsley

White Sauce:
1-1/2 cups butter
1-1/2 cups flour
6 cups milk

Arrange artichokes in bottom of buttered casserole. Add shrimp and chicken. Saute mushrooms in butter, drain and add to casserole. Combine ingredients for white sauce. Add Worcestershire, salt and pepper and sherry to white sauce. Pour over shrimp and chicken. Sprinkle top with cheese and dust with paprika and parsley. Bake uncovered at 350 degrees for 40 minutes. *Delicious! May be served over rice.* Serves 24.

Joan B. Thompson,
Moderator, Presbyterian Women 1992-93

Chicken Spaghetti

1 (8 ounce) package vermicelli
4 cups chicken, cooked and diced
1/2 cup celery, diced (optional)
Small onion, chopped
1 can mushroom soup

1 can cream of celery soup
1 cup chicken broth
1 pound sharp Cheddar cheese, grated
Salt and pepper to taste

Cook pasta according to directions on package; drain. Saute celery and onion in small amount of margarine until tender. Mix all ingredients thoroughly in large bowl. Place in casserole dish. Bake at 350 degrees for about 30 minutes. *This is a good recipe to use when cooking for large crowds or when you want to cook ahead of time and freeze until needed.* Serves 6 to 8.

Sue Deneke

Chicken Spaghetti

1 hen, cooked and cut up, reserving broth
8 strips bacon, chopped
1 bell pepper, chopped
1 button garlic, chopped
1 onion, chopped
3 stalks celery, chopped
1 (8 ounce) can mushrooms, drained

1 (15-1/2 ounce) can diced tomatoes
1 small can tomato paste
Stuffed olives, sliced
Cheddar cheese, grated
1 (12 ounce) package spaghetti

Cook bacon portions half done and remove from skillet. Saute celery, onion, pepper, and garlic in bacon fat; then add tomatoes, tomato paste, some chicken broth and the bacon. Cook slowly about 1 hour. Add chicken and mushrooms. Cook spaghetti in rich broth and drain. Serve spaghetti topped with sauce. Sprinkle with cheese and sliced olives. Serves 8.

Frances Howell Martin

Chicken Spaghetti

1 medium size hen
Small bottle chili powder
Large can sliced mushrooms

Cheddar cheese, grated
1 (14 ounce) package spaghetti
Swanson's chicken broth

Boil chicken until tender; cut into bite size pieces, and save broth. Cook spaghetti in chicken broth, saving broth. Mix spaghetti, chicken, chili powder and mushrooms. Add remaining chicken broth (adding Swanson's chicken broth if necessary) to make a rather juicy mixture. Cook 1 hour at 300 degrees. Remove from oven, stir and add grated cheese on top. Continue to cook for 30 minutes. *This recipe was made up by Gyp Railsback in the early 1930's and has been handed down in the family.*

In memory of Mrs. Glenn A. Railsback (Gyp)

Chicken Squares

1 (3 ounce) package cream cheese, softened
2 tablespoons melted butter
2 cups cooked chicken, diced
1/2 teaspoon salt
1/4 teaspoon pepper
2 tablespoons milk
1 tablespoon dried chives

1 tablespoon chopped pimento
1 (8 ounce) can crescent dinner rolls
1/4 cup crushed seasoned croutons
1/4 cup chopped fresh parsley (optional)

Combine first 8 ingredients, blending well. Separate rolls into 4 rectangles on an ungreased cookie sheet. Seal perforations. Spoon 1/2 cup chicken mixture into center of rectangle, fold and seal. Brush tops with butter and sprinkle with crushed croutons and/or parsley. Bake at 350 degrees for 20 to 25 minutes.

Sue Smith

Chicken Supreme

1 whole frying chicken, cut up, <u>or</u> 4 chicken breasts
1 package dry Lipton Onion Soup Mix

1 bottle Seven Seas Russian salad dressing
1 small jar apricot preserves

Place chicken in baking pan. Mix onion soup mix, Russian dressing, and apricot preserves together. Spread over chicken. Bake uncovered at 325 degrees for 1-1/2 hours or until done. Serves 4.

Margaret Hooten

Chicken Tetrazinni

4 pounds chicken breasts
2 cans chicken broth
1 cup celery, diced
Salt
Pepper
2 bell peppers, diced
2 onions, diced
20 ounces vermicelli

20 ounces grated Cheddar cheese
2 (10-3/4 ounce) cans cream of mushroom soup
1 (4 ounce) can sliced mushrooms, drained
1 (4 ounce) jar chopped pimento, drained

Place chicken in large pot, cover with 2 cans of chicken broth and water to cover. Add celery, salt and pepper and cook until tender. Cool, skin, debone chicken and cut into chunks. Bring broth in pot back to boil with peppers and onions and cook until tender. Strain. Next cook vermicelli in this broth. When done, drain, <u>reserving broth</u> (2 cups). Add vermicelli, celery, peppers, onions, grated cheese, mushrooms and mushroom soup to the 2 cups of reserved broth. Stir until cheese melts, then add chicken and pimento. Bake at 350 degrees, uncovered, for 30 to 40 minutes, after pouring into your favorite casserole. *Great with French bread, salad and light dessert!* Serves 12 to 16.

Leila Wilkins O'Keefe

Chicken Timbales with Mushroom Sauce

5 tablespoons butter
5 tablespoons flour
1 cup broth from chicken
1 cup milk
2 eggs
1/2 cup bread crumbs
A little scraped onion

Seasonings to taste: salt, red
pepper, black pepper, poultry
seasoning and about
1 teaspoon celery seed
Ground meat from 1 whole
chicken (about 3 cups)

Melt butter and stir in flour. Add milk and stock. Cook over low heat, stirring, until thick. Add seasonings. To the ground chicken add beaten eggs, bread crumbs, onion and sauce. Bake in greased ramekins or Pyrex custard cups set in about 1/4 inch of hot water. Cook at 350 degrees for 45 to 60 minutes or until firm and crusty on top. Serve with mushroom sauce (see recipe below). Serves 8 to 10.

In memory of Mrs. Hugh Humphreys

Mushroom Sauce

4 tablespoons butter
4 tablespoons flour
1 cup milk

1 cup of broth from chicken
Salt and pepper to taste
Mushrooms

Melt butter and stir in flour. Add milk and broth. Cook over low heat, stirring, until thick. Add salt and pepper to taste; then sliced mushrooms. Serve over Chicken Timbales.

In memory of Mrs. Hugh Humphreys

Creamed Chicken

6 tablespoons butter or chicken fat
6 tablespoons flour
1 teaspoon salt
1/8 teaspoon pepper
1-1/2 cups seasoned chicken broth

1 cup cream or Pet milk
1 cup cooked chicken, cut up
1 (8 ounce) can sliced
mushrooms

Melt butter or fat, add flour, salt and pepper, stirring constantly. Cook over low heat until bubbling. Remove from heat and stir in broth and milk. Bring to a boil and slowly boil 1 minute, stirring constantly. Stir in gently, chicken and mushrooms. Serve hot over toast points or Pepperidge Farm puff pastry shells. Serves 6.

Leila Wilkins O'Keefe

Crunchy Chicken Bake

2 cups wheat wafers, crushed
2 cans cream of chicken soup
1/2 cup mayonnaise
1-1/2 cups cooked chicken, diced
2 cans asparagus spears, drained

1 (8 ounce) can water
  chestnuts, drained
2 (2-1/2 ounce) cans sliced
  mushrooms, drained
1/4 cup margarine, melted

Spread 1/2 of wheat wafers in a greased 9x13 casserole. Combine soup and mayonnaise, spread 1/2 over wafers. Top with chicken, water chestnuts, asparagus and mushrooms. Spread remaining soup mixture over this. Combine remaining wafers with melted oleo - sprinkle on top; cover with foil loosely. Cook at 350 degrees for 30 minutes covered and 15 minutes uncovered. *This is delicious with a green salad.*

Joan B. Thompson

Devilish Chicken

1 pound chicken breasts,
  (split, boned and skinned)
2 tablespoons oil
1/3 onion, chopped
1 large clove garlic, chopped
5 ounces dry white wine

5 ounces chicken broth
1 tablespoon cornstarch or flour
1 tablespoon Dijon mustard
1 tablespoon capers
Parsley, chopped
Cooked noodles

Brown and cook chicken breasts in oil. Brown onion and garlic in remaining oil. Add the wine, chicken broth, cornstarch or flour, mustard and capers. Cook, stirring, until a sauce consistency. Pour sauce over cooked chicken breasts and garnish with parsley. Serve with buttered noodles. Serves 4.

Bobbye Nixon

In 1910, the treasurer of the Incidental Fund, Mr. R. W. Seymour, was authorized to pay 50 cents per month or $5.00 a year, to have the church's lot in Bellwood Cemetery kept in a neat condition, and if he had not sufficient funds in hand for this purpose, to go out and collect it from the members.

El Paso Chicken

1 pound boned skinless chicken
   breasts, cooked and cut up
2 chicken bouillon cubes
1 can condensed chicken broth
1 clove garlic, chopped
1 cup green pepper, chopped
1-1/2 cups onion, chopped
1/2 stick margarine
1 (7 ounce) package vermicelli

2 cans diced Ro-Tel
1 teaspoon Worcestershire
1 (8 ounce) can tiny English
   peas, drained
1 (8 ounce) can sliced
   mushrooms, drained
1 pound Velveeta, cut up
Coarse ground pepper to taste

Add can of condensed broth to reserved broth, making 1 quart. Saute peppers, onions and garlic in margarine. Cook vermicelli in broth and drain. Add Worcestershire, onion mixture, drained Ro-Tel, Velveeta and pepper. After cheese melts, add chicken, peas, and mushrooms. Place in casserole and bake at 350 degrees. (If you like hotter do not drain Ro-Tel). Serves 8.

Frances Toney Hall,
President, Women of the Church,
1964-65; 1982-83

Favorite Chicken

1 chicken, cooked and torn into
   pieces (reserving broth)
8 ounces fresh mushrooms
4 tablespoons butter
1 (12 ounce) package spaghetti

Salt and pepper to taste
Garlic powder (as desired)
2 cans cream of celery soup
1/2 cup sherry
Parmesan cheese

Cook and tear chicken. Saute mushrooms (sliced) in butter. Cook spaghetti in broth. Drain and add all ingredients except sherry and cheese. Place in oblong Pyrex pan and drizzle with sherry. Sprinkle well with Parmesan. Bake at 350 degrees for 25 minutes or until bubbly. May be prepared ahead. Serves 8.

Gail Morschheimer

Grilled Chicken

1 cup olive oil
1/2 cup fresh lemon juice
3 cloves garlic, minced
3 bay leaves
1 tablespoon dried rosemary, crumbled

1 teaspoon salt
1/2 teaspoon pepper
8 chicken quarters

Combine olive oil, lemon juice, garlic, bay leaves, rosemary, salt, and pepper. Mix thoroughly. Arrange chicken quarters in a shallow dish and pour marinade over them. Cover and refrigerate overnight, turning occasionally. Grill chicken, basting frequently, about 15 to 20 minutes or until juices from pricked chicken run clear. Garnish with lemon wedges and parsley. Serves 8.

Monte Atkins

Hot Chicken Salad

24 cups cooked diced chicken
3 cans cream of chicken soup
6 cups celery, chopped
1-1/2 cups green peppers, chopped
1-1/2 cups grated onion
1-1/2 cups lemon juice

1-1/2 cups toasted almonds
Salt and pepper
6 cups mayonnaise
6 cups grated Cheddar cheese
12 cups crushed potato chips
Parmesan cheese

Mix all ingredients together except crushed potato chips and Parmesan cheese. Place in lightly sprayed casseroles. Top with chips and sprinkle with Parmesan. Cook at 350 degrees for 30 to 35 minutes or until hot. Serves 42.

Debbie Robinson

Mr. and Mrs. Fain Ezell and Mr. and Mrs. John Lewis were married in the first double wedding in the new Presbyterian Church at Fifth and Walnut. They were married by Dr. John L. Caldwell on December 18, 1900. Mrs. Ezell and Mrs. Lewis were sisters.

Summer Hot Chicken Salad

2 cups cooked chicken
1/2 cup toasted nuts (pecans are best)
2 cups finely chopped celery
1/2 teaspoon salt
1/4 teaspoon white pepper

2 teaspoons chopped onion
2 tablespoons fresh lemon juice
1 cup mayonnaise
1/2 cup grated Cheddar cheese
1 cup crushed potato chips

Cook chicken in well seasoned water until tender. Remove from bone and chop (white meat makes a prettier dish). Add all other ingredients except cheese and potato chips. Toss lightly. Place in very lightly greased individual baking dishes or a single casserole as you prefer. Sprinkle with grated cheese and then potato chips. Bake in 400 degree oven for 10 minutes. If you use single casserole, bake a few minutes until hot. This needs to be served hot. Garnish with fresh parsley. Serves 6.

Mrs. Trulock was on the Board of Women's Work of Southern Presbyterian Church from 1950 to 1960. She was also Synodical President and District President, Women of the Church.

In memory of Mrs. Walter N. Trulock, Jr.,
President, Woman's Auxiliary, 1935-37

Jefferson Chicken

16 skinless and boneless chicken breasts
1 jar dried beef
Bacon strips to wrap chicken
1 (8 ounce) package cream cheese

2 cans cream of chicken soup
1 small carton sour cream

Line baking pan with chopped dried beef. Pepper chicken. (DO NOT SALT). Roll up chicken, then wrap with bacon. Place chicken on dried beef. Mix other ingredients in a bowl and pour over chicken. Lightly cover baking dish with aluminum foil (do not seal). Bake at 325 degrees for about 2 hours. Remove foil and cook about 10 more minutes. If dish is prepared in advance and has been refrigerated it will take a little more than 2 hours of cooking before removing foil. Can be made day ahead. Serve with rice.

RICE

2 cups uncooked rice (cook according to package directions). While rice is hot, add 1 cup chopped bell pepper, 1 cup chopped parsley, 3 chopped garlic cloves, 1 cup milk, 1 cup grated sharp cheese, 1/2 cup Wesson oil and mix. Place in casserole and bake about 25 minutes at 350 degrees. Arrange chicken on platter around rice.

Jean Traylor

177

King Ranch Chicken

3 to 4 pound hen or chicken breasts
1 onion, cut up
2 ribs of celery
Salt and pepper
1 onion, chopped
1 large bell pepper, chopped
Flour tortillas

1 can cream of mushroom soup
1 can cream of chicken soup
Cheddar cheese, grated
Chili powder
Garlic salt
2 cans diced Ro-Tel, undrained

Cook chicken in water seasoned with cut up onion, celery ribs, salt and pepper. Cool and cut into bite size pieces. Strain and reserve broth. Chop onion and bell pepper. Soak flour tortillas in warm broth until pliable. Layer in sprayed 9x13 casserole; tortillas, chicken, onion, and bell pepper. Combine soups and grated cheese. Sprinkle with chili powder and garlic salt. Repeat layers. Top casserole with Ro-Tel. Bake at 375 degrees for 30 minutes. Serves 8 to 10.

In memory of Linda List Tanner,
Moderator, Presbyterian Women 1993-95

Lory's Chicken

4 raw boneless and skinless chicken
  breasts
8 slices Swiss cheese
1 can cream of chicken soup

1/4 cup dry white wine
1 cup herb seasoned stuffing
  mix
1/4 cup melted butter

Place raw chicken breasts in casserole. Top with 8 slices Swiss cheese. Mix cream of chicken soup undiluted with 1/4 cup dry white wine. Pour over chicken and cheese. Sprinkle with herb seasoned stuffing mix and drizzle the melted butter over it. Bake at 350 degrees for 45 to 55 minutes. Serve over rice. *Given to me by my daughter, Lory Hall.* Serves 4.

Frances Toney Hall

Mexican Chicken

4 boneless chicken breasts, cooked
  and diced
Nacho cheese flavored Dorito chips
  (large bag)

1 can cream of chicken soup
1 can cream of mushroom soup
1 can cheddar cheese soup
1 can diced Ro-Tel tomatoes

Crush bag of chips and place on bottom of 9x13 or large casserole dish. (Save a few whole chips to sprinkle on top). Place diced chicken meat on top of chips. Heat in saucepan: Cream of chicken soup, cream of mushroom soup, cheddar cheese soup and Ro-Tel. Stir. Do not add water. Pour hot soups and Ro-Tel over chicken and chips. Stir. Top with remaining whole chips. Bake uncovered at 350 degrees for 25 minutes. *Simple but good!* Serves 10.

Melissa Cook

Oven Barbecued Chicken

8 to 10 chicken breasts

Sauce:
1/2 pound butter
1 pint catsup
1 pint vinegar
1 tablespoon Tabasco
1 small bottle Worcestershire

1 tablespoon brown sugar
1 tablespoon onion juice
1-1/2 cloves garlic, chopped fine
Dash red pepper
Dash black pepper
1 to 3 tablespoons salt

Wash chicken and pat dry. Put in 9x13 pan. Cover with barbecue sauce. Cover with foil and bake 45 minutes at 350 degrees; uncover and cook on top rack of oven for last 15 minutes. Sauce: Bring all ingredients to a boil; stir and simmer for 5 minutes. Pour over chicken. Makes almost 2 quarts; save and refrigerate excess. Serves 8.

Cookbook Committee

Presbyterian Chicken

8 cooked chicken breasts, boned
  and skinned
8 slices baked ham
8 slices bacon
1 (10-3/4 ounce) can cream of
  chicken soup

1 (8 ounce) can sliced water
  chestnuts
1 (4 ounce) can sliced
  mushrooms
1 (8 ounce) carton French
  onion dip

Flatten chicken breasts and wrap around ham. Wrap bacon around breasts and ham "barber pole" style. Place in 9x13 casserole. Mix last ingredients and pour over chicken. Bake at 325 degrees for 2 hours. May be made up ahead and baked later. Serves 8.

Angela Ross

Ranch Chicken

1 pound boneless chicken breasts
1/2 cup melted butter
3/4 cup grated Parmesan cheese

3/4 cup cornflake crumbs
1 package Hidden Valley Ranch
  dressing mix (original milk)

Mix together cheese, cornflake crumbs and Ranch dressing mix. Dip chicken in melted butter and dredge in dry mixture, coating well. Bake uncovered in dish sprayed with Pam at 350 degrees for 50 to 60 minutes until golden brown. Serves 4.

Frances Toney Hall

Rock Cornish Hen

4 hens
Salt
White pepper

1/4 cup melted butter
1/2 cup apple jelly mixed with
1/4 cup soy sauce

Wash hens and pat dry. Sprinkle with salt and pepper inside and out. Brush with melted butter and bake 45 minutes at 350 degrees. Brush with apply jelly mixture and bake 15 more minutes. Serves 4.

Betty Leibenguth

Rock Cornish Hen with Rice Stuffing

6 Rock Cornish hens
1/4 cup butter
1/4 cup onion, chopped
1-1/3 cups rice, pre-cooked
1 cup water
1/2 cup orange juice
2 teaspoons orange rind, grated

2 tablespoons parsley, chopped
1 cup pecans, chopped
1/2 teaspoon sugar
1/4 teaspoon poultry seasoning
1-1/2 teaspoons salt
Melted butter or margarine

Thaw hens, rinse, and pat dry. Melt butter or margarine in saucepan; add onion and saute until tender, but not browned. Add rice, water, orange juice, orange rind, parsley, nuts, and sugar. Mix just to moisten rice. Bring to a boil quickly over high heat. Cover, remove from heat, and let stand 5 minutes. Add poultry seasoning and salt and mix lightly with a fork. Lightly salt inside cavity of each hen. Use approximately 1 cup of dressing for each hen, packing lightly. Place hens breast side up in uncovered pan; baste frequently with melted butter or margarine. Cook one hour at 425 degrees. *Served at Presbyterian Women's Christmas Luncheon, 1989.* Serves 6.

Cookbook Committee

Tallerine Chicken

1 hen or large fryer, cooked and cut up
2 tablespoons butter
1 onion, chopped
2 cloves garlic, chopped
1 cup celery, chopped
1 medium bell pepper, chopped
1/2 teaspoon curry powder

1/2 cup sliced stuffed olives
1 (4 ounce) can sliced
   mushrooms, drained
2 cans crushed tomatoes
1 package wide noodles
1/2 cup grated American cheese
Reserved chicken broth

Saute onion, garlic, celery, and bell pepper in butter. Add curry powder and olives along with the chicken. Cook the noodles in reserved seasoned broth. Drain and add noodles to mixture with mushrooms and tomatoes. Pour into casserole with grated cheese on top. Bake at 350 degrees for 25 to 30 minutes. Serves 10.

In memory of Lillian Sloan,
President, Women of the Church 1937-39

Tarragon Baked Chicken

2 (3-1/2 pound) fryers, cut up
1/4 cup melted butter or margarine
2 teaspoons salt
1 teaspoon tarragon
1/4 teaspoon garlic powder

1/8 teaspoon pepper
2 tablespoons parsley, chopped
1/2 cup cider vinegar
2 tablespoons tarragon vinegar
1/2 cup chicken broth

Wash chicken and pat dry. Arrange skin side up in roasting pan. Brush with butter. Mix seasonings and sprinkle over chicken parts, adding parsley. Cover and bake at 350 degrees for 30 minutes. Uncover, adding vinegars and bake at 400 degrees until chicken is golden brown and tender, basting often. Drain fat off drippings, stir in broth and heat until bubbly. Pour over chicken placed on platter and serve. *The best!* Serves 8.

Pat Lile,
President, Women of the Church 1978-80

Turkey-in-a-Sack

1 teaspoon pepper
2 teaspoons salt
3 teaspoons paprika

4 teaspoons hot water
1 cup peanut oil
1 (14 to 16 pound) turkey

Combine first 4 ingredients and let stand 10 minutes. Add peanut oil and mix thoroughly. Wash and dry turkey. Rub oil mixture inside and outside of turkey. Take a large grocer's sack and rub remaining oil mixture in sack being sure sack is completely coated. Place turkey in sack and seal by rolling open end of sack at least twice and stapling it together. Be sure there are no holes in sack. Place in baking or broiler pan uncovered and cook 10 minutes per pound at 325 degrees. Gravy may be made by browning 6 tablespoons of flour in grease from turkey when it is done and adding water until desired thickness. Giblets which have been cooked in salted water and chopped can be added to gravy. *Do not substitute peanut oil with other oil. Do not substitute paper bag! Be careful opening bag when done as it is full of steam!* Serves 18 to 20.

In memory of J. G. Smith

White Chili

1 pound small white beans
6 cups chicken broth (may need more)
2 cloves garlic, minced
2 medium onions, chopped
  and divided
1 tablespoon oil
2 (4 ounce) cans chopped green chilies
1-1/2 teaspoons dried oregano

2 teaspoons cumin
1/4 teaspoon ground cloves
1/4 teaspoon cayenne pepper
4 cups diced cooked chicken
breasts
3 cups grated Monterey Jack
cheese

Quick soak beans according to directions. Drain water and combine beans, chicken broth, 1/2 the onions and garlic in large pot. Simmer until beans are soft, 2 to 3 hours, add more broth if needed. Saute onions in oil. Add chilies and seasonings. Mix and add to bean mixture. Add chicken and simmer 1 hour, adding broth when needed. Top with grated cheese when serving. Can use chopped tomatoes, chopped parsley, sliced ripe olives, chopped scallions, sour cream, tortilla chips, salsa, or avocado. *Serve in tureen with variety of topping choices and jalapeno cornbread.*

Cookbook Committee

Basting Sauce for Chicken

1/4 cup red wine vinegar
2 tablespoons lemon juice
2 garlic cloves, crushed
1-1/2 teaspoons oregano or rosemary

2 tablespoons <u>fresh</u> parsley
1/2 cup water
1/4 cup olive oil
Salt and pepper

Blend all ingredients and baste while broiling or baking. Chicken should be patted dry and brushed with olive oil (additional) inside and out. Place 3 tablespoons of sauce in cavity then baste often with remainder of sauce. Bake 1 hour and 15 minutes at 350 degrees or until done. You may cook one pound <u>rigatoni pasta</u> according to directions. Drain and toss with roasting pan juices. Serve with chicken and a salad. *Very good!*

Kitty Rubenstein

Mornay Sauce

1/4 pound butter
1 cup flour
4 cups milk

2 pounds Velveeta cheese
1 can beer

Melt butter, add flour and cook until bubbly. Add milk and cook until smooth. Boil 1 minute. Cut cheese in small pieces and beat into hot cream sauce. Add beer a little at a time to obtain consistency desired. If you make the sauce and keep it several days, beat it again to restore its light consistency. Serve over chicken breasts. Makes 1-1/2 quarts. *For a group!*

Ann Rogers

Brunswick Stew

3 squirrels or 2 rabbits
6 to 8 chicken thighs, skinned
1 pound salt pork, cut in strips
2 large onions, chopped
2 (14-1/2 ounce) cans whole tomatoes,
 chopped
2 cups lima beans
2 cups whole kernel corn

2 to 8 medium potatoes, diced
2 tablespoons salt
1 teaspoon black pepper
1/8 teaspoon cayenne (optional)
4 teaspoons sugar (optional)
1/2 cup margarine
4 tablespoons flour

Cut up squirrels (or rabbits), chicken, salt pork, and onions and drop in boiling water. Simmer 2 hours or until meat comes off bone. Remove meat from bones. Add meat to vegetables and seasonings and bring to a boil. Cover and simmer 1 hour or more. Mix margarine and flour to make a smooth paste. Add to mixture. Boil 10 minutes to make a smooth stew. Add more seasoning if necessary. Makes about 1 gallon!

Martha Halbert

Rare Marinated Duck Breasts

8 boneless duck breasts
1 cup Wishbone Italian dressing
 (may use fat-free)
2 tablespoons Worcestershire sauce

Juice of 2 lemons
1/2 teaspoon garlic powder
1/2 teaspoon ground cloves
Bacon slices, halved

Soak duck breasts in salt water for 3 hours. Drain, dry and place in a Ziploc bag. In small bowl, combine marinade ingredients. Pour over ducks, seal and marinate at least 3 hours, turning bag. When ready to cook, get grill to slow-fire stage. Wrap each breast with half piece of bacon and secure with toothpick. Cook 7 minutes per side or until bacon is done. May serve whole as a steak or thinly sliced with barbeque sauce, as an hors d'oeuvre. *This recipe is for those who "think" they don't like duck - it tastes like beef filet.*

Jane G. Starling

Versatile Wild Duck

2 or 3 ducks
Choice of chicken broth, beef broth,
   or onion soup

Worcestershire sauce
Red wine as desired
Bacon

Simmer ducks one hour in choice of broths. Drain and place in oven pan. Douse liberally with Worcestershire and red wine. Place bacon slice on breast. Cover with foil and bake at 250 degrees for 3 hours. Duck will fall off bones. Cover meat with pan juices. May be frozen. When heated, add some butter. May be served on roll as an hors d'oeuvre; add rice and mushrooms for casserole; or add barbecue sauce and serve on buns. Serves 6 to 8.

Wilma Jane Gillespie

Wild Duck Gumbo

2 dressed ducks
1/2 cup butter
1 cup sifted flour
3 cups chopped onion
3 cups chopped celery
3 cloves chopped garlic
1 (6 ounce) can tomato paste
1 (20 ounce) can tomatoes, undrained
2 teaspoons Accent
3 cups chopped green pepper

1 bunch green onions, chopped
1 bunch parsley, chopped
1 teaspoon oregano
1 teaspoon thyme
1 teaspoon salt
1 tablespoon pepper
1/2 tablespoon red pepper
2 pounds shrimp, cooked and
   peeled
Wild and white rice, cooked

Boil dressed ducks until tender (2 hours or so) in slightly salted water to cover. Drain, reserving stock. Melt butter in a heavy iron pot and add flour to make roux the color of an Indian squaw. Stir constantly over medium heat. When roux is ready, add onions and celery. Cook with reduced heat until onions and celery brown. Add garlic, tomato paste, tomatoes, Accent, green onions, parsley, and seasonings. Add 2 quarts of reserved duck stock and boil rapidly for 1/2 hour. Remove meat from duck carcasses and cut into bite-size pieces. Add meat to pot. More stock may be added to make a rich gumbo. Add cooked and peeled shrimp. To serve, pour gumbo in soup bowl over scoop of rice using an ice cream scoop. Place sprig of fresh parsley on top of rice. Serves a bunch.

Susan Norton

Donald Locke's Duck

Wild duck
Salt and pepper
Sliced onion
Bay leaf

1 can cream of mushroom soup
1 can Ro-Tel
Rice (judge amount by amount
of broth)

Cover duck generously with salt and pepper. Put in pan with onion and bay leaf, cover with water and simmer until the meat falls off the bone. Remove duck from broth (strain and save broth). Remove meat from bones. Add soup, Ro-Tel and duck meat to broth. Add rice and cook covered, until rice is done.

The Cookbook Committee

Wild Ducks in Marnier Sauce

3 to 4 wild ducks
Lemon juice
1-1/2 cups dry white wine
Celery leaves
1 onion, sliced
1 tablespoon honey

1/2 cup sugar
1 tablespoon wine vinegar
Juice of 2 oranges
1/2 cup Grand Marnier
Grated rind of orange

Trim the wing tips and cut off the necks of 3 or 4 wild ducks. Wash thoroughly, inside and out, with cold water; dry. Rub cavities with lemon juice, and in each put a few celery leaves and onion slices. Place ducks "breast up" on rack in shallow baking pan. Cook birds in 325 degree oven 1/2 hour. Drain fat from pan and add wine. Baste ducks and continue cooking 1-1/2 hours, basting with pan juices every 20 minutes. If a very crisp skin is desired, brush ducks with honey about 15 minutes before taking from the oven and <u>do not</u> baste again. Remove ducks to hot serving platter, and keep warm. Skim excess fat from juices in roasting pan.

<u>Sauce:</u> In heavy saucepan combine sugar and wine vinegar. Cook mixture over medium heat until sugar melts and begins to caramelize. Add juice of oranges, Grand Marnier, and grated rind of 1 orange. Stir well and cook 5 minutes. Combine this mixture with juices in roasting pan and add 1/4 cup orange peel cut in Julienne strips, which have been cooked in a little water for 5 minutes and drained. Season to taste and pour sauce over ducks on serving platter.

Gen Kennedy Wilkins

FAVORITES FROM THE MANSE

When Dr. John Livy Caldwell came to Pine Bluff in 1893, the church rented a house for him and his family at 714 West 5th until this manse at 205 West 5th (across the street from First Methodist Church) could be built. Dr. Caldwell supervised the building of the new manse and the Caldwells moved to their new home in November of 1893.

The two ministers and their families who lived in this manse were Dr. Caldwell, 1893-1903 and Dr. Joseph I. Norris, 1905-1922.

To The Wives of Our Ministers

It is with deep gratitude that we salute the strong Christian women, wives of our ministers. Through the past 138 years each, in her own way, has faithfully carried forward the program of our church.

We are grateful for the many times they have spoken words of encouragement and extended the hand of Christian friendship to us. We dedicate this section to them with love and appreciation for the many blessings they have given us.

Chicken Marengo

2-1/2 pounds chicken parts
1 teaspoon salt
1/8 teaspoon pepper
2 tablespoons flour
1/2 teaspoon dried thyme
4 tablespoons olive oil
1 chopped onion

1 clove garlic, minced
1 cup chopped canned or
   fresh tomatoes
1/4 cup white wine
2 tablespoons lemon juice
1 cup sliced mushrooms
1/2 cup sliced ripe olives

Sprinkle chicken with salt, pepper, flour, and thyme; brown in oil, set aside. Saute onions and garlic in the same pan. Add chicken and the rest of the ingredients, cover and simmer on the range top for about 40 minutes. Serve with noodles or rice. *This recipe is best made ahead of time in order for the flavors to blend.* Serves 6.

Mrs. William Lee Kinney (Peggy), 1995-

As for me and my family, we will serve the Lord.

Joshua 24:15

Viennese Nutballs

1 cup butter
1 (8 ounce) package cream cheese
1/4 cup white sugar
1-1/2 cups all purpose flour

1 cup ground almonds
1 teaspoon vanilla
1/4 cup powdered sugar

Cream butter and cream cheese together. Add all other ingredients, except the powdered sugar. Mix well. Chill dough for 1 hour. Shape dough into large marble sized balls. Roll in confectioner's (powdered) sugar. Place on a lightly greased cookie sheet. Bake for 20 to 35 minutes in a 300 degree oven. Remove from cookie sheet immediately. After they are rack-cooled, roll in confectioner's sugar again. Baking time will vary greatly depending upon the size of formed cookies. *This recipe has been passed down for 5 generations.*

Mrs. William Lee Kinney (Peggy), 1995-

Hummus

3 green onions, sliced
3 to 4 cloves garlic
1 (19 ounce) can Garbanzo beans,
    drained
1/4 cup parsley, chopped

2 tablespoons lemon juice
1/2 teaspoon salt
1/4 teaspoon pepper
Dash Tabasco
1/4 cup olive oil

In blender add onions and garlic; pulse, then add remaining ingredients, except oil. Blend briefly and add oil slowly while blender is running. Serve with melba rounds. Serves 4 to 6.

Mrs. Lawrence A. Wood (Helen), 1983-1994

Howard's Favorite Chocolate Pie

2 squares unsweetened chocolate
1 cup milk
2 eggs, separated
2 tablespoons flour

3/4 cup sugar
1/2 teaspoon vanilla
1 baked pie shell
4 tablespoons sugar

In top of double boiler, melt chocolate and add milk. Separate eggs, saving whites. Combine yolks, flour and sugar. Add this mixture to chocolate and milk in double boiler. Cook, stirring constantly, until very thick and smooth. Add vanilla and pour into baked pie shell. Beat the two egg whites until very stiff. Add 4 tablespoons of sugar; beat in and spread over pie. Bake at 350 degrees until brown.

Mrs. John Howard Edington (Patricia), 1978-1982

Church Chicken

1 can cream of mushroom soup
1 can cream of celery soup
1 can cream of chicken soup

1-1/4 cups uncooked rice
Chicken pieces
Salt to taste

Combine soups and add rice. Place in oblong casserole. Top with as many pieces of chicken as your family can eat. Cover and bake at 275 degrees for as long as it takes to go to Sunday School and church!

Mrs. John Howard Edington (Patricia), 1978-1982

Slushy Punch

3 cups water
1 cup sugar
2 ripe bananas, cut up
3 cups pineapple juice
1 (6 ounce) can frozen orange juice

1 (6 ounce) can frozen lemonade
2 tablespoons lemon juice
1 (28 ounce) bottle carbonated drink (Sprite, 7-Up, Gingerale)

In a 3-quart saucepan, combine water and sugar. Bring to boiling, stirring until sugar is dissolved. Boil syrup gently, uncovered, for 3 minutes; remove from heat and cool. Meanwhile, in a blender, combine cup up ripe bananas and half of the unsweetened pineapple juice. Cover and blend until smooth. Stir banana mixture into cooled syrup. Stir in remaining pineapple juice, the thawed orange juice and lemonade concentrate and lemon juice. Turn fruit mixture into a 13x9x2 inch dish. Freeze. To serve: Remove from freezer and let stand at room temperature for 30 minutes. To form a slush, scrape a large spoon across the surface of the frozen mixture. Spoon into punch bowl. Slowly pour in carbonated soda. Stir gently to mix. Garnish with fresh mint leaves. *Delightfully refreshing.* Makes 15 six ounce servings.

Mrs. Richard Allison Dodds (Betty), 1973-1976

Blessed are the peacemakers: for they shall be called the children of God.
Matthew 5:9

Turkey-Dressing Casserole

4 cups stuffing mix
(Pepperidge Farms)
1 cup melted margarine
1 (10 ounce) package frozen
chopped broccoli, cooked
3 cups cooked turkey or chicken, cut up

2 cans cream of mushroom
soup
1 large can evaporated milk
Dash of pepper

Mix stuffing mix with melted margarine. Pat one-half in bottom of 9x13 inch pan. Spread cooked broccoli over stuffing mixture. Mix soup, milk, turkey/chicken, and pepper together and pour over broccoli layer. Spread remaining stuffing mix on top. Bake at 350 degrees for 45 minutes. *This casserole has gone to many a potluck supper and the dish always come home clean.* Serves 12 to 15.

Mrs. Richard Allison Dodds (Betty), 1973-1976

Citrus Salad

2 (3 ounce) packages orange Jell-O
1 (15 ounce) can orange and
grapefruit sections
1 (15 ounce) can crushed pineapple

1 (12 ounce) can Royal Anne
cherries
2 (7-1/2 ounce) cans
mandarin oranges

Drain all fruit, use juice for liquid for Jell-O, plus water as needed to make 3 cups. Add fruit. Mold in individual molds or ring mold. *Refreshing and not too sweet.* Serves 10 to 12.

Mrs. William Lewis McColgan (Allie Mae), 1947-1973

Virginia Spoon Bread

1 cup sweet milk
1/2 cup corn meal
1/2 teaspoon salt

1 egg, separated
1 teaspoon baking powder

Let 1 cup sweet milk come to a boil. Remove from fire and stir in 1/2 cup corn meal. When lukewarm, add 1/2 teaspoon salt, yolk of 1 egg, 1 teaspoon baking powder, add beaten egg white. Place in hot, greased baking dish. Bake quickly (about 15 minutes) in 450 degree oven. Serve immediately. This is not a "pick-up" bread. It is served with a spoon and eaten with a fork. *Came from Lewis' home in Norton , Virginia. A favorite of his there as well as in our home.*

Mrs. William Lewis McColgan (Allie Mae), 1947-1973

Lemon Chess Pie

2 cups sugar
1/2 cup butter
4 eggs

1 rounded tablespoon flour
2 large fat lemons
Very best pastry

Cream sugar and butter. Beat in eggs. Add flour and lemon juice. Fill a pastry shell half full and bake in a moderate oven until done.

In memory of Mrs. Charles Edgar Newton (Betty), 1931-1947

Chicken Salad

Hen, cooked, diced or ground
6 hard boiled eggs, finely chopped
2 cups celery, chopped
1/4 onion, finely chopped
1/2 to 3/4 cup rich chicken broth
Mayonnaise
Juice of 1/2 lemon
Salt and white pepper to taste

Broth:
Water to cover hen
3 to 4 ribs celery
Celery leaves (some)
Large onion, quartered
2 teaspoons salt
1/4 teaspoon white pepper

Cook chicken with celery, onion, salt, and pepper (adding salt last 45 minutes) until tender. Cool and dice or grind. Cook broth down until good and rich. Cool and add 1/2 to 3/4 cups broth to diced chicken, chopped eggs, chopped celery, onion, and lemon juice. Use enough mayonnaise to hold together.

In memory of Mrs. Charles Edgar Newton (Betty), 1931-1947

Ribbon Sandwiches

2 loaves fresh bread, sliced thin
Filling:
3 small packages cream cheese
1 cup finely chopped green olives
Lemon juice to taste
Worcestershire sauce to taste

Onion juice to taste
Mayonnaise
  (1/3 cup approximately)
1/2 cup finely chopped pecans

Mix cream cheese and mayonnaise until smooth, add Worcestershire, lemon juice and onion juice to taste. Stir in olives and pecans. Remove crusts from bread. Spread with filling and roll up like jelly roll. Tie a pastel narrow ribbon around sandwich to make a bow. *They are very pretty and were used for luncheons or teas.*

In memory of Mrs. Robert Excell Fry (Mary), 1922-1930

Oatmeal Cookies

1 cup sugar
1 cup shortening
2 eggs
1 scant teaspoon soda dissolved
   in 4 tablespoons sweet milk
2 cups flour

2 cups oatmeal
1 heaping teaspoon cinnamon
Pinch salt
1 teaspoon vanilla
1 cup raisins
1 cup chopped pecans

Cream sugar and shortening. Add eggs, one at a time. Still beating, add soda-milk mixture alternately with flour. Stir in remaining ingredients. Drop by teaspoonfuls on greased baking sheet. Bake in slow oven until done.

In memory of Mrs. Robert Excell Fry (Mary), 1922-1930

Maids of Honor

1/2 pound blanched almonds
4 eggs
1 cup sugar
Juice of 1 lemon
Grated rind of 1 lemon

1 teaspoon vanilla
1/2 cup melted butter
1 small jar strawberry preserves
Best pastry

Grind blanched almonds. Beat eggs well. Add sugar, lemon juice and grated rind, gradually. Beat after each addition. Stir in ground almonds, vanilla and melted butter. Blend well. Line muffin tins with pastry leaving a fairly high fluted edge. Spoon in strawberry preserves. Pour egg mixture over to cover the preserves well. Place in cool oven and turn to 425 degrees and bake until brown and filling is set. Cool and remove from tins. Serve with whipped cream.

In memory of Mrs. Joseph Ingles Norris (Ernestine), 1905-1922

Date Roll

3 cups sugar
1 cup milk

1 package dates (40 dates)
1 cup chopped pecans

Stone (pit) the dates. Boil the sugar, milk and dates until it makes a soft ball when dropped in a cup of cold water. Beat well and add pecans. When firm roll the candy in a damp kitchen towel. Put in icebox and cool and then slice.

In memory of Mrs. Joseph Ingles Norris (Ernestine), 1905-1922

Cream of Corn Soup

1 large can cream style corn
1-1/2 quarts sweet milk
1 tablespoon onion juice
6 tablespoons butter
1 teaspoon salt

1 teaspoon sugar
1 teaspoon pepper
4 tablespoons flour
4 egg yolks

Put the corn, milk, onion juice and two tablespoons of the butter into a double boiler. Cook ten minutes. Strain. Add the salt, sugar, and pepper. Rub the flour and remainder of the butter to a paste and thicken the soup stirring well as it cookes smooth (double boiler again). Remove from fire and add well beaten yolks which have been strained after beating. Serve in soup cups with teaspoon of whipped cream on top and dash of paprika.

In memory of Mrs. John Livy Caldwell (Amanda), 1893-1905

Cream Charlotte

1 quart very thick cream
1 cup pulverized sugar
1 package gelatin
1/4 cup water

1 wine glass of sherry wine
12 lady fingers
Almonds, chopped
Maraschino cherries, chopped

Whip very stiff 1 quart thick cream. Sweeten with 1 cup pulverized sugar. Soak gelatin in water. Melt, cool and fold into whipped cream. Flavor with wine glass of sherry wine. Dip lady fingers in wine and line a bowl. Pour in whipped cream mixture and sprinkle chopped almonds or cherries over the top. You can color the cream a delicate green and sprinkle with pistachio nuts chopped fine.

In memory of Mrs. John Livy Caldwell (Amanda), 1893-1905

Watermelon Preserves

Ripe melon
Sugar

Cinnamon bark

Use the inside of a ripe melon, take out the seeds and cut into small pieces. Use half as much sugar as melon. Boil slowly until juice is thick. Before it cools down add a little cinnamon bark to flavor. Pour into hot jars and seal.

In memory of Mrs. Joseph Alexander Dickson (Catherine), 1881-1893

Bread Pudding

1-1/2 cups milk
2 eggs, separated
1/2 cup bread crumbs
1/2 cup sugar

1 teaspoon vanilla
Tart jelly
4 tablespoons sugar
Almonds, chopped

Scald 1-1/2 cups of milk. After it has cooled, add the yolks of 2 eggs well beaten. Stir into this 1/2 cup of bread crumbs, 1/2 cup of sugar. Flavor with 1 teaspoon vanilla. Bake 20 minutes in greased dish. Cover with jelly; then beat the whites of eggs and 4 tablespoons of sugar and put over the top. Set inside the oven and brown slowly. Add chopped almonds or pecans to the pudding, if desired.

In memory of Mrs. Joseph Alexander Dickson (Catherine), 1881-1893

Saith the Lord of Hosts, I will open you the windows of heaven, and pour you out a blessing, that there shall not be room enough to receive it.

Malachi 3:10

DESSERTS

Dr. Robert Excell Fry came as minister in 1922 and the manse at 1310 Olive Street was built for him and his family. They lived there until Dr. Fry left in 1930.

Dr. Charles Edgar Newton and his wife lived there from 1931-1947.

In 1947 Dr. William Lewis McColgan and his family came and lived there until his retirement in 1974. Upon his retirement the house was given by the church to Dr. and Mrs. McColgan for their home.

Amaretto Dessert

Crust:
1 cup flour
1/4 cup brown sugar
1/2 cup slivered almonds
1/2 cup butter

Filling:
1/2 cup amaretto
1/2 pound marshmallows
1 cup whipping cream,
  whipped

Mix first 4 ingredients with pastry blender. Crumble into a 9 inch pie plate. Bake at 375 degrees for 30 minutes, stirring often. Save some crumbs to sprinkle on top. Cool. Melt marshmallows in amaretto in double boiler. Cool and fold in whipped cream. Put in cooled crust and top with reserved crumbs. Refrigerate.

Joan B. Thompson

Almond Bavarian with Apricot Sauce

Almond Bavarian:
1 envelope Knox gelatin
1/2 cup sugar
1/8 teaspoon salt
2 eggs, separated
1-1/4 cups milk
1/2 to 1 teaspoon almond extract
1 cup whipping cream
Almonds, toasted

Apricot Sauce:
1-1/2 cups apricot nectar
1/2 cup sugar
1 teaspoon fresh lemon juice
1/2 cup dried apricots,
  chopped

Combine gelatin, 1/4 cup sugar and salt. Mix egg yolks and milk. Add to gelatin mixture and beat until gelatin is dissolved and mixture coats spoon. Stir in almond extract and chill. Beat egg whites and gradually beat in the remaining 1/4 cup sugar until stiff. Fold into gelatin custard mixture. Whip the 1 cup cream and fold into the mixture. Put in individual molds. Before serving, top with apricot sauce and slivered almonds. Apricot Sauce: Combine apricot nectar, sugar and lemon juice. Add apricots and simmer until tender. Pour into blender and blend until smooth. Chill. Be sure to taste sauce for sweetness before using. Also taste Bavarian to see if it has enough almond. (May need 1 teaspoon extract instead of 1/2 teaspoon.)

Frances Toney Hall

Peppermint Bavarian

50 marshmallows
2 cups milk
1 tablespoon peppermint flavoring
2 envelopes Knox gelatin

1/2 cup <u>cold</u> water
1 pint whipping cream
Pink or green food coloring

Melt marshmallows in milk. Add peppermint flavoring. Add gelatin soaked in 1/2 cup cold water. Cool and add cream which has been whipped. Color as desired. Serve with chocolate sauce. *This dessert of Hortense Jones was served often.*

In memory of Mrs. Jimmy Alexander

Almond Rocca

4 eggs, separated
1 cup sugar
1 cup whiskey
3 tablespoons gelatin, dissolved in
1/2 cup hot water
1 pint whipping cream, whipped

Lady Fingers
1/2 pint whipping cream,
whipped
1/3 cup slivered almonds,
parched
1/3 cup sugar

Mix egg yolks and sugar; beat well. Add whiskey and gelatin and beat until thick. Fold in whipped cream and beaten egg whites. Line springform pan with Lady Fingers. Pour in mixture. Ice with whipped cream and top with nut mixture. Nut mixture: Caramelize sugar in skillet, stirring constantly not to burn sugar. Add parched almonds and chop mixture when cold. Serves 8 to 10.

In memory of Corinne Smart West

Angel Berry Dessert

6 egg whites
1/2 teaspoon cream of tartar
1/4 teaspoon salt
1-3/4 cups sugar
2 (3 ounce) packages cream cheese,
softened
1 cup sugar
1 teaspoon vanilla

2 cups whipping cream, whipped
1 cup miniature marshmallows
Topping:
1 (21 ounce) can cherry pie
filling
1 teaspoon lemon juice
2 cups sliced fresh strawberries
(Combine ingredients)

Preheat oven and lightly grease 9x13 pan. Have eggs at room temperature. Beat eggs with cream of tartar and salt until fluffy. Gradually add sugar while beating. Scrape sides of bowl occasionally. Beat until stiff and glossy, about 10 minutes. Spread in pan and bake 1 hour at 275 degrees. Mix cream cheese with 1 cup sugar and vanilla. Gently fold in whipped cream and marshmallows; spread over <u>cool</u> meringue. Spoon topping over marshmallow mixture and cut in squares. Refrigerate several hours before serving. Serves 12 to 15.

Helen O'Keefe King

Angel Delight

1 angel food cake

Filling:
1-1/2 cups sugar
4 tablespoons cornstarch
1 cup water
1/2 cup fresh lemon juice
Grated rind of 2 lemons

3 egg yolks
2 tablespoons butter

Icing:
3 tablespoons powdered sugar
1/2 pint whipping cream
1 teaspoon vanilla
Pinch of salt

Split cake into 4 layers. Filling: Mix cornstarch in water; add sugar and rind, yolks and lemon juice. Cook very slowly on top of stove. When thick, add butter and cool. Spread between layers of cake, sparingly. Refrigerate. Icing: Whip cream, powdered sugar, vanilla, and salt. Ice cake and refrigerate. *I usually double icing for cake. Use mix or make from scratch.*

Frances Toney Hall

Baked Stuffed Apples

Apples, as many as needed
Brown sugar (1/4 cup per apple)
Butter or margarine (2 teaspoons
   per apple)

Cinnamon
Sugar
Nutmeg
Maple syrup

Wash and core apples. In each apple, stuff brown sugar and margarine; sprinkle with cinnamon, sugar and nutmeg. Pour maple syrup over each. Bake 1 hour at 350 degrees. *Best when served with whipped cream and chopped nuts!*

Sue Deneke

November, 1917: On motion the pastor was authorized to go before the city council and tell them that it is the sense and desire of the First Presbyterian Church Session that the Sabbath laws be strictly enforced.

Easy Strawberry Bonaparte

1 package (2 sheets) Pepperidge Farm
frozen puff pastry sheets
1 (3-1/2 ounce) package vanilla
instant pudding
1 cup milk
2 cups whipped cream or thawed
frozen non-dairy whipped topping

1-1/2 cups sliced strawberries
Milk
1/2 cup powdered sugar
1 cup whole strawberries
(for garnish)

Thaw pastry sheets at room temperature for 20 minutes. Preheat oven to 400 degrees. Unfold pastry on lightly floured surface. Cut each sheet into 3 strips along fold marks. Bake on baking sheet 15 minutes or until golden. Remove from baking sheet and cool on rack. Prepare pudding mix according to package directions with 1 cup milk. Fold in whipped cream. Cover and refrigerate. Split each pastry into 2 layers (12 total pastries). For icing, mix powdered sugar and 2 teaspoons milk. Spread on 4 top layers. Spread each remaining layer with pudding, top with sliced strawberries. For each dessert, assemble 2 layers and top with iced layer. Top with sliced or whole fresh strawberries. Refrigerate up to 4 hours. Slice and serve. Each dessert will serve 4. *Very easy and very elegant dessert!*

Debbie Robinson

Boston Cream Pie

7 eggs, separated
1 cup sugar
1 cup flour

1 teaspoon vanilla
1 teaspoon cream of tartar

Beat egg whites until stiff, slowly adding 2/3 cup sugar. Beat 4 yolks adding 1/3 cup sugar. Fold yellow mixture into whites, adding vanilla. Fold in flour. Grease and flour two 9 inch cake pans. Divide batter and bake at 300 degrees until light brown.

Custard for Boston Cream Pie

4 cups milk
3/4 cups sugar
1/2 cup flour
3 yolks (left from cake) <u>plus</u> 1 whole egg
2 teaspoons vanilla

1 pint heavy cream, whipped
and sweetened with 4 tablespoons confectioner's sugar
1-1/2 teaspoons vanilla

Scald milk in double boiler. Mix and beat other ingredients; add slowly to milk (beating as you add). Cook until thick stirring constantly. Let cake and custard stand separately until about 30 minutes before serving. Slice cake through the middle, making 4 layers. Divide custard and put between cake layers. Serve with whipped cream.

Frances Howell Martin

Boston Cream Pie with Chocolate Filling

4 egg yolks
1 tablespoon cold water
1-1/2 cups sugar
1/3 cup hot water
1-1/2 cups sifted flour

1-1/2 teaspoons baking powder
Pinch salt
1 teaspoon vanilla
4 egg whites
1/2 teaspoon cream of tartar

Beat until very light the yolks with 1 tablespoon water. Gradually add sugar and beat until smooth. Blend in 1/3 cup hot water. Add flour with baking powder and salt. Add vanilla. Hastily beat whites of eggs with cream of tartar. Fold in egg mixture. Bake in a slow oven (250 degrees) in 2 greased and floured pans about 25 minutes until done.

Chocolate Filling

2 tablespoons cocoa
1/2 cup sugar
4 heaping tablespoons flour

2-1/2 cups sweet milk
2 eggs, beaten
2 teaspoons vanilla

Mix dry ingredients together and gradually add milk. Heat in heavy pan or double boiler. Add a little hot mixture to beaten eggs and stir well. Add this to remainder in pan or boiler, stirring constantly. Cook over low heat until thick; add vanilla. Cool. Use as filling between cake layers. Dust top of cake with confectioner's sugar.

In memory of Mrs. A. M. Barrow
President, Women's Auxiliary, 1921-23

November 13, 1917:
The following resolution by Mr. V. O. Alexander was unanimously adopted by the Session:
Be it resolved by the Session of the First Presbyterian Church of Pine Bluff, Arkansas, that we as a branch of the church of Jesus Christ do humbly place ourselves on record as being emphatically opposed to the licensed saloon and liquor traffic in general and hope and pray that it may be driven out of our city, state, and nation.

Bread Pudding with Lemon Sauce

5 slices of day-old white or French bread
5 eggs
1 cup sugar
1/4 cup butter, melted

2 cups milk
1-1/2 teaspoons vanilla
1/4 teaspoon nutmeg
1/2 cup raisins (optional)

Remove crust from bread and cut into cubes. Beat eggs; add sugar, butter, milk, vanilla and nutmeg. Add bread and raisins, if desired, to mixture and mix well. Pour into a greased 2-quart casserole and bake at 350 degrees for 45 minutes. *Lemon Sauce is a must!*

Grace Hoffman

Lemon Sauce

1 cup sugar
1 tablespoon cornstarch
1/2 teaspoon salt
3 eggs, slightly beaten

Juice of 2 lemons
Rind of 2 lemons, grated
1 cup water
2 tablespoons butter

Mix sugar, cornstarch and salt in top of double boiler. Add eggs, lemon juice and rind, and water. Mix well. Cook in double boiler until thick, stirring constantly. Add butter and cool. *Good served with bread pudding, rice pudding and gingerbread.* Makes 2-1/2 cups sauce.

Grace Hoffman

Charlotte Russe

1 envelope gelatin, soaked in 1/4 cup
    cold water
1/4 cup boiling milk
1/2 pint whipping cream, whipped
2 egg whites

1/4 cup sugar
1 teaspoon vanilla or
    2 tablespoons whiskey or
    4 tablespoons sherry

Add soaked gelatin to boiling milk, stirring until dissolved. Cool. Fold into whipped cream. Beat egg whites until stiff, adding sugar and flavoring. Fold in whipped cream mixture. Chill for several hours. *Delicious old-fashioned dessert.*

In memory of Mrs. C. H. Triplett, Jr.
President, Women's Auxiliary, 1925-27

Cheesecake

Graham Cracker Crust:
2 cups crumbs (11-12 double crackers)
1/2 cup sugar
1/2 cup melted butter or oleo

{ Mix together and press in spring-form pan. Bake at 350 degrees just to set (10 minutes).

Filling:
2 (8 ounce) packages cream cheese
5 eggs, separated (whites stiffly beaten)
1 teaspoon vanilla
3 tablespoons lemon juice

Peel of 1 lemon, grated
1 cup sugar
2 cups sour cream

Beat cheese, egg yolks, vanilla, lemon juice, peel, and sugar until smooth. Add sour cream; beat only till blended. Fold in stiffly beaten egg whites. Pour into baked crust. Bake 45 minutes at 350 degrees; turn off oven and leave 1 hour in oven. *Almost a souffle. Serve with whipped cream or your favorite sauce.*

Ellen Nuckolls

Pumpkin Cheesecake

Pumpkin Mixture:
1 cup granulated sugar
3/4 cup pumpkin
3 egg yolks, lightly beaten
1 tablespoon cinnamon

1/2 teaspoon ginger
1/2 teaspoon salt
1/2 teaspoon mace

Blend all the above ingredients well and set aside.

Cream Cheese Mixture:
1-1/2 pounds cream cheese
1/2 cup sugar
2 whole eggs
2 tablespoons heavy cream

1 tablespoon cornstarch
1/2 teaspoon lemon extract (optional)
1/2 teaspoon vanilla extract

1 box of graham cracker crumbs (make crust according to directions, for a 9 to 10 inch springform pan)

Cream the sugar and the cheese until smooth and fluffy. Add eggs, beating well after each addition. Add the heavy cream, cornstarch and extracts. Fold pumpkin mixture into cream cheese mixture. Pour into baked graham cracker crust and bake at 475 degrees for ten minutes, then turn oven down to 250 degrees and bake for 1-1/2 hours. Cake will still be soft in center. Chill at least 3 hours before serving. Serves 10

Connie Mullis

Chocolate Angel Dessert

1-1/2 cups milk
2 eggs, beaten
1/2 cup sugar
1/4 teaspoon salt
1 envelope Knox gelatin
1/3 cup cold water
3/4 cup semisweet chocolate chips
2 tablespoons bourbon

1-1/2 cups heavy cream, whipped
1 angel food cake (may be made
 from mix)
1/2 cup sliced almonds
Whipped cream
Maraschino cherries with stems
*Rum flavoring may be
 substituted for bourbon

Mix milk, eggs, sugar and salt. Cook in double boiler until it coats a spoon. Soften gelatin in cold water and add to hot custard. Remove 1 cup custard and add chocolate chips, stirring until melted. Cool remaining custard and add bourbon. Whip cream and fold into bourbon custard. (You have divided the custard into 2 portions, chocolate and bourbon or rum). Rub crumbs off cake and tear into pieces. Fold into bourbon custard and pour into 9x13 pan. Pour chocolate custard over top and sprinkle with almonds. Serve with additional whipped cream and stemmed Maraschino cherry.

Frances Toney Hall

Gingerbread with Orange Sauce

1/2 cup butter or oleo
3/4 cup sugar
3/4 cup syrup or molasses
2 eggs
1/2 cup buttermilk
1 teaspoon soda
1 teaspoon ginger
Dash cinnamon, nutmeg, cloves
2 cups flour

Sauce:
1 cup sugar
Juice of 2 oranges (1/2 to 3/4
 cup) and a little grated rind
Boil until thickens (about 10
minutes); remove from fire, add
1 tablespoon butter.

Cream butter and sugar, then add other ingredients (eggs one at a time, beating well). Pour into 9x13 pan. Bake in 350 degree oven until done, about 30 minutes. Sauce: Combine ingredients in order and spoon over gingerbread while warm. *Cut in squares and serve with orange sauce.* Serves 8 to 10.

In memory of Esther Triplett Williamson
President, Women's Auxiliary, 1933-35

202

English Toffee Refrigerator Dessert

1-1/2 cups vanilla wafer crumbs
2 cups powdered sugar
1/4 teaspoon salt
4 tablespoons cocoa
1/2 cup butter or oleo

2 eggs, separated
1 cup nuts, broken up
1 teaspoon vanilla
Whipped cream

Spread half of vanilla wafer crumbs in bottom of buttered 8 or 9 inch square pan. Sift sugar; measure; sift again with sugar, salt and cocoa. Cream butter, add sugar mixture, creaming till light and fluffy. Add unbeaten egg yolks, one at a time, beating well after each. Stir in nuts and vanilla. Fold in stiffly beaten egg whites. Pour into prepared pan. Top with remaining crumbs. Chill in refrigerator overnight. Cut into squares and serve with whipped cream. Serves 9.

Helen Clement

Frozen Toffee Dessert

<u>Butter Crunch Crust:</u>
1 stick margarine
1/4 cup light brown sugar
1 cup flour
1/2 cup chopped pecans

Hot Fudge Sauce

<u>Filling:</u>
2 tablespoons instant coffee
1 tablespoon boiling water
2-1/2 packages Heath Bar chips
1 quart vanilla ice cream
1/2 cup whipping cream
2 tablespoons Cream de Cacao

Prepare the crust and put in pan, baking for 15 minutes at 400 degrees. Stir with spoon. Reserve 3/4 cup for topping. Line bottom and sides of a 9x13 inch pan. Set aside. Filling: Dissolve coffee in hot water. Combine 2 packages Heath Bar chips with ice cream and dissolved coffee. Spoon mixture into crust and freeze until firm. Whip cream with Cream de Cacao until stiff. Spread over ice cream mixture. Sprinkle remaining Heath chips over whipped cream. Freeze until firm. *Serve with your favorite Hot Fudge Sauce.*

Mabel Sloan Williams

Lemon Charlotte

3 egg yolks
1/4 cup sugar
1 tablespoon corn syrup
1/2 cup milk
Juice and rind of 1 lemon, grated
1 cup powdered sugar

1/2 cup butter
3 egg whites
2 packages Lady Fingers
1/2 pint whipping cream
Mandarin orange sections
Grated rind of 1 lemon

Beat egg yolks, add sugar, corn syrup and milk. Cook over low heat until thick. Cool and add lemon juice and grated rind. Chill. Cream together butter and powdered sugar. Add chilled lemon custard and beat until smooth and fluffy. Beat egg whites until stiff. Fold custard and butter mixture into egg whites. Line a cut glass bowl with Lady Fingers - bottom and sides. Pour mixture into bowl and chill overnight. Whip cream adding a little sugar. Pour over Charlotte inside Lady Finger edging and decorate with Mandarin orange sections and grated lemon rind.

In memory of Mrs. Samuel Caldwell Alexander

Lemon Dessert

2 eggs, separated
1 cup sugar
2 tablespoons flour
3 tablespoons melted butter
1 cup milk

1/4 cup of lemon juice or
   juice of 2 lemons and grated
   peel
Cool Whip (optional)

Separate eggs. Beat whites until stiff. Mix all other ingredients; then fold in whites. Bake for 45 minutes in a 325 degree oven putting a pan of water under the baking dish. Serve hot or chilled. Turn servings upside down. Serve with Cool Whip topping if desired. *Instant dessert for guests or family. You almost always have these ingredients on hand.*

In memory of Tippie Puddephatt

Robert Cherry, who joined the church in 1916, had a perfect attendance record in Sunday School until age 15 when he went away to school. He pumped the bellows for the organ on Sunday mornings and was often called upon very early on Sunday mornings to start the coal furnace so the church would be warm for the congregation.

Frozen Lemon Mousse

30 lemon wafers, crumbled
1/2 cup melted butter
4 eggs, separated
1/2 cup lemon juice
1/4 cup sugar
1-1/2 tablespoons lemon peel, grated

1/8 teaspoon cream of tartar
1/8 teaspoon salt
3/4 cup sugar
1-1/2 cups whipping cream,
    whipped

Combine wafer crumbs and butter; line bottom of springform pan. Combine the 4 egg yolks, lemon juice, sugar and lemon peel and let stand at room temperature. Beat 4 egg whites until foamy; add cream of tartar and salt. Beat until soft peaks form. Add remaining 3/4 cup sugar, gradually - beat until stiff. Gently fold egg whites and whipped cream into mixture. Spoon into pan, cover with foil and freeze. Serves 12 to 16.

Joan B. Thompson

Orange Clouds

1 cup sugar
1/2 stick butter
2 eggs, beaten
1 cup crushed pineapple, drained

1 small box orange Jell-O
1 cup chopped pecans
Graham cracker crumbs

Cream butter and sugar; add beaten eggs and pineapple; cook, stirring constantly, until thickened. Prepare Jell-O as directed on box; let gel until slightly thick; pour into bowl and beat with electric mixer until fluffy (about 10 minutes). Butter bottom of 8x8 Pyrex dish slightly; add cooked ingredients, pecans and top with whipped Jell-O. Sprinkle top with graham cracker crumbs. Serve in squares. Serves 4 to 6.

In memory of Mildred Buck Daniel

Orange Fluff

6 eggs, separated
1-1/2 cups sugar
1 cup orange juice
2 tablespoons grated orange rind

1 package gelatin, dissolved
    in 1/4 cup cold water
1 angel food cake

Beat egg yolks and 1 cup of the sugar. Add orange juice and orange rind. Cook in double boiler until thick. Add gelatin and let cool. Beat egg whites and add remaining 1/2 cup sugar. Fold into cooled orange mixture. Layer with torn up angel food cake in 9x13 Pyrex pan. Serve with whipped cream. Can use frozen undiluted orange juice concentrate for part of cup of juice or add a little lemon juice to make it tart. Serves 6 to 8.

In memory of Mrs. H. K. Toney

Oreo Dessert

1 large package Oreo cookies
1/2 gallon vanilla ice cream
1 small carton Cool Whip

1/2 to 1 cup chopped pecans,
if desired

In long baking dish, crumble one row of cookies. In a large bowl, mix ice cream, Cool Whip, and 1 row of crumbled cookies. Pour over the cookies in dish. Top with remaining row of cookies crumbled. Sprinkle with pecans if desired. Freeze. Cut into square to serve. Serves 12 to 15.

Sharon Norton

Eggnog Pudding

2 eggs, separated
1/2 cup sugar
1/2 cup whiskey
1 envelope Knox gelatin
2 tablespoons cold water

2 tablespoons hot milk
1/2 pint whipping cream
1 dozen Lady Fingers
Ground blanched almonds

Beat the yolks of eggs and add sugar. Add whiskey and beat well. Soak the gelatin in the cold water. Add to very hot milk and dissolve thoroughly. Let cool and stir into mixture. Whip the cream and fold in carefully. Do not stir. Split the Lady Fingers and make two layers of Lady Fingers and two layers of mixture in bowl. Whip cream and season with whiskey. Ground blanched almonds sprinkled on top adds to the dessert.

In memory of Mrs. Samuel Caldwell Alexander

Fudge Batter Pudding
(from "Woman's Day" - 1950)

2 tablespoons margarine or butter, melted
1 cup sugar
1 teaspoon vanilla
1 cup sifted flour
8 tablespoons cocoa

1 teaspoon baking powder
3/4 teaspoon salt
1/2 cup milk
1/2 cup chopped nuts
1-2/3 cups boiling water

This pudding when baked has a chocolate sauce on the bottom and cake on top. Mix margarine, 1/2 cup sugar and vanilla together. Sift flour, 3 tablespoons cocoa, baking powder and 1/2 teaspoon salt. Add milk. Add alternately to first mixture. Mix well and stir in nuts. Mix together remaining 1/2 cup sugar, 5 tablespoons cocoa, 1/4 teaspoon salt, and boiling water. Pour into 10x6x2 inch pan. Drop first batter by tablespoons onto top. Bake in moderate 350 degree oven for 40 to 45 minutes. Serve warm. Spoon out a portion of cake and cover with your favorite chocolate sauce. If served cold, add whipped cream or poured cream, as the sauce becomes quite thick. Serves 6.

Katherine Ramage Love

Jeannie's Baked Fudge Pudding

2 eggs
1 cup sugar
1/2 cup melted butter
2 tablespoons flour

2 heaping tablespoons cocoa
Pinch salt
1/2 teaspoon vanilla
1 cup nuts, broken up

Beat eggs well with electric mixer. After they begin to thicken, gradually add in sugar, continuing to beat. Stir in melted butter. Sift together flour, cocoa, and salt and add to mixture. Add vanilla and nuts.. Pour into buttered 8x12 inch Pyrex pan. Put this pan in larger pan and add about an inch of hot water. Bake 45 minutes in 325 degree oven. Remove from oven and remove dessert from pan of water. Cut into 8 squares. Serve warm or at room temperature with ice cream or whipped cream. Will be crusty on top and gooey inside. *A real favorite in our family - my sister, Jean F. Noble's recipe.*

Helen Clement

Quaking Pudding

1 tablespoon gelatin
1/2 cup cold water
2 cups milk, scalded
4 eggs, separated

3/4 cup sugar
1 tablespoon brandy
2 cups whipped cream
Maraschino cherry halves

Soak gelatin in cold water until dissolved. Scald milk. Beat egg yolks and sugar until light in color. Slowly pour into hot milk, stirring. Cook until it begins to thicken over low heat. Pour over gelatin and season with brandy. Let cool. Fold in 1 cup whipped cream and stiffly beaten egg whites. Pour into mold. Chill. Remove from mold. Cover with remaining cup of whipped cream and garnish with cherries. *This recipe came from Chester, South Carolina, when the family moved to Arkansas on a land grant in 1856. Mary Taylor was Ed Brown's great grandmother.* Serves 4.

In memory of Mary Taylor

Queen's Pudding

4 cups bread crumbs (8-10 slices)
4 eggs (save 2 egg whites)
1/2 cup sugar
1/4 teaspoon salt
1 teaspoon vanilla
3 cups milk
Apricot preserves

Beat
until
stiff
{

Meringue:
2 (reserved) egg whites
1/4 teaspoon cream of tartar
4 tablespoons sugar

Use stale bread, if desired and remove crusts. Place in greased, buttered 2-quart casserole dish. Mix remaining ingredients and pour over bread crumbs. Stir to mix well. Place casserole in a container with about 1 inch water. Bake at 350 to 375 degrees until firm (30 to 40 minutes). The middle can be a little shaky. Spread thin layer of preserves and cover with meringue. Set back into water container and bake until slightly browned (8 to 10 minutes). Serves 6 to 8.

Dolly Capps Skipper

Brandy Alexander

1/2 gallon vanilla ice cream
1/4 cup Kahlua

1/3 cup bourbon

Half fill blender with ice cream; then Kahlua, and bourbon. Add rest of ice cream till blender is full. Taste it. Put in plastic container and stir every so often. Keep in freezer until ready to serve. Beat with egg whipper (wire whisk) before serving. Serves 5.

Corinne Hunter

Fresh Peach Ice Cream

4 pounds fresh peaches
2-1/2 cups sugar
2 cups whipping cream
4 cups Half and Half

1/4 teaspoon salt
2 teaspoons vanilla
1/2 teaspoon almond extract
Dash lemon juice

Peel the peaches and chop finely in the food processor (or blender). Add other ingredients and freeze in freezer. Serves 12.

Pat Lile

Chocolate Sauce

1 box confectioner's sugar
1 (13 ounce) can evaporated milk
4 squares bitter chocolate

1 stick margarine
1/4 teaspoon vanilla

Mix all ingredients together and blend in a double boiler. Cool until thickened. Serve over ice cream or cake. *His mother, Eura Beisel, says this sauce is wonderful on ice cream or cake!*

Dr. Larry Beisel, Evansville, Indiana

Hot Fudge Sauce

1 cup butter (no substitute)
4-1/2 cups powdered sugar
1-1/3 cups evaporated milk

4 (1 ounce) squares
unsweetened chocolate

Melt butter in double boiler. Add sugar and milk and stir until dissolved. Add chocolate and melt, stirring until smooth. Continue to cook over hot water for 30 minutes <u>without stirring</u>. Remove from heat; stir until creamy smooth. May be refrigerated and reheated over boiling water. *This was in "Southern Accent" and is being reprinted in our cookbook because it is one of the best chocolate sauces we have ever eaten --Cookbook Committee.*

Pat Lile

Praline Sauce

1 cup brown sugar, packed
1/4 cup white Karo syrup
1/2 cup margarine
2 tablespoons butter

1 teaspoon vanilla
Pinch of salt
1 cup pecans, chopped

Mix all ingredients in a saucepan. Bring to boil and cook for 10 minutes.

Helen Claire Brooks

Angel Food Cake

18 egg whites
Pinch of salt
1-1/2 teaspoons cream of tartar
2-1/4 cups sugar

1-1/2 cups flour
1 teaspoon vanilla
1 teaspoon almond extract

Beat egg whites to a froth, add pinch of salt, then add cream of tartar. Next fold in sugar (sifted 3 times); then fold in flour (sifted 3 times). Add flavoring. Bake in a stemmed angel food cake pan for 1 hour at 325 degrees. When done turn pan upside down and let cake cool. Ice with favorite frosting. *Mrs. A. M. Barrow was president of the Ladies Auxiliary, 1921-1923. Her food trays to her neighbors and friends were legendary in Pine Bluff. She was a lovely Christian lady.*

In memory of Mrs. A. M. Barrow

Apple Cake

1 can apple pie filling
2 cups flour
2 cups sugar
1/2 cup oil
2 eggs
1 teaspoon cinnamon
1 teaspoon salt

2 teaspoons baking soda
1/2 cup raisins (optional)
Icing:
3 ounces cream cheese
1 cup powdered sugar
1/2 stick butter, softened
1 teaspoon vanilla

Mix thoroughly in any order. Grease and flour 9x13 pan. Batter is very thick. Spread evenly in pan. Bake for 50 minutes at 350 degrees. Check - it may need 5 more minutes. Don't overbake. Ice while warm

Cathy Kennedy

Fresh Apple Cake

2 eggs
2 cups sugar
1-1/2 cups oil
1 teaspoon vanilla
3 cups all purpose flour, sifted
1/4 teaspoon salt
1 teaspoon baking soda
1 teaspoon baking powder

1 teaspoon cinnamon
1 teaspoon nutmeg
2-1/2 cups peeled chopped apples
Glaze:
1/2 cup apple juice
1-1/2 cups powdered sugar
Grated rind and juice of
1 lemon

Grease and flour a tubepan. In a large mixing bowl, beat together the eggs, sugar, oil and vanilla. Sift together the flour, salt, soda, baking powder, cinnamon, and nutmeg. Add to sugar and egg mixture and beat until well blended. Stir in apples. Bake about 1-1/2 hours at 300 degrees. Prepare glaze and pour over the cake while warm. Glaze: In a saucepan, heat apple juice, sugar, lemon juice, and rind. Beat until smooth.

Debbie Robinson

Carrot Cake Cupcakes

3 cups flour
2 teaspoons baking powder
1-1/4 teaspoons salt
1-1/2 teaspoons baking soda
2 teaspoons cinnamon
1 (20 ounce) can crushed pineapple
4 to 5 eggs
2 cups sugar
1-1/2 cups oil
3 cups grated carrots

1 cup chopped pecans
2 teaspoons vanilla
Icing:
1 stick margarine, softened
1 (8 ounce) package cream
  cheese
1 box powdered sugar
1 teaspoon vanilla
A little Half and Half or milk
  to smooth mixture

Mix dry ingredients. Drain pineapple, reserving juice. Beat eggs. Add sugar, oil and juice. Make a well in dry ingredients; add liquids, mixing well. Stir in pineapple, carrots, pecans and vanilla. Pour into foil cups, 1/2 full. Bake at 350 degrees for about 20 minutes. Ice when cool. Makes about 48 cupcakes.

Helen O'Keefe King

Chocolate Cake

Cake:
2 cups flour
2 cups sugar
1 stick oleo or butter
1/2 cup Crisco
4 tablespoons cocoa
1 cup water
1 teaspoon soda
2 eggs, slightly beaten
1/2 cup buttermilk or 2 tablespoons
  vinegar to milk to make 1/2 cup
1 teaspoon vanilla

Icing:
1 stick oleo
4 tablespoons cocoa
6 tablespoons milk
1 box powdered sugar
1 teaspoon vanilla
1 cup pecans, chopped

Sift flour and sugar together in large bowl. Combine oleo, Crisco, cocoa, and water and bring to rapid boil. Pour this mixture over sugar and flour and stir well. Dissolve soda in buttermilk. Then add buttermilk, eggs, and vanilla to other ingredients. Mix until well blended. Pour into a 9x13 inch greased pan. Bake at 375 degrees for 35 minutes. For a very rich, gooey brownie, bake in jelly roll pan 325 degrees for 30 minutes. Icing: Melt oleo, cocoa, and milk together and bring to a boil. Pour over powdered sugar. Beat well. Add vanilla and pecans. Mix and pour over cake in pan while cake is still hot. Makes 16 to 32 squares.

Ruth Ingram and Grace Hoffman

Florence's Chocolate Cake

2 squares unsweetened chocolate
2 cups sugar
3/4 cup (1-1/2 sticks) butter
5 eggs
2 cups flour

1 cup buttermilk mixed with
1 teaspoon soda
1 teaspoon vanilla
1/4 teaspoon salt

Melt chocolate and add sugar and cool. Cream butter with sugar and chocolate. Add eggs one at a time, beating after each egg; then add flour and buttermilk mixed with soda alternately. Add vanilla and salt. Grease and flour 3 round cake pans and cook at 350 degrees about 30 minutes. Do not overcook. No substitutes. *This is my cousin Florence Toney Cummins' chocolate cake. It is the best that I have ever eaten. It was always chosen for our birthday cakes at home.*

Icing

2 squares Baker's unsweetened chocolate
2 cups sugar
3/4 cup Half and Half
3 ounces white Karo

1/8 teaspoon salt
1/2 stick butter
1 teaspoon vanilla

Melt chocolate in pan. Add sugar to chocolate, stirring to blend. Add Half and Half, Karo, and salt. Cook, stirring until 238 degrees on candy thermometer. Add butter and vanilla. Cool until bottom of pan is warm. Beat with electric mixer until creamy and thick enough to ice cake. No substitutes.

Frances Toney Hall

Chocolate Chip Bundt Cake

1 Duncan Hines yellow cake mix
   (butter recipe)
1 cup oil
1/4 cup water
1 small package Jell-O instant chocolate
   pudding mix

4 eggs
1 teaspoon vanilla
1 (8 ounce) carton sour cream
1 (6 ounce) package chocolate
   chips
1 cup chopped pecans (optional)

Combine all ingredients except chocolate chips and pecans. Mix well. Stir in chips and pecans. Bake in greased and floured bundt pan at 325 degrees for 50 to 60 minutes. Do not overbake - if toothpick comes out clean, you've overdone it!

Elizabeth Henry

Church Circle Cake

1 Duncan Hines Lemon Supreme
  cake mix
1 box lemon instant pudding
1 cup orange juice
4 eggs

1/2 cup oil
1 teaspoon orange extract
Glaze:
2 tablespoons lemon juice
1 cup powdered sugar, sifted

Mix all ingredients together, beating for 10 minutes. Pour mixture into greased and floured bundt pan. Bake at 350 degrees for 45 to 60 minutes. Cool slightly and turn out on rack. Glaze. *Given to me by Miss Mary Will Winters at Church Circle.*

Frances Toney Hall

Five Flavor Cake

2 sticks butter or oleo
1/2 cup Crisco
3 cups sugar
5 eggs, beaten
3 cups flour
1/2 teaspoon baking powder
1 cup milk
1 teaspoon coconut flavor
1 teaspoon rum extract
1 teaspoon butter flavor

1 teaspoon lemon extract
1 teaspoon vanilla

Serve with fruit mixture:
1 can peach pie filling
1 large can chunk pineapple,
  drained
1 (10 ounce) package frozen
  strawberries, juice and all
2 large sliced bananas

Cream butter, shortening, and sugar until light and fluffy. Add eggs, which have been beaten until lemon colored. Combine flour and baking powder and add to creamed mixture alternately with milk. Stir in flavorings. Spoon mix into greased and floured 10 inch tube pan (angel food pan may be used) and bake at 325 degrees about 1-1/2 hours or until done. Serves 15 to 16.

Frances Stone

Heavenly Host Cake

Cake:
2 cups sugar
1/4 cup oil
2 cups flour
2 eggs
2 teaspoons soda
2 cups crushed pineapple, including juice

Icing:
1 cup sugar
1 stick oleo
1 small can Pet milk
1 cup nuts (pecans)
1 cup coconut

Combine ingredients in order listed. Mix by hand or by electric mixer just until blended well. Grease and flour 9x13 pan. Bake 40 minutes at 350 degrees. Ovens vary so 60 minutes could be required. Let cake cool in pan and then pour icing over cake. Icing: Boil together for 10 minutes the sugar, oleo, and Pet milk. Remove from fire. Add pecans and coconut. Beat until thick enough to spread on cake. Serves 12.

Lois Lea

Hummingbird Cake

2 cups sugar
2 cups all purpose flour
1 teaspoon salt
1 teaspoon baking soda
3 eggs
1-1/2 cups Mazola oil

1-1/2 teaspoons vanilla
2 cups chopped bananas
1 (20 ounce) can crushed
  pineapple, drained
2 cups chopped pecans

Grease and flour bundt pan and preheat oven to 350 degrees. Sift dry ingredients and add remaining ingredients. Mix with fork, pour into prepared pan and bake for 1 hour and 10 minutes. Remove from oven and cool in pan for 2 hours. Remove from pan and ice. Serves 12 to 15.

ICING

1 (8 ounce) package softened
  cream cheese
1 box powdered sugar

1 stick softened butter
1 teaspoon vanilla

Cream all together and frost.

Isabelle Monroe

Kahlua Cake

1 (18-1/2 ounce) package Swiss
   chocolate cake mix <u>without</u> pudding
1 cup pecans, chopped
1 (4 ounce) package chocolate
   instant pudding

4 eggs
1/2 cup cold water
1/2 cup vegetable oil
1/2 cup Kahlua

Grease and flour a 10 inch tube pan or bundt pan. Sprinkle nuts over bottom of pan. Combine cake and pudding mixes, eggs (one at a time), water, oil, and liqueur. Beat thoroughly on medium speed. Pour batter over nuts. Bake for 1 hour at 350 degrees. Before removing from pan, pour some of glaze over cake while it is still hot.

Frances Toney Hall

Kahlua Cake Glaze

1/4 cup butter
1/4 cup water

1 cup sugar
1/2 cup Kahlua

Melt butter. Stir in water and sugar. Boil 5 minutes. Remove from heat and stir in Kahlua. Place cake on serving plate with rounded sides. Prick top of cake and drizzle over top and sides letting it absorb the mixture. Use all the glaze. (Rum or Amaretto may be substituted for Kahlua).

Frances Toney Hall

Lemon Ice Box Cake

6 eggs, separated
3/4 cup lemon juice
Grated rind of 1 lemon
1-1/2 cups sugar
1 envelope gelatin

1/4 cup cold water
1 angel food cake (either home-
   made or made with a mix.
   Do not use bought cake.

Separate eggs. Beat yolks slightly and add lemon juice, grated rind and 3/4 cup sugar. Cook in double boiler, stirring constantly until mixture coats spoon. Add the gelatin which has been soaked in the 1/4 cup cold water. Mix well and cool. Beat egg whites until stiff, adding the remaining 3/4 cup sugar gradually. Fold into cooled lemon mixture. Pour half in a 9x13 dish and cover with small pieces of cake. Add the remaining lemon mixture. Serve with whipped cream and stemmed cherry.

In memory of Mrs. H. Roddy Jones

Lemon Nut Cake

2 cups margarine
2 cups sugar
6 eggs
4 cups flour

1 teaspoon baking powder
1 (15 ounce) box golden raisins
1 pound pecan halves
2 ounces lemon extract

Preheat oven to 275 degrees. Cream margarine and sugar. Beat in eggs one at a time. Add remaining ingredients. Bake 2 hours in two 9x5x3 greased and floured loaf pans at 275 degrees. *This was my grandmother's "white fruit cake" recipe.* Serves 15 to 20.

Mabel Sloan Williams

Mounds Cake

1 box chocolate cake mix
30 large marshmallows
1 cup sugar
2/3 cup milk

1 teaspoon vanilla
1 (14 ounce) package coconut
1 package chocolate fudge icing

Prepare cake mix according to box directions, using two 8 inch pans. Cool. Split cake layers. Melt marshmallows, sugar, milk, and vanilla together over low heat. Add coconut to filling mixture. Spread filling between cake layers. Ice top and sides of cake with fudge icing.

Margaret Dial Dawson

Orange Cake

1 cup butter
2 cups sugar
4 eggs
3 cups flour
1 teaspoon soda
1-1/4 cups buttermilk

1 tablespoon grated orange rind

Glaze:
2 cups sugar
1 cup freshly squeezed orange
   juice

Combine butter, sugar, and eggs. Add flour and soda alternately with buttermilk. Add orange rind. Pour into greased and floured tube pan and bake at 350 degrees for 50 to 60 minutes. While cake is warm, pour glaze over it.

In memory of Helen Alexander

Buttermilk Pound Cake

1-1/2 cup Crisco
2-1/2 cups sugar, sift 3 times
4 eggs
1/2 teaspoon baking soda
1 tablespoon hot water
1 cup fresh buttermilk

3-1/2 cups flour
1 tablespoon lemon extract

Glaze:
1/2 cup sugar
1/2 cup orange juice

Cream Crisco and sugar well. Add eggs, one at a time. Beat well after each egg. Add soda to hot water. Mix well with buttermilk. Add alternately with flour and beat well. Add flavoring. Bake in an ungreased tube pan 1-1/2 hours at 325 degrees. Let sit in pan for 10 minutes before removing. Pour glaze mixture over the warm cake. *This was my mother's recipe, Mrs. Van Davis.*

Becky Thomasson

Chocolate Pound Cake

1 cup butter
1/2 cup shortening
2-1/2 cups sugar
5 eggs
3 cups flour

1/2 teaspoon baking powder
1/2 teaspoon salt
4 tablespoons cocoa
1 cup milk
1 tablespoon vanilla

Cream together butter and shortening. Add sugar and eggs, blending well. Sift dry ingredients together. Add alternately with milk to creamed mixture. Add vanilla; mix thoroughly. Bake in a greased and floured tube pan for 80 minutes at 325 degrees. Serves 18 to 20.

CHOCOLATE ICING

1/4 cup butter
2 ounces bitter chocolate
1 pound box powdered sugar

1 teaspoon vanilla
Cream to moisten

Melt butter and chocolate. Add sifted sugar and vanilla, adding cream as needed to achieve spreading consistency.

Susan Norton

Easy Pound Cake

Duncan Hines Butter Yellow Cake Mix
2/3 cup oil
4 eggs
1 (8 ounce) carton sour cream

1/2 cup sugar
1 teaspoon vanilla extract
1 teaspoon almond extract
1 teaspoon lemon extract

Mix all ingredients together. Pour in greased bundt pan and bake at 350 degrees for 50 to 55 minutes.

Mrs. Norwood Brown, Jr.

Old Fashioned Pound Cake

1/2 pound butter
3 cups sugar
6 eggs, whipped until thick
3 cups flour

1/2 pint whipping cream
1 teaspoon lemon flavoring
1 teaspoon vanilla flavoring
1 teaspoon almond flavoring

Cream butter and sugar; add beaten eggs; mix well. Add flour alternately with whipping cream. Add flavorings. Grease and flour tube or bundt pan. Bake at 325 degrees for approximately 1 hour and 10 minutes.

Lynn McGehee Stewart

Pound Cake

1/2 pound (2 sticks) butter
1-2/3 cups sugar
5 eggs

2 cups cake flour (sifted, then measured)
1 teaspoon lemon flavoring

Cream butter well with electric beater. Gradually add sugar. Beat until white and creamy. Add eggs, one at a time, beating well after each. Add flour in several amounts (not all at once). Add lemon flavoring. Place in greased angel food tube pan or in loaf pans. Tap on counter to remove air. Bake at 300 degrees for 1 hour or longer.

In memory of Annie B. Brown

Pearl's Pound Cake

1/2 pound (2 sticks) margarine, softened
1/2 cup shortening
3 cups sugar
2 teaspoons lemon or any flavoring

5 large eggs
1 cup milk
3 cups cake flour, sift once
before measuring

Cream margarine, shortening, and sugar well. The secret is creaming this very well. Add flavoring. Add eggs one at a time, beating after each addition. Add milk, alternating with flour. Pour in 10 inch tube pan or large (15x5x4) loaf pan. I prefer a loaf pan. Put in cold oven. Set oven at 325 degrees and bake about 1 hour and 25 minutes. Wait 10 minutes before removing from pan. *Served to friends and family.* Serves 25.

Jean Deal

Spice Prune Cake

2 cups sugar
1 cup Wesson oil
3 eggs
1 cup cooked, mashed prunes
1 cup chopped pecans
2 cups flour
1 teaspoon allspice
1 teaspoon cloves
1 teaspoon cinnamon

1 teaspoon nutmeg
1 teaspoon soda
1 teaspoon salt
1 cup buttermilk

Icing:
1/2 stick butter
1/2 cup sugar
1/4 cup buttermilk

Mix all ingredients together well. Pour in well greased and floured tube pan. Bake at 350 degrees for 55-60 minutes. Cool and ice. Icing: Mix all ingredients and cook five minutes. Drip on cake while warm.

Anna Bess Westerfield

Punch Bowl Cake

1 yellow cake mix
2 large cans crushed pineapple, drained
2 cans cherry pie filling
1 large vanilla pudding, prepared as
box directs

2 large bowls of Cool Whip
Banana slices
Chopped pecans

Bake the cake mix according to directions on box. Let it cool. Crumble 1 layer in bottom of bowl. Layer 1/2 of pineapple, 1 can of pie filling, 1/2 pudding, 1 bowl of Cool Whip, bananas, and chopped pecans. Repeat the layers ending with Cool Whip. *Served at the 1994 M/M dinner hosted by the Young Adults.* Serves 25.

Jo Neal

Sunshine Cake

1 box yellow cake mix
1 (11 ounce) can Mandarin oranges,
  with juice
4 eggs
1/2 cup vegetable oil

Icing:
1 (20 ounce) can crushed
  pineapple, with juice
1 (8 ounce) container Cool Whip
1 (3 ounce) package instant
  vanilla pudding, uncooked

Combine cake mix and oranges with juice, eggs, and oil with electric mixer until fluffy - about 3 minutes. Pour into 3 greased and floured 9 inch cake pans. Bake at 350 degrees about 20 minutes or until cake tests done. Cool on rack. Ice between layers and on top. Icing: Blend pineapple with juice, Cool Whip, and vanilla pudding mix until mixed well. Keep cake refrigerated.

Jean Atwood

Tropical Breeze Cake

1 package butter recipe yellow cake mix
1 (20 ounce) can crushed pineapple,
  in own juice
3/4 cup sugar
2 (3-1/2 ounce) packages instant
  vanilla pudding mix

3 cups milk
1 cup heavy or whipping cream
1/4 cup powdered sugar
1 teaspoon vanilla extract

In a 9x13 inch pan, bake cake according to package directions. Meanwhile, in medium saucepan combine pineapple with its juice and sugar; cook over medium heat, stirring occasionally, until thick and syrupy, about 20 minutes. When cake is done, remove from oven and pierce top with a fork at 1 inch intervals. Pour on pineapple mixture and spread evenly over cake. Cool completely. In medium bowl, combine pudding mix with milk; blend until thick. Spread over cake. In medium bowl beat cream until soft peaks form. Add powdered sugar and vanilla; continue beating until stiff. Spread over cake. Refrigerate 24 hours. Serves 16.

Sue Deneke

Snow on the Mountain

1/2 cup sugar
1/4 cup white corn syrup
2 tablespoons water

2 egg whites
Pinch salt

Mix thoroughly dissolving the sugar. Put all ingredients in top of double boiler and mix with electric mixer until stiff and will stand in peaks. Easily doubled. *This was my Aunt Ida Toney's recipe. I used it often during the war when sugar was scarce. It made 1/2 cup sugar go a long way. It does not cream or get hard, makes a beautiful cake and never fails.*

Frances Toney Hall

Blackberry Cobbler

Pastry for 1 pie
4 cups blackberries
1 tablespoon lemon juice
1-1/4 cups sugar

4 tablespoons flour
3/4 cup water
1/4 stick butter or margarine

Wash and cap blackberries. Drain. Combine lemon juice, blackberries, sugar, flour and water. Place in oven-proof 8x2 inch Pyrex dish. Cut pastry in 8x1 inch strips. Place small pieces of pastry into berry mixture, saving enough strips to cover top of berries. Top with pats of butter or margarine. Bake at 400 degrees until crust is golden brown, approximately 45 minutes. Serve hot with ice cream or whipped cream. *Have a few "not so ripe" berries for a "taste of tart".* Serves 8.

Novelle Clark

Easy-Mix Fruit Cobbler

1 stick margarine
1 cup flour
1 cup sugar
2 teaspoons baking powder

1 teaspoon salt
1 cup milk
Can of your favorite fruit -
    apples, cherries, peaches, etc.

Melt stick of margarine in oblong cake pan or Pyrex dish (13x9). Mix flour, sugar, baking powder, salt and milk together. Pour batter in pan of melted margarine. Pour your favorite can of fruit on top of batter. Bake in 375 degree oven until crust is brown (about 30 minutes). Serves 8.

Betty Perryman

Caramel Pie

2 baked pie crusts
2 egg yolks
2-1/2 cups milk
2 tablespoons butter, melted
2 cups sugar
2 tablespoons cornstarch

1 teaspoon vanilla

Meringue:
4 egg whites
8 tablespoons sugar
1 teaspoon vanilla

Beat egg yolks. Add 2 cups milk and melted butter. Heat to boiling point being careful not to scorch. Melt sugar in iron skillet stirring constantly. When melted pour into milk mixture which should be at boiling point. Stir cornstarch into 1/2 cup cold milk and stir into first mixture. Stir until thick. Cool and add vanilla. Pour into baked pie crusts. Cover with meringue. Bake in 350 degree oven until light brown. Meringue: Beat 4 egg whites until frothy. Gradually add 8 tablespoons sugar. Beat until stiff. Add vanilla and beat well. Makes 2 pies, each pie serves 6 to 8. *Mrs. Tucker taught a Bible class on the 4th Monday of every month for 30 years.*

In memory of Mrs. Everett Tucker

Chocolate Marshmallow Mousse Pie

1 9-inch pie crust, unbaked
Filling:
1/4 cup firmly packed brown sugar
3 tablespoons cornstarch
1/4 teaspoon salt
1-1/2 cups milk
6 ounces (6 squares) semi-sweet
  chocolate, chopped
2 teaspoons vanilla

1 cup miniature marshmallows
1 cup whipping cream, whipped
1/4 cup powdered sugar
1/2 cup pecans, chopped
Topping:
Whipping cream, whipped,
  sweetened
8 pecan halves

Heat oven to 450 degrees. Prepare pie crust and bake 9 to 11 minutes. Cool. In medium saucepan, combine brown sugar, cornstarch, and salt; mix well. Gradually add milk and cook over medium heat until mixture boils and thickens; using wire whisk, stir constantly. Remove from heat; stir in chocolate and vanilla until smooth. Cool mixture 5 to 10 minutes. Stir in marshmallows. Refrigerate about 25 minutes. In small bowl, beat 1 cup whipping cream until soft peaks form. Add powdered sugar, beating until stiff peaks form. Fold whipped cream into cooled chocolate mixture. Stir in 1/2 cup pecans. Pour into cooled pie crust. Refrigerate for 2 hours. Garnish with whipped cream and pecan halves. Store in refrigerator. *Reminiscent of an all-time favorite, Rocky Road ice cream.* Serves 8.

Margaret Dial Dawson

Ann's Cherry Jubilee Pie

1 pie shell, unbaked
1 can pie cherries, drained,
  reserving juice
3/4 cup sugar
3 tablespoons flour
1/2 teaspoon almond extract

1 (8 ounce) package cream
  cheese
2 eggs
1/2 cup sugar
1/2 teaspoon vanilla
1 cup sour cream

Bake pie shell until half done. Drain pie cherries. Mix flour and sugar in saucepan. Stir in cherry juice and cook until thickened. Add cherries and almond extract. Pour into pastry shell. Mix cream cheese, eggs, sugar, and vanilla. Pour over cherries. Bake at 375 degrees for 30 to 35 minutes or until it puffs around edges only. Remove from oven and cool. Spread with sour cream. Chill. *Delish! This recipe was given to me by one of my sisters, Ann F. Kurth, who was a wonderful cook.*

Helen Clement

Divinity Pie

1 (9 inch) baked pie crust, cooled
Filling:
1/2 pint whipping cream
3 tablespoons white Karo syrup
1 tablespoon sugar
1/2 teaspoon vanilla

Meringue:
3 egg whites
3 tablespoons sugar
1 tablespoon water
Pinch of salt
1/2 teaspoon lemon juice

Beat 1/2 pint whipping cream. Add 3 tablespoons white Karo syrup, 1 table-spoon sugar, 1/2 teaspoon vanilla, beating until stiff peaks form. Fill pie shell. Beat 3 egg whites until stiff peaks form. Add 3 tablespoons sugar, 1 tablespoon water, pinch of salt, and 1/2 teaspoon lemon juice. Beat thoroughly. Cover pie with meringue and quickly brown in 350 degree oven. The pie must be thoroughly chilled when placed in the oven to avoid melting the cream. *There was always a place set at the Toney table for Dr. J. I. Norris for dinner. This was Dr. Norris's favorite dessert.* Serves 6 to 8.

In memory of Mrs. W. M. Toney

Egg Custard Pie

10 inch unbaked pie shell
1 cup sugar
Pinch of salt
2 tablespoons butter, melted

1 teaspoon vanilla
6 eggs
2 cups milk
Nutmeg

Mix sugar and salt with butter. Add 1 teaspoon vanilla. Add eggs one at a time (slightly beaten). Add milk and mix together. Pour into pie shell. Sprinkle with nutmeg on top. Bake 7 minutes at 425 degrees. Lower heat to 325 degrees for 25 to 45 minutes until custard is set.

Susan Norton

Heavenly Fruit Pie

2 (9 inch) graham cracker crusts
1 can Eagle Brand milk
1/3 cup lemon juice
1 (15-1/2 ounce) can crushed pineapple, drained
1 (11 ounce) can Mandarin oranges, drained

1/2 cup pecans, chopped
1 (12 ounce) whipped topping, thawed
Optional: toasted slivered almonds

Combine milk, lemon juice, pineapple, oranges and pecans. Stir well. Fold in whipped topping. Pour mixture into pie crusts. Chill several hours before serving. Option: Leave pecans out of pie; but sprinkle top with toasted slivered almonds. Makes 2 pies.

Leah "Pud" Harris

Hypocrite Pie

2 (8 or 9 inch) pie crusts
1 (8 ounce) package dried peaches
1/2 cup sugar
<u>Custard:</u>
1 cup sugar

2 tablespoons butter, melted
Pinch salt
Pinch of nutmeg (optional)
4 large or 5 medium eggs
2 cups milk

Using your favorite pie crust recipe, make two 8 or 9 inch pie shells. Set aside. Rinse peaches, barely cover with cold water and simmer, covered, over low heat until tender, approximately 20 to 30 minutes. Mash peaches and then add sugar. Cool. Custard: Mix sugar, butter, salt, and nutmeg. Add eggs. Beat well. Add milk and continue beating. To assemble pie: Put 1/2 of peaches in bottom of unbaked pie crust, pour 1/2 custard on top of peaches. Preheat oven to 425 degrees. Bake pie 7 minutes; reduce heat to 325 degrees and bake for 30 minutes. Pie is done when custard "shimmies". Can be topped with Cool Whip or whipping cream, if desired. Makes 2 pies. *Shared by Melba Crass.*

Debbie Robinson

Quick and Easy Fudge Pie

3 eggs
1 cup sugar
5 tablespoons flour, sifted
1 stick butter

2 squares chocolate,
    unsweetened
1/2 cup pecans, chopped
1 teaspoon vanilla

Butter and flour an 8 or 9 inch pie pan. Beat eggs and combine with sugar and flour. Melt butter (what is left from 1 stick after greasing pie pan), and chocolate in top of double boiler and add to first mixture. Add nuts and vanilla. Pour into pie pan. Bake at 325 degrees for 20 to 25 minutes. Do not overbake. It should settle into a fudge brownie consistency when removed from oven. Serve with ice cream and chocolate sauce topping.

Susan Norton

Jeff Davis Pie

1 unbaked pie shell, 10 inch pie
1 cup sugar
2 tablespoons flour
1 teaspoon cinnamon, ground
1/2 teaspoon allspice, ground
1/2 teaspoon nutmeg, ground
1/2 teaspoon cloves, ground
1-1/2 cups milk
4 eggs, separated
1/2 teaspoon salt
4 tablespoons sugar

Mix together in mixer sugar, flour, spices, and 1/2 cup milk. Separate eggs. Add egg yolks one at a time to spice mixture, beating between each yolk. Add salt and balance of milk. Pour in pie shell and bake in slow (325 degree) oven 1 hour. Let cool. Beat egg whites with 4 tablespoons sugar until stiff peaks are formed. Spoon meringue over pie and return to oven until browned. *This pie is good warm or cold. My grandmother Howell's recipe. I have never had this pie outside of our family.* Serves 6 to 8.

Joanne S. Smith

Key Lime Pie

2 (8 inch) baked pie shells
1 envelope unflavored gelatin
1/2 cup sugar
1/4 teaspoon salt
4 egg yolks
1/2 cup lime juice, 2 limes
1/4 cup water
1 teaspoon lime peel
2 drops green food coloring
4 egg whites
1/2 cup sugar
1 cup heavy cream, whipped
Optional: Pistachio nuts and
    lime wedges

Thoroughly mix gelatin, 1/2 cup sugar, and salt in saucepan. Beat together egg yolks, lime juice, and water. Stir into gelatin mixture. Cook and stir constantly over medium heat just until mixture comes to boiling. Remove from heat and stir in grated peel and food coloring for a pale green color. Chill, stirring occasionally, until the mixture mounds slightly when dropped from a spoon. Beat egg whites until soft peaks form; gradually add 1/2 cup sugar, beating to stiff peaks. Fold gelatin mixture into egg whites. Fold in whipped cream, pour into baked pastry shell, and edge with grated lime peel. Garnish the center of pie with chopped pistachio nuts and edges of the pie with lime wedges. *Delicious! This is Marjorie (Mrs. Hershel) Sturdivant's recipe.*

Joan B. Thompson

Lemon Pie

1 can Eagle Brand milk
3 lemons, juice of

1/2 pint whipping cream,
whipped

Combine Eagle Brand milk and juice of lemons. Stir well. Fold in whipping cream. Pour mixture into a graham cracker crust. Chill for 3 hours.

Jane Eddins Stone

Mac's Favorite Lemon Ice Box Pie

Vanilla Wafer Pie Crust:
Vanilla wafers
1/4 cup margarine or butter melted
Filling:
1 (14 ounce) can Eagle Brand
   sweetened condensed milk
1 teaspoon lemon peel, grated

1/2 cup lemon juice (fresh,
   reconstituted or frozen)
2 egg yolks
Meringue:
3 egg whites, room temperature
1/4 teaspoon cream of tartar
6 tablespoons sugar

Vanilla wafer crust: Line bottom of pan with 1 cup crushed vanilla wafers combined with 1/4 cup melted margarine or butter. Line sides with whole wafers. Filling: In medium sized mixing bowl blend together condensed milk, lemon peel, lemon juice, and egg yolks until thickened. Pour into pie pan. Meringue: In small mixing bowl beat egg whites with cream of tartar until they hold soft peaks. Gradually add sugar. Continue beating until whites are stiff. Pile onto pie filling and seal to inside edge of pie shell. Bake in 325 degree oven until top is golden brown, about 15 minutes. Cool before serving. Serves 6 to 8.

Susan Norton

Lemon Tarts

1/2 cup butter
2 cups sugar
4 eggs

1 tablespoon flour
1/3 cup fresh lemon juice
Grated lemon rind, optional

Cream together butter and sugar. Beat in eggs, one at at time. Blend in flour. Add lemon juice and rind. Fill tart shells about 2/3 full. Bake at 350 degrees about 30 minutes.

In memory of Josephine Martin

Osgood ("Oh So Good") Pie

1 (9 inch) unbaked pie shell
4 eggs, separated
2 cups sugar, sifted
1 teaspoon cinnamon
1 teaspoon cloves

6 tablespoons butter, melted
1 cup raisins
1 cup chopped nuts
3 tablespoons vinegar
3 tablespoons whiskey

Separate eggs, beat yolks until light. Beat whites until stiff. Mix all ingredients, folding in beaten whites last. Pour into unbaked pie shell. Bake in moderate (350 degree) oven until done (50 or 60 minutes). *This was served by me to Mrs. Bill Fullbright who requested the recipe and served it in Washington. It was my mother's recipe from South Carolina.* Serves 7 or 8.

Mrs. Robert Dickins,
President, Women of the Church 1953

Fresh Peach Orange Pie

Crust:
1-1/2 cups graham cracker crumbs
1/2 cup butter, melted
3 tablespoons sugar

Filling:
100 tiny marshmallows
1/4 cup orange juice
3 cups fresh peaches, peeled
    and sliced
1/2 pint whipping cream
1/4 cup Maraschino cherries
1/3 cup powdered sugar
1/4 cup walnuts, chopped

Crust: Mix all 3 ingredients and press to sides and bottom of a 9 inch pie pan. Bake at 350 degrees for 8 to 10 minutes. Cool. Filling: Put marshmallows in juice and let stand. Stir. Put sliced peaches into pie shell. Whip the cream. Fold in the cherries, sugar, walnuts, and marshmallow mixture. Pour over the peaches. Chill at least 2 hours. *If using bought pie crust, use less peaches as it won't be 9 inches.* Serves 6 to 8.

In memory of Helen K. Ferranti

Pecan Pies

2 pie crusts, unbaked
3 eggs
1/2 cup sugar
1-1/2 cups dark Karo syrup
2 cups pecans, broken in large pieces

1/2 teaspoon salt
1 teaspoon vanilla
1 stick margarine, softened

Beat eggs. Add sugar and syrup. Using 2 pie crusts of your choice rolled thin, cover bottom of pie crusts (uncooked) with broken pecans. Add salt, vanilla and margarine to eggs, sugar and syrup mixture. Divide mixture and pour into pie shells of nuts. This makes a thin pie. Bake in 350 degree oven for 45 to 50 minutes. *I like to use one 9 inch pottery pie pan and one 8 inch throw away pan I can take to someone or send home with my out-of-town children. This recipe came from a nurse I worked with in Charlotte, N.C. before I was married in 1949, and it has been a favorite of my family for years.* Makes 2 pies.

Corinne Hunter

Pecan Tartlets

1 cup butter or margarine
2 (3 ounce) packages cream cheese
2-1/2 cups flour
3/4 teaspoon salt
1-1/2 cups chopped pecans

1 cup brown sugar (packed)
2 eggs, slightly beaten
2 tablespoons butter
1/2 teaspoon vanilla
1/2 cup light corn syrup

Soften the butter and cheese. Blend in 1/2 of flour at a time and 1/2 teaspoon salt. Shape pastry into 2 inch diameter rolls. Wrap and chill overnight. Slice pastry into 36 portions. Press into 2 inch muffin tins. Line cups not making rims. Place 1/2 of the nuts in the lined cups. Beat sugar into eggs. Add melted butter and remaining 1/4 teaspoon salt. Add vanilla, stir in syrup. Pour into shells and sprinkle in remaining nuts. Bake at 350 degrees for 20 minutes. *These are wonderful for pick-up desserts.* Makes 3 dozen.

Joan B. Thompson

Strawberry Pizza

Layer 1:
1 cup flour
1/4 cup powdered sugar
1 stick butter, melted

Mix together and press into pizza pan. Crust will be very thin. Bake at 350 degrees for 10 minutes or until golden brown. Cool.

Layer 2:
1 can Eagle brand milk
1/4 cup lemon juice

Spread over the crust.

Layer 3:
1 quart fresh strawberries, sliced
3 tablespoons or more sugar
1 tablespoon cornstarch

Cook in saucepan until thick and glossy. Cool. Pour over Layer 2.

Cover the entire pizza with Cool Whip and refrigerate. Serves 12.

Debbie Robinson

Sweet Potato Pie

1 (10 inch) pie crust, unbaked
3 medium sweet potatoes
1/2 stick butter
3 eggs
1/2 cup milk
1 cup evaporated milk
1 cup light brown sugar
1-1/2 teaspoons cinnamon
1/4 teaspoon nutmeg
Pinch of salt

Peel and cube sweet potatoes. Cook in small amount of boiling water until tender. Drain. Add butter and beat until smooth with electric mixer. Add remaining ingredients and blend thoroughly. Pour into prepared, unbaked pie crust. Bake at 400 degrees for 10 minutes. Reduce heat to 350 degrees and bake 30 minutes or until filling is set.

Grace Hoffman

Sweet Potato Pies

2 (9 or 10 inch) unbaked pie crusts
2 cups cooked, mashed sweet potatoes
2 cups sugar
6 eggs
1-1/2 cups buttermilk
1 teaspoon soda
1/2 cup butter or margarine, melted
1 teaspoon lemon flavoring

Mix ingredients in order listed. To make only one pie, cut ingredients in half. Put mixture in unbaked pie crust. Bake at 325 to 350 degrees until crust is brown at edges and knife inserted in middle comes out clean. Can be used as sweet potato custard if not put in pie crust. This *recipe was given to Mrs. Hogg, my mother, by her mother-in-law, Mrs. G. A. Hogg. It was printed as Sweet Potato Custard in 1900 Cookbook of Woman's Hospital Association of Pine Bluff.* Makes 2 pies. Serves 6 to 8 per pie.

Lois Lea

Chocolate Crinkle Cookies

1/2 cup Mazola oil
4 squares unsweetened chocolate,
    melted
2 cups sugar
4 eggs

2 teaspoons vanilla
1/2 teaspoon salt
2 teaspoons baking powder
2 cups flour
Powdered sugar

Using a metal mixing bowl, combine oil, melted chocolate, and sugar. Add one egg at a time; mix well. Add vanilla. Stir in combination of salt, baking powder, and flour. Chill mixture in refrigerator overnight. Roll dough into 1/2 teaspoon size balls, then roll balls in powdered sugar. Place on greased cookie sheet. Bake at 350 degrees for 6 minutes. Cookies may dry out if not stored in airtight container. *For convenience, place mixing bowl in freezer between each cooking. It will make dough easier to handle.* Makes 4 to 6 dozen.

Oralee Leslie

Cocoons

7 tablespoons butter
2 tablespoons confectioner's sugar
1 cup flour
1 teaspoon vanilla

1/2 teaspoon water
1/2 cup finely chopped,
    toasted pecans

Cream butter and sugar. Add flour, a little at a time. Add water and vanilla as needed to work in the flour. When dough is smooth add chopped nuts and shape into cocoons. Bake on lightly greased cookie sheet at 300 degrees about 20 to 25 minutes. Cool and roll in powdered sugar.

Sally Cook

Cornflake Cookies

1 cup white Karo
1 cup sugar

1-1/2 cups crunchy peanut butter
6 cups cornflakes

Let Karo and sugar come to a boil. Remove from stove while hot, add peanut butter, and stir until smooth. You may need to return to stove to reheat to get smoothness. Quickly add cornflakes and stir. Batter is very thick. Drop by spoon on pan or cabinet top. Do not put in refrigerator! When firm, place in storage tin, over layers of wax paper. Delicious and so easy. Makes 3 dozen.

Cathy Kennedy

Crybabies

3 sticks butter or margarine
2 cups sugar
2 eggs
1/2 cup molasses
4 cups flour, all purpose, sifted

4 teaspoons baking soda
2 teaspoons ginger
2 teaspoons cinnamon
2 teaspoons salt
Sugar

Preheat oven to 325 degrees. Cream butter and sugar. Beat in eggs and molasses. Sift together dry ingredients. Mix all together and chill for at least an hour. Roll mixture into 3/4 inch diameter balls and roll in sugar. Place on greased baking sheet and bake for 10 to 12 minutes. Makes about 10 dozen cookies.

Gail Bellingrath

Debbie's Cookies

2 cups butter flavored Crisco
  (can use the Crisco sticks)
1-1/2 cups brown sugar
1-1/2 cups granulated sugar
4 eggs

2 teaspoons hot water
3 cups self-rising flour
1 teaspoon baking soda
4 cups oatmeal
1 teaspoon vanilla

Mix the above ingredients and then add: 6 ounces chocolate chips, 6 ounces butterscotch chips, and 1 cup chopped nuts. Bake at 350 degrees for 10 to 12 minutes. Makes 4 dozen.

Debbie Robinson

Ginger Cookies

1/2 cup molasses
2 cups sugar
2 eggs
1-1/2 cups margarine, melted
4 cups flour

4 teaspoons soda
2 teaspoons cinnamon
1 teaspoon cloves
1 teaspoon ginger
Sugar

Preheat oven to 350 degrees. Add molasses, sugar, and eggs to margarine. Beat well. Sift together and add to this mixture the flour, soda, and spices. Refrigerate the dough for 3 to 4 hours. Make into small balls. Roll in sugar. Bake until firm and brown, about 8 to 10 minutes. *These are Richard Henry's favorite!* Makes 6 dozen.

Elizabeth Henry

Graham Cracker Cookies

1 stick margarine
1 stick real butter
1/2 cup sugar

Graham crackers
Chopped pecans, if desired

Melt 1 stick margarine, 1 stick real butter and 1/2 cup sugar. Bring to a boil and boil for 2 minutes. Line a cookie sheet with aluminum foil and bring up on sides of pan. Line the pan with single graham crackers close together. Pour the hot mixture over the crackers and sprinkle chopped pecans on top. Bake for 9 to 10 minutes at 350 degrees. Allow to cool before breaking the crackers apart. *Do not substitute for the 1 stick margarine and 1 stick real butter!* Makes 36 cookies.

Sharon Norton

Miss Ruth's Just the Best Cookies

1 cup butter, softened
1 cup sugar
1 cup light brown sugar
1 egg
1 cup vegetable oil
1 cup oats
1 cup crushed cornflakes

1/2 cup coconut
1/2 cup chopped pecans
3-1/2 cups flour
1 teaspoon soda
1 teaspoon salt
1 teaspoon vanilla
Powdered sugar

Preheat oven to 325 degrees. Cream butter and sugar until light and fluffy. Add egg and blend. Add oil, stirring until well blended. Add oats, cornflakes, coconut and nuts. Stir until mixed. Add flour, soda, salt, and vanilla and mix well. Form into balls about the size of a walnut. Place on ungreased cookie sheet and flatten with a fork dipped in water. Bake for 12 minutes. Allow to cool before removing. Sprinkle with powdered sugar. Makes 4 to 5 dozen.

Joan B. Thompson, Grace Hoffman,
and Mabel Sloan Williams

No-Bake Cookies

1 stick butter or margarine
2 cups sugar
1/4 cup cocoa
1/2 cup milk

1/2 cup creamy peanut butter
1 teaspoon vanilla
Pinch salt
3 cups quick cooking oats

Bring first 4 ingredients to rapid boil on top of stove. Boil 1 to 1-1/2 minutes. Remove from heat. Add remaining ingredients. Stir well. Drop by spoonfuls on waxed paper. *These delicious cookies can be made from start to finish in 15 minutes or less.*

Melissa Cook and Sharon Norton

Easy Peanut Butter Cookies

1 cup creamy peanut butter
1 cup sugar

1 egg
1 teaspoon vanilla

Mix ingredients with spoon. Form into 1 inch balls and place on slightly greased cookie sheet. Criss-cross with moistened fork. Bake at 375 degrees for 10 to 12 minutes. Cookies may appear too soft when removing from oven but will firm after sitting. *Recipe may be doubled. This is a delicious and easy recipe. Great for children learning to cook.* Makes 3 dozen.

Melissa Cook

Practically Perfect Cookies

2-1/4 cups flour
1 level teaspoon baking soda
1 level teaspoon salt
3/4 cup white sugar
3/4 cup dark brown sugar, packed

2 sticks sweet butter, softened
1 teaspoon vanilla extract
2 large eggs
1 (12 ounce) package Nestle's semi-sweet chocolate chips

Preheat oven to 375 degrees. Mix the flour, baking soda, and salt in a bowl and set aside. Use an electric mixer to mix the 2 sugars briefly at low speed. Add the butter in small bits, mixing first at low and then at high speed. Beat the mix until it's pale, light and very fluffy. Add the vanilla at the mixer's lowest speed, then beat it at high speed for a few seconds. Add the eggs, again at the lowest speed, switching to high speed for the final second or so. The eggs should be well beaten in, and the mix should look creamed, not curdled. Add the flour, baking soda, and salt, 1/2 cup at a time, mixing at low speed for about 1 minute, then at high speed for a few seconds. Scrape down the bowl's sides with a spatula, add chocolate chips, and mix at low speed for about 10 seconds. Put tablespoonfuls of the mix on an ungreased cookie sheet. Bake until the cookies are pale golden brown (9 minutes in an electric oven, 10 to 11 minutes in a gas one). All the mixing done in this recipe makes for a really light cookie, especially if you make the cookie size smaller. *Recommended for chocoholics!* Makes 40 medium-sized cookies.

Sue Deneke

Rocks

1-1/2 cups sugar
1 cup butter
3 eggs
3 cups flour
1/4 teaspoon salt
1/2 cup warm water

1 teaspoon soda
1 teaspoon cinnamon
2 teaspoons allspice
1 teaspoon ground cloves
1 pound nuts, chopped
1 pound raisins or chopped dates

Cream sugar and butter, adding eggs one at a time. Add flour sifted with salt. Dissolve soda in warm water. Add to mixture. Add spices, then chopped nuts and fruit. Drop by teaspoonfuls on ungreased baking sheet. Bake at 350 degrees for 10 to 15 minutes or until set and brown. Do not overcook.

In memory of Leila Coles Wilkins

Scotch-a-roos

1 cup sugar
1 cup light Karo syrup
1 cup peanut butter
5 cups Rice Krispies

Icing:
1 (12 ounce) package chocolate chips
1 (12 ounce) package butterscotch chips

Bring sugar and Karo to boil on stove. Remove from heat and add peanut butter. Stir until peanut butter is melted. Add Rice Krispies. Mix and press onto buttered 9x13 pan or 11x16 jelly roll pan. Icing: Melt chocolate chips and butterscotch chips together in microwave or over double boiler on stove. Spread over Rice Krispies mixture and cool in refrigerator. When cool, cut in squares. Makes 2 dozen.

Jana Roberts

Scots Shortbread

4 cups flour
1 cup sugar

1/2 teaspoon salt
1 pound (4 sticks) butter

Mix flour, sugar, and salt. Add butter. (It helps to soften butter). Knead until blended. At this point, divide in half to make it easier to handle. Continue to knead until smooth and satiny. Make into rolls. Chill in refrigerator for 30 minutes or more to firm up. Slice into 1/4 inch slices. Place on greased cookie sheets leaving plenty of room as they will grow in oven. Prick with a fork. Bake at 300 degrees for 25 to 30 minutes. Store in tight tins. *Wonderful with a glass of milk at night when counting sheep doesn't help.*

Donald Angus Tatman

Holiday Sugar Cookies

1-1/2 cups powdered sugar, sifted
1 cup butter
1 egg
1 teaspoon vanilla extract

1/2 teaspoon almond extract
2-1/2 cups all purpose flour
1 teaspoon soda
1 teaspoon cream of tartar

Mix sugar and butter. Add egg and flavorings; mix thoroughly. Measure sifted flour. Stir in dry ingredients. Refrigerate 2 to 3 hours. Heat oven to 375 degrees. Work with 1/2 of dough; refrigerate remainder until ready to use. Roll out on lightly floured surface until 3/16 inch thick and cut with cookie cutters of your choice. Place on lightly greased cookie sheet and bake 7 to 8 minutes or until golden brown. If you use self-rising flour, omit soda and cream of tartar. Decorate with colored sugar or colored powdered sugar icing. *I have wonderful childhood memories helping Mom in the kitchen making these cookies at Christmas time. Children love to make these.* Makes 5 to 6 dozen.

Lisa Mills Wilkins

Mama's Sugar Cookies

2-1/4 cups flour, sifted
1/4 teaspoon salt
2 teaspoons baking powder
1/2 cup shortening

1 cup sugar
2 eggs, beaten
1/2 teaspoon vanilla
1 tablespoon milk

Sift flour, salt, and baking powder together. Cream shortening and sugar together. Add eggs, vanilla, and milk. Then add sifted ingredients. Roll and cut. Sprinkle with sugar. Bake on baking sheet at 375 degrees for 12 minutes. *I add food coloring right before adding the dry ingredients. We do pink hearts for Valentine's Day, orange pumpkins for Halloween, pink bunnies at Easter, green and red Santas for Christmas. These cookies made wonderful childhood memories for me and now for my children!* Makes 2-1/2 dozen cookies.

Susan Norton

Virginia Clement's Cut Glass Sugar Cookies

1 cup butter or oleo
1 cup sugar
2 eggs
4 to 5 cups sifted flour

1/2 teaspoon salt
1/2 teaspoon ground nutmeg
1 teaspoon soda

Cream butter and sugar. Add eggs, one at a time, beating well after each. Gradually work in flour with spoon. Amount of flour governed by size of eggs - it usually takes 4-1/2 cups for large eggs. Add salt, nutmeg and soda to last cup of flour. If mixture is too thick to work with spoon, work in with hands. Make into balls the size of a walnut and roll in sugar. Place on ungreased cookie sheet. Flatten each cookie with bottom of a cut glass which has been dipped in sugar. Bake at 350 degrees for 12 to 15 minutes. Don't overcook - they should be light and crisp and as thin as possible; the edges should just barely change color. *Joe's mother used to make these often and everyone loved them.* Makes 5 dozen.

In memory of Virginia C. Clement,
President, Women of the Church 1947-48

Papoose Cookies

1 (8 ounce) package cream cheese
2 sticks butter (no substitutes)
2-1/2 cups flour
1/2 pound ground pecans

1 cup sugar
3 tablespoons crushed Zwieback
4 tablespoons honey
1 jigger whiskey

Cream together cream cheese, butter, and flour. Put in refrigerator to chill until firm enough to handle. Take out small amounts at a time. Roll thin. Cut dough into 2 inch squares. Fill with nut mixture. Mix pecans, sugar, Zwieback, honey and whiskey. Blend well. Put ball of this mix into center of each square of dough. Fold over the 2 opposite corners and secure with wooden toothpick. Cook at 350 degrees about 25 minutes or until golden brown. When cool, roll in powdered sugar. Store in well sealed metal box. Keeps well. *This takes time and is trouble, but is extra good.* Makes 3 or 4 dozen.

Sue Trulock,
President, Women of the Church 1963-64

Shortbread Cookies

2 sticks margarine
3/4 cup sugar
1 egg yolk

2-1/4 cups flour
Dash of salt

Let margarine soften about 1 hour out of refrigerator. Cream with sugar. Add beaten egg yolk, flour and salt. Roll into small balls and press down with a fork. Bake on cookie sheet at 350 degrees for 15 minutes or until brown. Makes 5 dozen.

Frances Martin

Teacakes

1 heaping cup sugar
1 stick butter
2 eggs
1 cup flour or more if needed
1/2 teaspoon soda

1 teaspoon nutmeg
1 teaspoon baking powder
2 tablespoons buttermilk
2 teaspoons vanilla

Cream butter and sugar. Add eggs - then add flour sifted with dry ingredients. Add buttermilk and vanilla. Roll out on floured board and cut with round cookie cutter. Bake at 350 degrees for 8 to 10 minutes. *During World War I the ladies of Pine Bluff made cookies and took them down to the troop trains as they went through Pine Bluff. Mrs. Hugh Fox was the chairman and this was the recipe given to the ladies to use. My mother used it all her life.* Makes 50 cookies.

In memory of Mrs. William L. Toney

Since the home address of our first four ministers, Mr. John Boozer, Mr. Evander McNair, Mr. William Dabney, and Dr. Joseph Dickson, was the same, Bonne, S. W. Corner West James, we believe this was the church manse from 1862 - 1892. It was the frame house next door to the church owned by the church.

Brownies

2 tablespoons butter
1-1/2 squares semi-sweet chocolate
1 cup sugar
2 beaten eggs

1 teaspoon vanilla
1/2 cup flour
1/2 cup nuts

Melt butter and chocolate together. Add sugar, beaten eggs, vanilla, flour, and nuts. Stir well. Pour into 8x8 pan. Bake at 350 degrees for 20 minutes. *I melt butter and chocolate in double boiler and add other ingredients - one pan preparation. Easy to double recipe.* Makes 24 brownies.

Mrs. Peter Ahlgrim

Mary's Brownies

1/2 cup Crisco
2 ounces unsweetened chocolate
2 eggs
1 cup sugar
3/4 cup sifted flour
1/2 teaspoon baking powder
3/4 teaspoon salt
1 teaspoon vanilla
2 tablespoons white Karo

1 cup chopped pecans or
  walnuts
Icing:
2 tablespoons water
1 tablespoon butter
1/4 teaspoon vanilla
1/2 ounce (1/2 block)
  chocolate, melted
1 cup sifted powdered sugar

Melt Crisco and chocolate in double boiler. Cool. Beat eggs until light. Add sugar; beat until light and fluffy. Add cooled chocolate mixture. Blend in flour, baking powder, and salt. Blend in vanilla, Karo, and nuts. Spread in greased 7x9 inch pan. Bake 30 to 35 minutes at 350 degrees. Test in center with toothpick - should not coat toothpick but don't overbake. Icing: Heat water and butter together in saucepan. Heat until butter melts, add vanilla and melted chocolate. Add powdered sugar. Beat until smooth. Spread on brownies. Cut when cool.

Mary Snavely

Quick Brownies

1/2 cup butter or margarine
1 cup sugar
2 eggs
1/2 teaspoon vanilla

4 tablespoons cocoa
1/2 cup flour
1/4 teaspoon salt
Nuts, if desired

Cream butter and sugar. Add eggs, beaten. Stir well. Add remaining ingredients and mix. Bake in a greased 8x8 inch pan at 350 degrees for 25 minutes. *I prefer to leave them a bit soggy - perhaps cook about 20 minutes. I took these to our Circle luncheon and was asked to submit the recipe to the Cookbook.* Makes about 16.

Mrs. Collins Andrews, Jr.

Super Brownies

— too much! make ½ recipe

2 sticks butter or margarine
2 cups sugar
1/2 cup cocoa
4 eggs
1-1/2 cups flour
1-1/2 cups chopped nuts (optional)
3 teaspoons vanilla
1/2 teaspoon salt

Icing:
1 stick butter or margarine
4 tablespoons cocoa
6 tablespoons milk
1 teaspoon vanilla
1 box powdered sugar
1 cup chopped nuts (optional)

Melt butter, add sugar, and cocoa. Mix well. Add eggs, blending well. Add flour, nuts, vanilla, and salt. Mix well. Pour into greased and floured 9x13 pan. Bake at 325 degrees for 30 to 35 minutes. Five minutes before brownies are done, bring to a boil the butter or margarine, cocoa and milk. Remove from heat, add vanilla, powdered sugar, and nuts (optional). Beat and spread on hot brownies.

Ellen Nuckolls

Black Forest Squares

1 chocolate cake mix
1 (8 ounce) carton sour cream
1 (3-1/2 ounce) package instant
   chocolate pudding mix
1 cup milk
1/4 cup Creme de Cassis
1 (16 ounce) can Bing cherries, pitted

2 tablespoons sugar
1 tablespoon cornstarch
1/2 cup whipping cream,
   whipped
1/4 cup sliced almonds,
   toasted

Make cake and pour into a greased and floured 9x13 pan. Bake about 12 to 15 minutes. Cool. Beat sour cream, pudding mix, 1/3 cup of the milk, and Creme de Cassis until fluffy. Gradually add other 2/3 cup milk. Pour over cooled cake, cover and refrigerate. Drain cherries (may be halved) reserving 3/4 cup liquid. In saucepan, combine sugar and cornstarch, gradually adding juice. Cook until thick. Cook 1 additional minute, add cherries and cool. Spread over pudding mixture. Refrigerate. Add whipped cream and toasted almonds to squares before serving. Makes 12 to 16.

Frances Toney Hall

Brown Sugar Bars

2 cups all purpose flour
1 box brown sugar
2 teaspoons baking powder

2 eggs
2 sticks margarine or butter
2 cups chopped pecans

Mix all ingredients together and spread on a greased jelly roll pan or cookie sheet. Bake at 300 degrees for 25 minutes. Let cool in pan and then cut into bars. Makes 30 to 36 bars.

Susan Norton

Creole Pecan Praline Bars

Shortbread Layer:
1 stick unsalted butter, room temperature
1 cup (packed) light brown sugar
1/4 teaspoon salt
2 cups sifted all purpose flour
2-1/2 cups large pecan halves

Praline Topping:
1-1/2 sticks unsalted butter
1/3 cup (packed) light brown sugar

Pan preparation: Pour 1 tablespoon water in 9x13x2 pan. Line pan with foil covering bottom and sides, leaving water in pan. Beat butter with electric mixer until soft. Add sugar and salt and beat to mix. Add flour and beat for 1 to 2 minutes. Dough will form tiny crumbs. Press dough in pan with hands to form an even layer. With pecan halves, flat side down, form straight lines across the width and length of pan pressing pecans slightly into dough. Prepare praline topping: Melt butter and sugar over high heat. Stir until mixture comes to a rolling boil. Continue stirring for 30 seconds. Pour over pecan layer. Bake at 350 degrees for 22 minutes. Cool. Refrigerate for at least 1 hour or up to 2 days before slicing. To slice bars - invert pan on flat board to remove foil. Invert back so pecans are on top. Cut each bar with one pecan by 3 pecans down approximately 1x3 inches. Serve at room temperature. Make 32 or 64 bars.

Ann Rogers

Rachel's Lemon Bars

1 package lemon cake mix
1/2 cup melted Parkay (light)
1 egg
1 package lemon frosting mix

1 (8 ounce) package cream
  cheese (light)
2 eggs

Mix cake mix, Parkay, and egg with mixer. Spread into 13x9 greased pan. Open frosting mix and remove 3/4 cup of dry mix. Set aside in small bowl. To the remainder add 2/3 of cream cheese and 2 eggs and cream together with mixer. Pour onto cake mixture and bake at 350 degrees for about 30 minutes or until light brown. Remove and cool. Mix remaining cream cheese and frosting mix well and spread on top. Cut into squares and serve. *Cannot eat just one!* Makes 36 to 48 bars.

Lisa Mills Wilkins

Caramel Fudge

3 cups sugar
1 cup Pet milk
1 teaspoon vanilla

Lump of margarine
1 cup nuts, halved or smaller pieces

Mix 2 cups of sugar and 1 cup Pet milk, heat to a boil. Melt 1 cup of sugar in iron skillet. Add to milk mixture slowly. (Do not heat sugar too hot but just until melted). Stir constantly. Cook until reaches soft ball stage tested in cold water. Add margarine and beat well. Add nuts. Pour onto platter greased with margarine.

Oralee Leslie

Corinne's Chocolate Fudge

2 cups sugar
1/3 cup white Karo syrup
1/2 cup Half and Half
1/2 stick butter
Pinch of salt

2 squares bitter chocolate
2 squares semi-sweet chocolate
1 teaspoon vanilla
1 cup chopped nuts

Place all ingredients except vanilla and nuts in a heavy pan and melt thoroughly. Stir with wooden spoon. Bring to a hard boil and let boil 3-1/2 minutes by timer. Take from heat and beat with regular spoon. Add 1 teaspoon vanilla and 1 cup nuts when fudge starts to lose shine. Pour up immediately in buttered Pyrex. Don't beat too long! There is a magic moment to pour it up. Cut into squares while hot. *Be sure pan is heavy in order to melt chocolate slowly. This is a delicious fudge. Corinne West gave me this recipe.* Makes 12 to 15 squares.

Mary Snavely

In 1867, two years after the Civil War ended, the first women's organization was founded in our church. It was called the Mite Society and Miss Estelle Holland (later Mrs. Charles Triplett, Sr.) was the first president. The dues were 10 cents a month.

Light Peanut Brittle

1 cup white corn syrup
2 cups granulated sugar
1/2 cup water
1 cup shelled peanuts
2 tablespoons butter or margarine

2 teaspoons vanilla
2 teaspoons soda
1/2 teaspoon salt

I use a candy thermometer to eliminate guesses. Combine syrup, sugar, and water and bring slowly to 230 degrees (soft ball) stirring as mixture heats. Add peanuts and take to 300 degrees (hard crack), continuing to stir slowly so peanuts will not burn but cook evenly. Remove from heat. Add margarine, vanilla, soda, salt and stir until well blended. DO NOT STIR TOO LONG. Pour into well buttered jelly roll pan (15-1/2x10-1/2x1 inch). Try to pour continuously and distribute in pan as well as possible. Place pan on cooling rack and cool thoroughly before breaking. This peanut brittle is honeycombed and light and easy to eat. The best peanut brittle is made on dry days. *I have had this recipe 30 years and have never had a failure.* Recipe makes about 1-1/2 pounds.

James W. Leslie

N & M Pralines

1 cup dark brown sugar
1/2 cup light brown sugar
1 small (5 ounce) can condensed
  milk
1-1/2 cups white sugar

3 tablespoons white Karo
1 tablespoon margarine
3-1/2 cups pecans
1/3 stick margarine
1 tablespoon vanilla

Cook in 8 quart kettle (or iron skillet). Combine the first 6 ingredients in the kettle. Cook over medium heat 5 minutes, stirring frequently and scraping the bottom and crevices of kettle. Turn fire to medium high and cook, stirring constantly to a rolling boil. Add the 1/3 stick margarine and remove from fire. Set pan in cold water for 10 minutes without stirring. Beat by hand 5 minutes, add pecans and vanilla. Drop by tablespoon on waxed paper that rests on newspaper sheets. This helps removing without breaking praline. *The hardest thing is not stirring while cooling. Pick a good day. Evelyn Shirley, 80 years old, Minden, LA, original recipe.* Makes 22.

Novelle B. Clark

Orange Pecans

3/4 tablespoon flour
1 cup sugar
1/2 cup freshly squeezed and strained
   orange juice

1 tablespoon butter
Pecan halves

Stir flour into sugar, add orange juice and cook to soft ball stage. Remove from heat and add butter. Beat until creamy. Stir in pecan halves. Pour on waxed paper. Cool and separate into small chunks. *A German holiday favorite given to Mary Cathryn in 1938 while studying piano in Heidleburg.*

In memory of Mary Cathryn Eden

Peanut Butter Fudge

2 cups sugar
1 cup evaporated milk
2 tablespoons butter

1-1/2 teaspoons vanilla
1/2 cup peanut butter

Cook and stir sugar and milk to soft ball stage over medium heat. Remove from heat and add butter, vanilla, and peanut butter. Beat with wooden spoon until mixture becomes thick. Pour into a buttered 8 inch square pan. Cool. Cut into squares.

Grace Hoffman

Puppy Chow

1 stick margarine
1 cup chocolate chips
1/2 cup peanut butter

8 cups Rice Chex
2 cups powdered sugar

Melt margarine and chocolate chips over low heat. Add peanut butter and stir together. Pour over Rice chex and mix together. Put in large paper bag and add powdered sugar. Shake well to coat. *A great snack - kids love it. Makes a nice "home-made" gift at Christmas or for teachers. Keeps well in jars or tins. It looks like puppy chow, but really tastes great!*

Leah "Pud" Harris

Benediction

The Lord bless you and keep you:
The Lord make His face to shine upon you,
and be gracious unto you:
The Lord lift up His countenance upon you,
and give you peace.

Numbers 6:24-26

INDEX

INDEX

INDEX

INDEX

INDEX

INDEX

INDEX

INDEX

INDEX

INDEX

INDEX

INDEX

INDEX

INDEX

INDEX

INDEX

ORDER FORM
𝕭lessings

717 West 32nd
Pine Bluff, Arkansas 71603
870-534-7831

_____ copies at $16.95 each   _____

Postage and handling, $3.05 per book _____

TOTAL _____

ENCLOSED IS MY CHECK OR MONEY ORDER FOR $_____.

NAME_____

STREET_____

CITY_____STATE_____ZIP_____

TELEPHONE NUMBER _____

CHARGE TO MY: VISA OR MASTERCARD

ACCOUNT NUMBER: _____

EXPIRATION DATE:_____

CUSTOMER'S SIGNATURE _____

ORDER FORM
𝕭lessings

717 West 32nd
Pine Bluff, Arkansas 71603
870-534-7831

_____ copies at $16.95 each   _____

Postage and handling, $3.05 per book _____

TOTAL _____

ENCLOSED IS MY CHECK OR MONEY ORDER FOR $_____.

NAME_____

STREET_____

CITY_____STATE_____ZIP_____

TELEPHONE NUMBER _____

CHARGE TO MY: VISA OR MASTERCARD

ACCOUNT NUMBER: _____

EXPIRATION DATE:_____

CUSTOMER'S SIGNATURE _____